Frommer's 97

Bermuda

**by Darwin Porter
and Danforth Prince**

Macmillan • USA

ABOUT THE AUTHORS

A native of North Carolina, Darwin Porter was a bureau chief for the *Miami Herald* when he was 21, and later worked in television advertising. A veteran travel writer, he is the author of numerous bestselling Frommer guides, notably to England, France, Germany, Italy, and the Caribbean. When not traveling (which is rare), he lives in Georgia. Working with Darwin is Danforth Prince, formerly of the Paris bureau of the *New York Times*. Both of these journalists discovered Bermuda during their various spring break College Weeks, and have been frequent visitors ever since.

MACMILLAN TRAVEL

A Simon & Schuster Macmillan Company
1633 Broadway
New York, NY 10019

Find us online at **http://www.mcp.com/mgr/travel** or
on America Online at Keyword: **Frommer's.**

ISBN 0-02-860924-7
ISSN 1069-3572

Editor: Charlotte Allstrom
Production Editor: Denise Hawkins, Jama Carter, and Michael Thomas
Digital Cartography: John Decamillis
Design by Michelle Laseau
Page Creation by Linda Quigley, Bill Levy, Natalie Hollifield, Jerry Cole, John Carroll, Sherri Fugit, Sean Decker and Heather Pope
Maps copyright © by Simon & Schuster, Inc.

SPECIAL SALES

Bulk Purchases (10+ copies) of Frommer's travel guides are available to corporations at special discounts. The Special Sales Department can produce custom editions to be used as premiums and/or for sales promotion to suit individual needs. Existing editions can be produced with custom cover imprints such as corporate logos. For more information write to: Special Sales, Simon & Schuster, 1633 Broadway, New York, NY 10019.

Manufactured in the United States of America.

Contents

List of Maps

AN INVITATION TO THE READER

In researching this book, we discovered many intriguing places—hotels, restaurants, shops, and more. We're sure you'll find others. Please tell us about them, so we can share the information with your fellow travelers in upcoming editions. If you were disappointed with a recommendation, we'd love to know that, too. Please write to:

Darwin Porter/Danforth Prince
Frommer's Bermuda '97
Macmillan Travel
1633 Broadway
New York, NY 10019

AN ADDITIONAL NOTE

Please be advised that travel information is subject to change at any time—and this is especially true of prices. We therefore suggest that you write or call ahead for confirmation when making your travel plans. The authors, editors, and publisher cannot be held responsible for the experiences of readers while traveling. Your safety is important to us, however, so we encourage you to stay alert and be aware of your surroundings. Keep a close eye on cameras, purses, and wallets, all favorite targets of thieves and pickpockets.

WHAT THE SYMBOLS MEAN

✪ Frommer's Favorites

Hotels, restaurants, attractions, and entertainment you should not miss.

⑤ Super-Special Values

Hotels and restaurants that offer great value for your money.

The following abbreviations are used for credit cards:

AE	American Express	EU	Eurocard
CB	Carte Blanche	JCB	Japan Credit Bank
DC	Diners Club	MC	MasterCard
DISC	Discover	V	Visa
ER	enRoute		

The Best of Bermuda

You've come to Bermuda to relax—not to exhaust yourself trying to figure out where you should go or searching for the best deals. With this guide in hand, you can spend your vacation in peace and let us do the work. Below you'll find our carefully compiled lists of the islands' superlative beaches, dive sites, restaurants, sports, sightseeing, and nearly anything else your heart might desire.

1 The Best Beaches

One of your first priorities on your Bermuda vacation will be to lounge on the beach. But which beach to choose? Hotels often have their own private beaches, which we've described in each accommodation review to help you choose a place to stay. There are many fine public beaches as well. Here are our picks for the top 10, arranged clockwise around the island, beginning with the south shore beaches closest to the city of Hamilton. See Chapter 9 for additional details on all of these.

- **Elbow Beach:** Pale pink sand stretches almost a mile at Paget Parish's Elbow Beach, one of the most consistently popular beaches in Bermuda. At least three hotels have swimming facilities along the beach's perimeter. There's a $3.50 fee for visitors who are not staying at one of these hotels. The beach, because of the protective coral reefs that surround it, is one of the safest on the island. During the Easter period, it tends to be packed with college students who are vacationing on Bermuda. The Elbow Beach Hotel/A Wyndham Resort (☎ 441/236-3535) offers facilities and rentals.
- **Astwood Cove:** In Warwick Parish, at the bottom of a steep and winding road that intersects with South Shore Road, this beach is so remote that it's rarely overcrowded. The trees and shrubbery of Astwood Park provide a verdant backdrop.
- **Warwick Long Bay:** This popular beach features a half-mile stretch of sand, one of the longest on the island. Against a backdrop of scrubland and low grasses, the beach lies on the southern side of South Shore Park, in Warwick Parish. Despite the frequent winds, the waves are surprisingly small because of an offshore reef. Less than 200 feet offshore a jagged coral island appears to float above the water.

- **Chaplin Bay:** At the southern extremity of South Shore Park, straddling the boundary between Warwick and Southampton Parish, this small but secluded beach almost completely disappears during storms or particularly high tides. An open-air coral barrier partially separates one-half of the beach from the other.
- **Horseshoe Bay Beach:** This is Bermuda's most famous beach. It's at Horseshoe Bay, South Shore Road, Southampton Parish, where the Beach House (☎ 441/238-2651) offers complete facilities, including rental equipment, for beachgoers.
- **Church Bay:** If you like to snorkel, this is the beach for you. The relatively calm waters, sheltered by offshore reefs, harbor a variety of marine life. Sunbathers love to nestle within the beach's unusually deep pink sands.
- **Somerset Long Bay:** The waters off this beach are often unsafe for swimming, but its isolation will appeal to anyone who wants to escape from the madding crowd. The undeveloped parkland of Sandys Parish shelters it from the rest of the island. The crescent-shaped beach—offering about a quarter-mile of sand—is ideal for beach-walking.
- **Shelly Bay Beach:** On the north shore of Hamilton Parish, you'll discover calm waters and soft pink sand.
- **Tobacco Bay Beach:** A popular stretch of pale pink sand, this is the most popular beach on St. George's Island and it offers lots of facilities.
- **John Smith's Bay:** The only public beach within Smith's Parish. Long, flat, and boasting the pale pink sand for which the south shore is famous, this beach usually has a lifeguard—a plus for families with children. There are toilet and changing facilities on site.

2 The Best Outdoor Activities

Sports and beaches are what Bermuda is all about. Any one of the activities below would be reason enough to visit the island. See Chapter 9 for more details.

- **Golfing:** Known for its outstanding golf courses, Bermuda attracts the world's leading golfers and those who'd like to be. In the past these have included such luminaries as President Eisenhower, President Truman, and the Duke of Windsor. Rolling, hummocky fairways characterize the greens. Many avid golfers come to Bermuda to play all the courses; they call this "collecting courses." Some holes are from hell, as golfers say. That includes Port Royal's notorious 16th hole. Both the tee and the hole are placed high on cliff edges with the rich blue water looming a dizzying 100 feet below.
- **Boating and Sailing:** As yachties around the world agree, Bermuda is in the premier class for this pastime. With the fresh wind of the Atlantic blowing in your hair, you can set out upon your own voyage of discovery, perhaps sailing Great Sound with its tiny islets that take in Long Island and Hawkins Island. Tiny secluded beaches beckon frequently. Many people forget that Bermuda is not just one island, but a series of islands—an archipelago, really—waiting to be discovered. A novice at sailing? Try Mangrove Bay; it's protected and safer than some of the more turbulent seas.
- **Bicycling:** Since island law forbids you to rent a car, you might as well take up bicycling, even if you haven't been on two wheels since you were a kid. Let's be honest: Bermuda isn't the world's greatest cycling terrain. If you don't want to face narrow roads and heavy traffic, opt instead for the Railway Trail, the island's premier cycling route. The paved trail (formerly the route of Bermuda's railway line) runs almost the entire length of the island. It's a paradise for cyclists.

- **Horseback Riding:** Because this sport is so restricted, it's all the more memorable. Taking a horse through the dune grass and oleander of the island, especially at South Shore Park, is an experience you won't want to miss. As you ride along beaches looking out over coral bluffs, you and your fellow riders may agree it isn't Kentucky, but what it is, isn't bad. Horseback riding centers will guide you on trail rides through not only the best of the Bermuda countryside, but also to beautiful hidden spots along the north coast.
- **Diving:** Whatever is demanded on the scuba calendar, Bermuda has it. That includes the wrecks of countless ships that went aground in storm-tossed seas, underwater caves, coral and marine life almost unequaled in its part of the world, more reefs than most divers will ever see, and, for most of the year, warm, gin-clear waters. Many scuba experts cite Bermuda as one of the safest and best places to learn this sport. Over a period of time one expert explored the wrecks of nearly 40 ships, all of which were said to be in "good condition," although there may be more than 300 wreck sites in all. Depths begin at 25 feet or less, but can go up to 80 feet or more. Some wrecks are in about 30 feet of water, which would even put them within the range of snorkelers.

3 The Best Dive Sites

The following are some of the most exciting shipwreck and coral reef dives. See Chapter 9 for more specifics on diving.

- **The *Marie Celeste:*** A paddle wheeler that sank in 1964. Its 15-foot-diameter paddle wheel, located off the southern portion of the island, is overgrown with coral standing about 55 feet off the ocean floor.
- **The *North Carolina:*** One of Bermuda's most colorful wrecks, this English sailing barque foundered in 1879 and today lies in about 40 feet of water off the western portion of the island.
- **Tarpon Hole:** A coral reef dive located near Elbow Beach off the south shore.
- **South West Breaker:** A coral reef dive located off the south shore about 1 1/2 miles off Church Bay. Hard and soft coral decorate these sheet walls in depths of 20 to 30 feet.
- ***L'Hermanie:*** This first-class 60-gun French frigate was 17 days out of its Cuban port and heading back to France when it sank in 1838. The ship lies in 20 to 30 feet of water off the western side of the island with 25 cannons still visible.
- **The *Hermes:*** This 165-foot steamer ship about 1 mile off Warwick Long Bay on the South Shore, shipwrecked in 1985, lies in about 80 feet of water.
- **The *Rita Zovetta:*** A 360-foot Italian cargo ship, located in about 20 to 70 feet of water off the southern side of the island, ran aground off St. David's Island in 1924.
- **The *Tauton:*** This British Royal Mail steamer sank in 1914 and lies in 10 to 40 feet of water off the northern end of the island.
- **The *Constellation:*** Off the northwestern side of the island, about 8 miles west of the dockyard, this 200-foot, four-masted schooner, which was en route to Venezuela in 1943, now lies in 30 feet of water. The circumstances of this ship inspired Peter Benchley to write his book *The Deep*.
- **The *Cristóbal Colón:*** This 480-foot Spanish luxury liner is the largest known shipwreck in Bermuda's waters; it ran aground in 1936 on a northern reef between North Rock and North Breaker. It lies in 30 to 55 feet of water.

4 The Best Sailing Outfitters

As one of the major sailing capitals in the Atlantic, Bermuda has a great many sail-yourself boats that can be rented to qualified people. The best outfitters include the following:

- **Mangrove Marina Ltd.** (end of Cambridge Road, Mangrove Bay in Somerset; ☎ 441/234-0914): This is the best place to rent a Boston whaler, which can hold three or four passengers, depending on its size—an ideal craft for exploring some of the uninhabited islands of Bermuda. This outfitter rents both 11½-foot and 13-foot Boston whalers, along with a 15-foot Open Bowrider with 30 hp, which also accommodates four.
- **Pompano Beach Club Watersports Center** (Southampton Parish; ☎ 441/234-0222): The best outfitter in this tourist-laden parish. Open from May to late October, it offers a variety of equipment, including the O'Brien Windsurfer, which is suitable for one person (either a novice or experienced). Its fleet includes Dolphin paddleboats, Buddy Boards, Aqua-Eye viewing boards, Aqua Finn sailboats, and kayaks. These vessels hold one or two people and can be rented for up to four hours.
- **Southside Scuba Water Sports** (Grotto Bay Beach Hotel, Hamilton Parish; ☎ 441/293-2915): Here you will find an even better selection of self-drive boats, such as a Sunfish, Boardsailer, kayak, Paddle Cat, or Sun Cat. The Boardsailer and kayak hold only one person, but the other vessels can accommodate two. The vessels can be rented for up to eight hours.

5 The Best Golf Courses

See Chapter 9 for further information.

- **Belmont Hotel Golf & Country Club** (Warwick Parish): This is an 18-hole, par-70, 5,777-yard course designed by Emmett Devereux, a Scotsman, in 1923. It's been challenging golfers ever since, especially its par-five 11th hole, with a severe dogleg left with a blind tee shot. Trade winds play havoc with the listed lengths. Critics complain that the layout of the course is "maddening," yet they continue to return for a new challenge. The grass is dense because of the modern irrigation system.
- **Castle Harbour Golf Club** (Hamilton Parish): This 18-hole, par-71, 6,440-yard course is the only one in Bermuda requiring use of a golf cart. Known for its challenging tee shots, the course was designed by the noted golf architect Charles Banks. Trade winds sweeping in from the Atlantic make the course seem far longer than it actually is. Challenges abound in many places, especially at the 2nd and 17th holes. There are not as many sand traps here as on many Bermuda courses. It's expensive to play here, but much of the money collected is used for state-of-the-art maintenance.
- **Port Royal Golf Course** (Southampton Parish): A public golf course that offers an 18-hole, par-71, 6,565-yard challenge. It ranks among the very best on the island, public or private; in fact, it is rated as one of the greatest public courses in the world. Jack Nicklaus apparently agrees, since he likes to play here. Robert Trent Jones designed the course along an ocean terrain; the 16th hole here is the most famous in Bermuda, and photos of it have appeared in countless golfing magazines. Port Royal's greens fees are cheaper than those at some of the elitist courses, such as Castle Harbour.

- **Southampton Princess Golf Club** (Hamilton Parish): Although perhaps not the most scenic one on the island, this is an 18-hole, par-54, 2,684-yard course, with elevated tees and strategically placed bunkers. There's an array of water hazards here to challenge even the most experienced golfer. Of this course one golfer commented, "You not only need to be a great player, but have a certain mountaineering agility as well." A state-of-the-art irrigation system helps prevent summer "brown-outs."
- **St. George's Golf Club** (St. George's Parish): One of the island's newest courses—and one of its best—this 18-hole, par-62, 4,043-yard course was designed by the master himself, Robert Trent Jones. Within walking distance of historic St. George's, it lies on a windy headland at the northeastern tip of Bermuda. Although you can enjoy panoramic vistas, your game is likely to be affected by winds from the Atlantic. The greens are the smallest on the island, no more than two dozen feet across.

6 The Best Tennis Facilities

- **Southampton Princess** (Southampton Parish): This is the premier destination in Bermuda for the most avid tennis players. Its tennis court layout is not only the largest on the island but also maintained in a state-of-the-art condition. This deluxe hotel, one of the finest in Bermuda, offers 11 Plexipave courts, three of which are illuminated for night games. The courts are somewhat protected from the north winds, but at times swirling breezes can affect the final score in a tennis match.
- **Elbow Beach Hotel/A Wyndham Resort** (Paget Parish): A runner-up in the tennis sweepstakes, these courts lag far behind those of the Southampton Princess. Some of America's leading collegiate tennis players use these courts during spring break College Weeks. During that time you can often see future stars in action here. The first-class hotel offers five LayKold courts, one of which is reserved just for tennis lessons (given by an on-site pro).
- **Port Royal Golf Course** (Southampton Parish): Tennis is also played here, and these well-maintained courts are among the island's best. There are four Plexipave courts, and two are illuminated for night games. Racks and balls can be lent to players. Even golfing luminaries such as Jack Nicklaus have been spotted on these tennis courts. The golf course with its tennis courts overlooks the pink sands and blue waters of Whale Bay, one of the leading areas for fishing and boating in Bermuda.
- **Government Tennis Stadium** (Pembroke Parish): Although Bermuda has been known as the tennis capital of the Atlantic since 1873, players often complain that the trade winds swirling around the island affect their game, especially at courts close to the water. That's why many prefer one of the inland courts, such as this government-owned stadium, which offers three clay and five Plexicushion courts. Three of these courts are illuminated for night games. The facility, which is north of Hamilton, requires players to wear tennis attire. On site are a pro shop, a ball machine, and a pro who can give private lessons.

7 The Best Hiking

See also Chapter 8, "Bermuda Strolls."

- **Spittal Pond Nature Reserve Tour:** This 60-acre unspoiled sanctuary is the island's largest nature reserve, home to both resident and migratory waterfowl. Some 25 species of waterfowl can be seen here annually from November to May.

Scenic trails and footpaths have been cut through the property. You can either explore on your own or take one of the guided hikes offered by the Department of Agriculture.

- **The Bermuda Railway Trail:** Stretching for some 21 miles, this unique trail was created along the course of the old Bermuda Railway, which served the island between 1931 and 1948. Bermudians traveled on this train in lieu of cars, which were not allowed on the island until the late 1940s. Armed with a copy of the *Bermuda Railway Trail Guide,* available from the various visitors centers, you can set out on your own following the old rail route of what was called "Rattle and Shake." Most of the trail winds along a car-free route, and you can see and do as much of it as your stamina allows.

- **Royal Naval Dockyard to Somerset:** Hikers can also take a 4-mile walk from the dockyard—former center of the British navy on Bermuda—to Somerset Island. There are many good sandy beaches along this route, if you want to pause from your hike to relax on a beach for a while. From the southern entrance to the dockyard, follow Pender Road for about half a mile, crossing Cut Bridge leading to Ireland Island South. After crossing Grey's Bridge, the route continues west along Watford Island until you cross Watford Bridge, which leads eventually to Somerset Village in Sandys Parish.

8   The Best Views

There is a 1950s play called *I Am a Camera,* and that is how you'll feel as you stroll about Bermuda. It's a shutterbug's delight, with panoramas and vistas unfolding at nearly every turn. But some views are more panoramic than others. See Chapter 7 for additional information.

- **Warwick Long Bay:** The longest stretch of pristine pink sand in Bermuda—stretching for half a mile or so—makes this a dream beach of the picture-postcard variety. It is set against a backdrop of towering cliffs and hills studded with Spanish bayonet and oleander. A 20-foot coral outcrop, rising some 200 feet offshore and resembling a sculpted boulder, adds even more variety to this beachscape.

- **Fort Scaur:** From Somerset Bridge in Sandys Parish, head for this fort atop the highest hill in the parish. Walk the fort's ramparts, enjoying the vistas across Great Sound to Spanish Point. You can also gaze north to the dockyard to take in the fine view of Somerset Island. On a clear day, a look through the telescope will reveal St. David's Lighthouse, some 14 miles away on the northeastern tip of the island. After taking in the fantastic view from the fort, stroll through the 22 acres of beautiful gardens.

- **The Queen's View:** At Gibbs Hill Lighthouse in Southampton Parish, a plaque designates the spot where Queen Elizabeth II paused in November 1953 to take in the view of Little Sound. You can admire that same view today, which includes Riddells Bay Golf Course and Perot's Island. (Although Ross Perot has a home in Bermuda, the island is not named for him, but for the father of William Bennett Perot, Bermuda's first postmaster.)

- **Gibbs Hill Lighthouse:** For an even better view than the one enjoyed by Queen Elizabeth II, climb the 185 spiral steps of the lighthouse itself; built in 1846, it is one of the oldest cast-iron lighthouses in the world. At the top you can relish what islanders consider the single finest view in all of Bermuda. You can, that is, if the wind doesn't blow you away. Hang on to the railing. In heavy winds, the tower actually sways; on certain days you may want to retreat regardless of the view.

9 The Best Places to Discover Old Bermuda

Much of Bermuda is modern, but its history dates back to the arrival of its first settlers in 1609. The following places provide insights—often maritime—into the old way of life, which has now largely disappeared. See Chapter 7 for more details.

- **The Back Streets of St. George's:** The 17th-century stocks on King's Square in historic St. George's have been photographed by virtually every tourist who's ever been to the island. But it is in the narrow cobblestoned lanes such as Shinbone Alley and the back streets and alleyways that you can recapture the old spirit of this town. Arm yourself with a good map and wander at leisure through such places as Silk Alley (also called Petticoat Lane); Barber's Lane Alley (named for a former slave from South Carolina); Printer's Alley (where Bermuda's first newspaper was published); and Nea's Alley (former stamping ground of the Irish poet Tom Moore). Finally, walk through Somers Garden and head up the steps to Blockade Alley. On the hill lies the so-called Unfinished Church.

- **The Royal Naval Dockyard:** Nothing recaptures the maritime spirit of this little island colony more than this sprawling complex of several attractions on Ireland Island. Beginning in 1809, Britain began building this dockyard, perhaps fearing attacks on its fleet from warmongering Napoleon or from pirates. Convicts and slaves provided much of the labor that went into constructing a shipyard for the Royal Navy that lasted for almost 150 years. The shipyard closed in 1951, and the Royal Navy has little presence here today; but the Maritime Museum and other exhibits enable visitors to gain a feel for a largely vanished era.

- **St. David's Island:** Much of Bermuda looks pristine and proper—its old way of life largely replaced with pretty pink cottages and tourist hotels. Whatever rustic maritime life still remains (that's not in a museum) can be found on St. David's. Some islanders never even bother to visit neighboring St. George's. To some locals, visiting the West End of Bermuda would be like a trip to the moon. St. David's Lighthouse has been a local landmark since 1879. In order to see how people actually used to cook and eat, you could drop by Dennis's Hideaway. Dennis Lamb personifies the eccentricity of St. David islanders, and his grubby place, with its mussel stew, conch steak, conch fritters, and shark hash, will give you an idea of how Bermudians used to eat before all that New York strip steak started arriving by plane.

10 The Most Intriguing Historical Sights

See Chapter 7 for more details.

- **Fort St. Catherine** (outside St. George's): This fort towers over the beach where the shipwrecked crew of the *Sea Venture* first came ashore in 1609. Tunnels, cannons, and ramparts remind visitors of this fortification, which was completed in 1614. Extensive rebuilding and remodeling continued over the years, right up until the 19th century. An audiovisual presentation on St. George's defense system will help you better understand what you're looking at.

- **Verdmont** (Smith's Parish): This 1770s mansion is situated on the property once owned by William Sayle, founder of South Carolina and its first governor. The house offers a rare glimpse into a long-faded Bermudian life of style and grace, and is filled with portraits, antiques, and china. Resembling a small English manor house, it is the finest historic home still standing in Bermuda.

- **Fort Scaur** (Sandys Parish): Together with Fort St. Catherine, this was part of a ring of fortifications that surrounded Bermuda. Built by the British navy, the fort was supposed to protect the Royal Naval Dockyard from an attack that never materialized. During World War II U.S. Marines were billeted nearby. The fort overlooks Great Sound, offering some of the island's most dramatic scenery.
- **Royal Naval Dockyard** (Ireland Island): This historic area of Bermuda was actually used by the British navy until 1951. Now restored and a major tourist attraction, as well as a multimillion-dollar cruise-ship dock, its centerpiece is the Bermuda Maritime Museum, the most important on the island. Constructed by convict labor, this 19th-century fortress today houses major exhibits on the island's nautical heritage.
- **St. Peter's Church** (St. George's): This is the oldest Anglican house of worship in the Western Hemisphere. At one time virtually everybody was buried here—from governors to criminals. To the west of the church lies the graveyard of slaves. This is the site of the original church, which was built by the colonists in 1612. That church was destroyed in a hurricane in 1712, but some parts of the interior were salvaged. The church was rebuilt on its present site in 1713.

11 The Best Offbeat Travel Experiences

- **Exploring Crystal Caves or Leamington Caves** (Hamilton Parish): Bermuda is a paradise for spelunkers, since it has the highest concentration of limestone caves in the world. These great stalactites and stalagmites have a gothic grandeur. The two best caves are Crystal Caves and Leamington Caves, both at Bailey's Bay. Crystal Caves, discovered in 1907, includes the crystal-clear Cahow Lake, and Leamington Caves also has underground lakes. These caves form one of the major natural wonderlands of Bermuda; their surreal formations took millions of years to create.
- **Helmet Diving** (Bronson Hartley, 5 North Shore Rd., Flatts FL, BX, Bermuda; ☎ 441/292-4434): You can enjoy the greatest undersea walk on the island by calling Mr. Hartley. He'll place a helmet on your head and then you descend the ladder of a boat to begin your guided walk underwater. A wonderland will unfold before your eyes: the feeding of corals, the breathing of sponges, and an array of rainbow-hued fish. The walk is ideal for everyone, including nonswimmers and those who wear glasses.
- **Visiting Dennis's Hideaway** (Cashew City Rd., St. David's Island; ☎ 441/297-0044): At his little home on remote St. David's Island, Dennis Lamb would qualify as one of those *Reader's Digest* "most unforgettable characters." If you'd like to have dinner at his ramshackle place, you can call for a reservation. He'll not only feed you his shark hash, mussel pie, or other seafood dish, but he'll give you some insight into how life used to be lived on Bermuda long ago. When he's not tending his pots, cleaning fish, or throwing food to one of his yapping dogs, he might share his philosophy of life with you. Don't dress up to come to visit him.

12 The Best Honeymoon Resorts

Bermuda has long been one of the world's favorite destinations for honeymooners, offering peace, solitude, and seclusion. Apparently all those honeymoon packages offered by hotels, ranging from deluxe resorts to guesthouses, seem to attract people, since Bermuda is also a favorite destination for couples on their second honeymoon.

Although some honeymooning couples seek out small housekeeping cottages and guesthouses, most honeymooners seem to prefer a package offered by one of the splashy resort hotels. A travel agent will help you secure the best deal (so you'll have some money left when you return home). The following resorts not only offer the best choices for a honeymoon in Bermuda, but also feature some of the best inclusive deals. See Chapter 5 for more details.

- **Elbow Beach Hotel/A Wyndham Resort** (60 South Shore Rd.; ☎ 441/236-3535 or 800/882-4200 in the U.S.): This hotel promises "marriages made in heaven." Its "Romance Packages" include daily breakfasts plus a romantic candlelit dinner for two in your room on the first night. On departure, the newlyweds are offered a copy of the *Elbow Beach Cookbook.*

- **Marriott's Castle Harbour Resort** (2 South Rd., St. George's; ☎ 441/293-2040 or 800/223-6388 in the U.S. and Canada): The island's largest beach resort might be the spot for a perfect honeymoon, since it offers seclusion for couples when they want it plus a large range of activities and tours. There are five different honeymoon packages with offerings that include a champagne breakfast in your room the first day, parasailing rides, gourmet dinners for two, and moped rentals.

- **Grotto Bay Beach Hotel** (11 Blue Hole Hill, Hamilton Parish; ☎ 441/293-8333 or 800/582-3190 in the U.S.): This resort, which actively seeks honeymooners, features everything from midnight swims at a private beach to cozy lovers'-nest rooms with private balconies overlooking the ocean. The honeymoon packages include romantic dinners, arrangements for cruises and walking tours, as well as optional champagne, fruit, and flowers.

- **Sonesta Beach Resort** (South Shore Road, Southampton Parish; ☎ 441/ 238-8122 or 800/766-3782 in the U.S.): The chilled champagne is in your room awaiting your arrival. To enhance your romantic visit, the staff will arrange a horse and buggy ride for you in the old Bermuda tradition, although the following day they'll give you a motorized scooter. The sports director will also offer one free tennis or scuba lesson. Countless couples like the location of this hotel, right on the beach. There's also a fully equipped, professionally staffed health spa. Honeymooners can dance to live music at the Boat Bay Club and Lounge, with its views of moonlit Boat Bay.

- **Southampton Princess Hotel** (101 South Shore Road; ☎ 441/238-8000 or 800/ 223-1818 in the U.S., 800/268-7176 in Canada): This hotel does everything it can to attract honeymooners who are seeking seclusion. Its honeymoon packages, which start at four days and three nights, include breakfast and dinner on a MAP "dine around plan," a bottle of champagne, a basket of fruit, and even a special-occasion cake, plus a souvenir photo and watercolor print by a local artist and admission to the exercise club.

13 The Best Family Accommodations

- **Belmont Hotel Golf & Country Club** (Middle Road, Warwick Parish; ☎ 809/ 236-1301 or 800/225-5843 in the U.S. and Canada): The Kee Kee Club, one of the best children's programs on the island, costs $10 to enroll children ages 2 to 12. The plan provides them with full day-care services and all meals, among other offerings. There is a wide range of children's amusements, including miniature golf. Families usually enjoy the hotel's barbecues.

- **Grotto Bay Beach Hotel** (11 Blue Hole Hill, Hamilton Parish; ☎ 441/293-8333 or 800/582-3190 in the U.S.): With its excellent children's program, this hotel attracts many families. Those that stay here usually don't mind its relative isolation across from the airport since they can enjoy the tropical landscaping of 21 acres—everything from oranges to papayas. The swimming pool has been blasted out of natural rock, and there are subterranean caves to explore. Communal swimfests are staged here. Barbecues by the beach and other activities make this a lively place.

- **Sonesta Beach Resort** (South Shore Road, Southampton Parish; ☎ 441/238-8122 or 800/766-3782 in the U.S.): Offering one of the best family packages on the island, the luxurious accommodations feature private balconies. A maximum of four people, including two children, are accepted for the four-day, three-night packages. Children eat free, and a second guest room for children is provided at 30% off the regular rate. A "Just Us Kids" activities program for ages 5 to 12 is held daily in summer, with pizza parties, unlimited free ice cream, and children's games, among other diversions.

- **Southampton Princess** (101 South Shore Road; ☎ 441/238-8000 or 800/223-1818 in the U.S., 800/268-7176 in Canada): From June through Labor Day, this hotel features the best children's program in Bermuda. Not only that, but children under 16 stay free. If the parents choose the MAP, children also get free meals. The former Touch Club has been redesigned to serve as Lenny's Loft—the social center for children's activities. With all its many sports facilities, including two freshwater pools and 11 tennis courts, this Princess is definitely for families that enjoy the sporting life.

- **The Royal Palms** (24 Rosemont Ave., Hamilton; ☎ 441/292-1854 or 800/678-0783 in the U.S., 800/799-0824 in Canada): Although this hotel can't compete with the large resorts and their expensive children's programs, it does offer a cozy nest for families on a budget. They can enjoy communal life around the swimming pool, and the hotel is close to many island attractions. Children under 16 are accepted for $25 a night (children 2 and under stay free). The bedrooms (all with private baths) are spacious enough for a family. Many families like to rent the private cottage, which is equipped with a kitchenette.

14   The Best Hotel Bargains

- **Palm Reef Hotel** (1 Harbour Road; ☎ 441/236-1000 or 800/221-1294 in the U.S.): Once known as the Inverurie, this was Bermuda's first hotel, and its history goes back to the 17th century. Visitors from that era wouldn't recognize the place today; it has grown and expanded, and has recently undergone a renovation. It lies at the point where Warwick and Paget Parishes meet. The rooms, which are reasonably priced, overlook Hamilton Harbour. Many sports can easily be arranged nearby, while the hotel provides its own entertainment from May to October.

- **Astwood Cove** (49 South Shore Road, Warwick Parish; ☎ 441/236-0984): For families seeking a self-contained studio apartment with a fully equipped kitchenette and a private porch or patio, this is a leading choice. You prepare your own meals and use the hotel's English bone china and wine glasses. Studio apartments have "hide-a-bed" sofas that can accommodate a third person if necessary. A third person under 15 pays $25, and children 4 and under are charged $15. This place is definitely a good buy in pricey Bermuda.

- **Loughlands** (79 South Shore Road, Paget; ☎ 441/236-1253): Set on 7 acres of landscaped grounds, this guesthouse offers privacy, an old-fashioned kind of elegance, and plenty of Bermuda charm. Staying here is somewhat like living at a country house on Bermuda, with attractively appointed bedrooms. There's a swimming pool, and arrangements can be made to participate in many other activities nearby, including golf, tennis, deep-sea fishing, and waterskiing.

- **Rosemont** (41 Rosemont Avenue, Hamilton; ☎ 441/292-1055 or 800/367-0040 in the U.S.): Lying near the Hamilton Princess, this has long been a family favorite for those who want a central location at a good price. This site offers panoramic views of Hamilton Harbour and the Great Sound. The accommodations consist of self-contained housekeeping units. Guests often prepare their own meals here to avoid some of the overpriced restaurants of Bermuda.

- **Sky-Top Cottages** (65 South Shore Road, Paget; ☎ 441/236-7984): This cottage cluster stands on a hilltop overlooking the southern shoreline, close to Elbow Beach. This is one of the more moderately priced groups of cottages on the island; each unit is named for a flower that grows in the garden, such as "Morning Glory." Most of the accommodations—English-style cottages—have a kitchenette where you can prepare your own meals. The cottages display a certain charm and character, and the property is well maintained.

15 The Best Restaurants

Admittedly, cuisine is not the reason you came to Bermuda in the first place, but some places do offer a memorable meal. See Chapter 6 for more details.

- **Once Upon a Table** (49 Serpentine Road, city of Hamilton; ☎ 441/295-8585): Savvy Bermudians, including one critic who has dined "at every single place on the island, even the dives," claim this is the best restaurant on the island. Even if you don't agree, you'll like the atmosphere: a romantic setting of Victorian memorabilia softened with flamboyant flowers.

- **Plantation** (46 Harrington Sound Rd., Bailey's Bay; ☎ 441/293-1188): In-the-know locals always refer to this place as either "real" or "truly" Bermudian. Freshly caught seafood, including the famed Bermuda lobster, dominates the fare. On the site of Leamington Caves, guests are seated at tables with flickering candles inside or, in good weather, al fresco in the tropical garden.

- **Waterlot Inn** (in the Southampton Princess; ☎ 441/238-8000): Housed in a historic inn and warehouse, this is the most famous venue for Sunday brunch on the island, but it's also an ideal choice for dinner. Everybody from Eleanor Roosevelt to Mark Twain has praised the French cuisine here, after sampling such dishes as poached chicken breast stuffed with foie gras.

- **Newport Room** (In the Southampton Princess; ☎ 441/238-8000): Also part of the hotel complex, this nautically decorated restaurant attracts the elite, especially yachties. The glistening teak decor makes it the most expensively furnished restaurant in Bermuda. Its French cuisine is worthy of the decor. The rack of lamb with a mixed nut crust is the stuff of which memories are made.

- **Tom Moore's Tavern** (Walsingham Lane, Hamilton Parish; ☎ 441/293-8020): Situated in a home that dates from 1652, this restaurant overlooks Walsingham Bay. Reportedly, the Irish poet Tom Moore was a frequent visitor. The menu, however, is not a relic from the past—it's quite innovative. Duck is a specialty, as is Bermuda lobster, but who can forget the quail in puff pastry stuffed with foie gras?

- **Fourways Inn** (1 Middle Road, Paget Parish; ☎ 441/236-6517): In this 1700s Georgian house of cedar and coral stone, you'll dine as they did back in the plantation days with traditional crystal, silver, and china. While you listen to the best piano music on the island, introduce yourself to a bowl of Bermudian fish chowder, followed by a choice of French or Bermudian dishes.

- **Henry VIII** (South Shore Road, Southampton Parish; ☎ 441/238-1977): The restaurant's mock Tudor decor is a bit corny, but sometimes it's nice to have fun with dinner—and this is what you'll find here. In spite of the decor the food is really good, as you get your fill of mussel pie (sometimes available) and such old pub favorites as steak-and-kidney pie. Some diners actually manage to "tuck in" desserts like bananas flambé in dark mellow rum.

- **Lantana Restaurant** (Somerset Bridge, Sandys Parish; ☎ 441/234-0141): At the western tip of the island, this enclave of elegance and grace fusses over its guests and presents them with a frequently changing continental menu. French classical cuisine is impeccably served, and there's a wine cellar worthy of the menu. Wahoo with orange peppercorn sauce is something to write home about.

- **Lobster Pot and Boat House Bar** (6 Bermudiana Road, city of Hamilton; ☎ 441/292-6898): If you don't find the most food-savvy islanders at the places above, they'll surely be at this local favorite. Against a nautical decor backdrop, the island's best regional dishes will delight you here. Black rum and sherry peppers might be the secret ingredients of their fish chowder, and their baked fish and lobster will tempt your tastebuds.

- **Black Horse Tavern** (34 Great Bay Road, St. David's Island; ☎ 441/293-9742): When you crave good, plentiful, and hearty food, as well as a casual atmosphere, this is the place to come. Islanders fill up most of the tables at night ordering their favorite dishes—everything from shark hash to curried conch.

Introducing Bermuda 2

Only about two hours from the southeastern coastline of the United States, another, quite different world comes into view as you approach it from the air. It is a world of natural beauty, with lush green hills, crystalline blue waters, and pink-hued sandy beaches. It is also a world of striking incongruities, where the modern coexists in harmony with the traditional and even the antiquated. That world is the British Crown Colony of Bermuda, an island in the Atlantic Ocean about 570 miles ESE of Cape Hatteras, N.C.

In Hamilton, the capital, you'll see colorful horse-drawn carriages ambling through tree-lined streets, indifferent to the sleek foreign cars that pass by. You'll see bobbies and businessmen walking around in shorts and knee-high socks—normal attire on this semitropical island where the annual average temperature is 70° Fahrenheit. You'll even see judges still wearing their customary powdered wigs as they head to Sessions House (the Parliament Building), where the Supreme Court meets.

Such a blend of contrasts—evident also in the island's architecture, music, and cuisine—gives Bermuda its character and makes it an enchanting place to visit. With its large luxury hotels, fashionable shops, and evening entertainment—as well as its beaches and historical sites—Bermuda is one of the world's most popular resorts, without some of the dangers and potential hassles that may await visitors who go to some of the sunnier destinations in the south such as Jamaica, Haiti, or Nassau in the Bahamas.

1 The Lay of the Land

"Bermuda" is actually a group of some 300 islands, islets, and coral rocks clustered in a fishhook-shaped chain about 22 miles long and 2 miles wide at the broadest point. Together, they're known as the Bermudas and form a landmass of about 21 square miles. Only 20 or so of the islands are inhabited. The largest one, called the "mainland," is Great Bermuda; about 14 miles long, it's linked to the other nearby major islands by a series of bridges and causeways. The capital of this archipelago, Hamilton, is situated on the mainland.

The other islands bear such names as Somerset, Watford, Boaz, and Ireland in the west, and St. George's and St. David's in the east. This chain of islands encloses the archipelago's major bodies of water, which include Castle Harbour, St. George's Harbour,

What's Special About Bermuda

Beaches
- Elbow Beach, Paget, which some say made Bermuda a vacation legend—it's tops for fun in the sun.
- Horseshoe Bay, Southampton, one-quarter mile of pink sand—this is the beach that is often shown in Sunday travel supplements.
- Warwick Long Bay, the pinkest of the pink sandy beaches, and also the sun strip with the longest stretch of sand.

Great Towns/Villages
- Hamilton, the colony's capital, in pretty pastels and whites and the center for shopping.
- St. George's, Bermuda's first capital, founded in 1612—a town filled with historical sights.

Places to Explore
- Ireland Island, a cruise-ship dock and tourist village, site of the Royal Naval Dockyard and the Bermuda Maritime Museum.
- Bermuda Railway Trail, stretching along the old train right-of-way for 21 miles and crossing three of the islands that make up the Bermuda archipelago.
- Fort St. Catherine, at St. George's—now a museum—towers over the beach where the shipwrecked *Sea Venture* crew first landed in 1609.
- Verdmont, Smith's Parish, an 18th-century mansion built on land once owned by the founder of South Carolina.
- Fort Hamilton, a massive Victorian fortification overlooking the city of Hamilton and its harbor.

Natural Spectacles
- Crystal Caves, Bailey's Bay, translucent formations of stalagmites and stalactites, including a crystal-clear lake.
- Leamington Caves, also at Bailey's Bay, with a grotto with crystal formations and underground lakes—first discovered in 1908.

Events and Festivals
- Bermuda Festival, a six-week winter International Festival of the Performing Arts—drama, dance, jazz, classical and popular music, and more.
- Bermuda College Weeks during the spring break, a ritual that draws some 10,000 students from the United States.

Harrington Sound, and Great Sound. Most of the other smaller islands, or islets, lie within these bodies of water.

Bermuda is situated far north of the Tropic of Cancer, which cuts through the Bahamian archipelago—about 775 miles SE of New York City, some 1,030 miles NE of Miami, and nearly 3,450 miles away from London. It has a balmy climate year-round, with sunshine prevailing almost every day. The chief source of Bermuda's mild weather is the Gulf Stream, a broad belt of warm water formed by equatorial currents, whose northern reaches separate the Bermuda islands from North America and, with the prevailing northeast winds, temper the wintry blasts that sweep across the Atlantic from west and north.

Bermuda is based on the upper parts of an extinct volcano, which may date back 100 million years. Through millennia, wind and water have brought limestone deposits and formed the islands far from any continental landmass—the closest is Cape Hatteras.

The first recorded discovery of the islands was made by the Spanish in the early 1500s (see "History 101," below). The uncharted islands were a navigational menace to ships that followed the trade routes of the Atlantic, as Spanish vessels did on voyages from the New World. Bermuda's location is at a point where galleons from New Spain could easily run into trouble in stormy weather, and the eroded wreckage of many ships, scattered on the ocean floor amid reefs and shoals, bears mute testimony to such tragedies.

Until the mid-17th century or so, the Bermudas were known to seafarers as the "Isles of Devils." They had probably contributed to the popular pre-Columbian belief that ships sailing too far west from Europe fell over the edge of the earth into a monster-filled pit. Many ships sailing too close to these remote and uninhabited islands came to ruin on the treacherous reefs just below the ocean's surface. Even Shakespeare was familiar with the reputation of the Isles of Devils, making "the still-vex't Bermoothes" the setting for *The Tempest*.

THE PARISHES IN BRIEF

The islands of Bermuda are divided, for administrative purposes, into several parishes. They are:

Sandys Parish   In the far western part of the archipelago, Sandys (pronounced Sands) Parish is centered around Somerset Village. This parish, which is named for Sir Edwin Sandys, a major shareholder of the 1610 Bermuda Company, encompasses the islands of Ireland, Boaz, and Somerset. Somerset Long Bay is the biggest and best public beach in Bermuda's West End.

Southampton Parish   Going east, Southampton Parish (named for the third earl of Southampton) stretches from Riddells Bay to Tucker's Island, site of the U.S. Naval Air Station Annex. This parish, which is split by Middle Road, is known for its public beach stretching along Horseshoe Bay. The parish is the site of such famed resorts as the Southampton Princess.

Warwick Parish   Named in honor of another shareholder in the Bermuda Company (the second earl of Warwick), this parish lies between Southampton and Paget Parishes. Known for its golf courses and hotels, it also includes Warwick Long Bay (along the south shore), one of Bermuda's best public beaches.

Paget Parish   East of Warwick Parish, Paget Parish begins at Hamilton Harbour in the east and lies directly south of the capital city of Hamilton. Named after the fourth Lord Paget, it has many residences and historic homes. It is also the site of the 36-acre Botanical Gardens.

Pembroke Parish   This parish includes the capital city of Hamilton (the only full-fledged city in Bermuda), which is most often viewed as passengers arrive aboard cruise ships in Hamilton Harbour. Named after the third earl of Pembroke, the parish is home to one-quarter of Bermuda's population.

Devonshire Parish   Lying east of both Paget and Pembroke Parishes, near the geographic center of the archipelago, Devonshire Parish is green and hilly. It has some housekeeping apartments, a cottage colony, and one of Bermuda's oldest churches, the Old Devonshire Parish Church, which dates from 1716. Named for the first earl of Devonshire, the parish is traversed by three of Bermuda's major roads—the aptly named South Road, Middle Road, and North Road.

Smith's Parish   Directly east of Devonshire Parish, Smith's Parish opens onto Harrington Sound along its eastern flank. Its northern and southern coasts face the

Atlantic. Named after Sir Thomas Smith, another member of the Bermuda Company, the parish includes Flatts Village as well as two bird sanctuaries.

Hamilton Parish   Not to be confused with the city of Hamilton (which is in Pembroke Parish), Hamilton Parish lies directly north of Harrington Sound, opening onto the Atlantic. Named for the second marquis of Hamilton, the parish ropes itself around Harrington Sound, a saltwater lake stretching some 6 miles. On its eastern periphery, it opens onto Castle Harbour.

St. George's Parish   At Bermuda's extreme eastern end, this historic parish encompasses several different islands; the two largest are St. George's Island and St. David's Island. St. George's Island was the site of the *Sea Venture*'s wreck in 1609. Its major settlement, St. George's (founded in 1612), was once the capital of Bermuda. Among its many historic buildings is St. Peter's Church, the oldest continuously used Protestant house of worship in the Western Hemisphere. The parish is flanked by Castle Harbour on its western and southern edges and divided into two parts by St. George's Harbour. St. David's Island is linked to the rest of Bermuda by the Severn Bridge, which lies near the U.S. Naval Air Station Annex and the colony's international airport. Those who inhabit this most easterly part of Bermuda are long-time sailors and fishers. St. George's Parish also includes Tucker's Town, founded in 1616 by Governor Daniel Tucker on the opposite shore of Castle Harbour.

2   The Natural Environment

PLANT LIFE

Bermuda's temperate climate, abundant sunshine, fertile soil, and adequate moisture account for some of the most verdant gardens in the Atlantic. Some of the best of these, such as the Botanical Gardens in Paget Parish, are open to the public (see Chapter 7, "What to See & Do"). Without the Gulf Stream, which provides warm air currents, the normal climate would be much colder. Bermudian gardeners pride themselves on the mixture of temperate-zone and subtropical plants that thrive on the island, despite the salty air.

Bermuda's once proud cedar forests succumbed to the effects of commercialization (many trees were felled for their copper-colored wood, used in boatbuilding) and a disastrous blight that struck in the late 1930s. The loss of the cedar forests is said to have removed valuable nesting sites for birds, as well as some of the island's most effective windbreaks.

Today, those native stands have been replaced on a large scale with casuarinas (Australian pines) and an array of deciduous and evergreen trees and shrubs (an estimated 500 species) imported from the far corners of what used to be the British Empire. Recent attempts at reforesting Bermuda with scale-resistant hybrids of the native cedar have proved moderately successful.

No matter how poor the soil in certain places, Bermuda is blessed with copious and varied plants. Examples include the indigenous sea grape, which flourishes along the island's sandy coastlines, preferring sand and saltwater to more arable soil, and the cassava plant, whose roots resemble the tubers of sweet potatoes. When ground into flour and soaked to remove a mild poison, these roots comprise the main

Impressions

You go to heaven if you want to—I'd rather stay here in Bermuda.
                                                    —Mark Twain, in a letter to Elizabeth Wallace, 1910

ingredient for Bermuda's traditional Christmas pies. Also growing wild and abundant are prickly pears, aromatic fennel, yucca, and a spiked-leaf plant that bears, in season, a single white flower, known as a Spanish bayonet.

To the early colonial settlers, Bermuda's only native palm, the palmetto, proved particularly useful. Its leaves were used to thatch colonial roofs. When crushed and fermented, the leaves produced a strong alcoholic drink called bibby, whose effects were condemned by the early Puritans. Its leaves were also fashioned into women's hats during a brief period in the 1600s, when they represented the height of fashion in London.

The banana, which flourishes today in Bermuda and constitutes one of its most dependable sources of fresh fruit, was introduced to the island in the early 1600s. It is believed that Bermudian bananas were the first to be brought back to London from the New World. Immediately they created a sensation, leading to the cultivation of bananas in many other British colonies.

The plant that probably contributed most to Bermuda's renown was the Bermuda onion *(Allium cepa)*. Imported from England in 1616, and later grown from seed brought from the Spanish and Portuguese islands of Tenerife and Madeira, the Bermuda onion became so famous along the eastern coast of the United States that Bermudians themselves became known as "onions." Sadly, however, during the 1930s Bermuda's flourishing export trade in onions declined because of high tariffs, increased competition from similar species grown in Texas (and elsewhere), and the limited arable land on the island.

Today, what you'll see decorating Bermuda's gently rolling landscapes are oleander, hibiscus, royal poinciana, poinsettia, bougainvillea, and dozens of other flowering shrubs and vines. Of the island's dozen or so species of morning glory, three are indigenous; they tend to grow rampant and overwhelm everything else in a garden.

Popular trees include pine, pawpaw (used in olden days for treating warts and fungal diseases of the skin), the indigenous olivewood bark, palm, casuarina, fiddlewood, the ubiquitous bay grape, and a luxuriant fruit tree known as loquat, which was introduced to the island by one of its governors in 1850. Indigenous flowers include the Bermudiana (sometimes known as the Bermuda iris), Darrell's fleabane (a member of the daisy family), and the maidenhair fern. Today, nearly all of Bermuda's important plants are sheltered in the already mentioned Botanical Gardens in Paget Parish.

ANIMAL LIFE

From birders to scuba divers, many visitors come to Bermuda for a close encounter with its fish and animal life. Because of the almost total lack of natural freshwater ponds and lakes, Bermuda's amphibians have adapted to seawater or to slightly brackish water. Amphibians include the tree frog *(Eleutherodactylus Johnstonei and Eleutherodactylus Gossei)*, whose nighttime chirping is sometimes mistaken by newcomers for the song of birds. Small and camouflaged by the leafy matter of the forest floor, the tree frog may be spotted between April and November.

More visible are Bermuda's giant toads, or road toads *(Bufo marinus)*, which sometimes reach the size of an adult human's palm. Imported from Guyana in the 1870s in the hope of controlling the island's cockroach population, they search out the nighttime warmth of the asphalt roads, and are often crushed by cars in the process; they are especially prevalent after a soaking rain. The road toads are not venomous— and, contrary to legend, they do not cause warts.

Island reptiles include colonies of harmless lizards, often seen sunning themselves on rocks until the approach of humans or predators sends them away.

The best-known species is the Bermuda rock lizard *(Eumeces longirostris),* also known as a skink, which is said to have been the only nonmarine, nonflying vertebrate in Bermuda before the arrival of European colonists. Imported reptiles include the Somerset lizard *(Anolis Roquet),* whose black eye patches give it the look of a bashful bandit, and the Jamaican anole *(Anolis Grahami),* a kind of color-changing chameleon.

Partly because of its ample food sources, Bermuda is home to abundant bird life; many species nest upon the island's terrain during their annual migrations. Most of these birds arrive during the cooler winter months, usually between Christmas and Eastertime. Serious birders, often from the U.S. mainland, have recorded almost 40 different species of eastern warblers, which peacefully coexist with species of martin, doves, egrets, South American terns, herons, fork-tailed flycatchers, and even some species from as far away as the Arctic Circle. Two of the most visible imported species are the cardinal, probably introduced during the 1700s, and the kiskadee. Imported from Trinidad in 1957 to control lizards and flies, the kiskadee has instead wreaked havoc on the island's commercial fruit crops.

The once-abundant eastern bluebird has been greatly reduced in number since the depletion of the cedar trees, its preferred habitat. Another bird native to Bermuda is the gray and white petrel, known locally as a *cahow,* which burrows for most of the year in the sands of the isolated eastern islands; the rest of the year it feeds at sea, floating for hours in the warm waters of the Gulf Stream. One of the most rarely sighted birds in the world, and once regarded as extinct, it is now protected by the Bermudian government.

Also native to Bermuda is the cliff-dwelling tropic bird, which can be recognized by the elongated plumage of its white tail. Resembling a swallow, it is considered the island's harbinger of spring because of its annual appearance in March.

Although the gardens and golf courses of many of the island's hotels attract dozens of birds, some of the finest bird-watching sites are maintained either by the Bermuda Audubon Society or the National Trust. Isolated sites known for sheltering thousands of native and migrating birds include Paget Marsh, just south of Hamilton, the Walsingham Trust in Hamilton Parish, and Spittal Pond in Smith's Parish.

In the deep waters off the shores of Bermuda, photographers have recorded some of the finest game fish in the world, including blackfin tuna, marlin, swordfish, wahoo, dolphin, sailfish, and barracuda. Also prevalent are bonefish and pompano, both of which prefer sun-flooded shallow waters closer to shore. Any beachcomber is likely to come across hundreds of oval-shaped chitons *(Chiton tuberculatus),* a mollusk that adheres tenaciously to rocks within tidal flats (locally, this mollusk is known as "suck-rock").

Beware of the Portuguese man-o'-war *(Physalia physalis),* a floating colony of jellyfish whose stinging tentacles sometimes reach 50 feet in length. Washed up on Bermuda beaches, usually between March and July, it can sting even though it may appear dead. Give this dangerous and venomous marine creature a wide berth: Severe stings could require hospitalization.

The most prevalent marine animal in Bermuda is responsible for the formation of the island's greatest tourist attraction, its miles of pale-pink sand. Much of the sand is composed of broken shells, pieces of coral, and the calcium carbonate remains of other marine invertebrates. The pinkest pieces are shards of crushed shell from a single-celled animal called *foraminifer.* Its vivid pink skeleton is pierced with holes, through which the animal extends its rootlike feet *(pseudopodia),* which cling to the underside of the island's reefs during the animal's brief life and are then washed ashore.

3   Bermuda Today

Even though the island long ago attained self-governing status, its social life still reflects British traditions. A profound sense of decorum is the most noticeable social feature on the island; it accounts for the somewhat formal dress code, which requires that even in ordinary social gatherings men should wear jackets and neckties and women should wear casually elegant clothes. Such attire is common during afternoon tea, a ritual observed as punctiliously on the manicured lawns of Pembroke Parish as in the finest hotels of London. Adherence to ritual is evident also during family events, such as weddings and funerals, when one is careful to do things precisely as they are done back in Britain, in accordance with the rites and traditions of the Church of England.

Politeness and formality are the norm. Examples of formality include the island-ers' clean-cut style, as well as their well-kept cottages and carefully tended gardens, which serve to enhance the natural setting of Bermuda and give it an unmistakable stamp of civilized orderliness. It even extends to a love of animals, which is here regarded as a peculiarly English virtue.

THE PEOPLE

Islanders who live in more troubled areas to the south often look with envy upon the residents of Bermuda, who have a much higher standard of living than is found in the Caribbean, with no personal income tax and virtually no unemployment. Today's 60,000 residents are mostly of African, British, and Portuguese descent. Some Ber-mudians can even trace their ancestry back to the first settlers and some to success-ful privateers and slaves. The population density, one of the highest in the world, is about 3,210 per square mile. About 61% of the population is black, and 39% is white. Many other minority groups are represented, the largest and most established being the Portuguese. The color bar, which continued even after slavery was abol-ished, has almost disappeared, and African-Bermudians have assumed a prominent place in the island's civic and government affairs. There is no illiteracy, and you won't see any slums or poverty.

As mentioned, the British influence is prevalent in Bermuda, what with predomi-nantly English accents, police wearing helmets like those of London bobbies, and cars driving on the left. Schools are also run along the lines of the British system and pro-vide a high standard of preparatory education. Children 5 to 16 years of age must attend school. The Bermuda College, which offers academic and technical studies, boasts a renowned hotel and catering program.

POLITICS

Bermuda was accorded the right of self-government in 1968. It is therefore a self-governing dependency of Great Britain, with a governor appointed by the queen of England and representing Her Majesty's government in the areas of external affairs, defense, and internal security. The 12-member cabinet is headed by a premier. The elected legislature, referred to as the Legislative Council, consists of a 40-member House of Assembly and an 11-member Senate. Bermuda's oldest political party is the Progressive Labour Party, formed in 1963. In 1964 the United Bermuda Party was established and is the party currently in power. Bermuda's legal system is founded on common law. Judicial responsibility falls to the Supreme Court, headed by a chief justice. English law is the fundamental guide, and in court English customs prevail, such as the tradition of judges wearing wigs and robes.

Bermuda Shorts

Bermuda shorts originated with the British army in India. Later, when British troops were stationed in Bermuda, they were issued shorts as part of the military's tropical kit gear.

Bermuda shorts are now considered suitable attire for the Bermuda businessman and are worn with a blazer, collared shirt, tie, and knee socks. They should not be more than 3 inches above the knee and must have a 3-inch hem.

Each of the nine parishes into which the island is divided is managed by an advisory council. The capital, Hamilton, is located in Pembroke Parish.

THE ECONOMY

Bermuda's political stability has proved beneficial to the economy, which relies heavily on tourism and foreign investment.

For much of the island's early history, the major industry was shipbuilding, made possible by the abundant cedar forests. But when, in the second half of the 19th century, wooden ships gave way to steel ones, the island turned to tourism. Today tourism, with annual revenues estimated at $450 million, is the leading industry. Approximately 550,000 tourists visit Bermuda each year. An estimated 86% arrive from the United States, 4% from Britain, and 7% from Canada. Bermuda enjoys a 42% repeat-visitor rate.

Because Bermuda has enacted favorable economic measures, more than 6,000 international companies are registered there; these companies are engaged mostly in investment holding, insurance, commercial trading, consulting services, and shipping—but fewer than 275 companies are actually located on the island. Bermuda has no corporate or income tax.

The island's leading exports are pharmaceuticals, concentrates (primarily black rum and sherry peppers), essences, and beverages. Leading imports include foodstuffs, alcoholic beverages, clothing, furniture, fuel, electrical appliances, and motor vehicles. Bermuda's major trading partners are the United States, Great Britain, Canada, the Netherlands, and the Caribbean states.

RELIGION

About a third of Bermuda's population adheres to the Church of England, which historically has been the dominant religion in the colony. Indeed, the division of Bermuda into nine parishes dates from 1618, when each parish was required by law to have its own Anglican Church, to the exclusion of any other. That division still exists today, but more for administrative than religious purposes.

Religious tolerance is now guaranteed by law. There are some 10,000 Catholics, many of them from the Portuguese Azores. Many people also belong to Protestant sects whose roots trace back to former slave churches, such as the African Methodist Episcopal Church. Established in 1816 by African Americans, this sect took root in Bermuda around 1870. Today the church has about 7,000 members.

Also found in Bermuda are Seventh-Day Adventists, Presbyterians, Baptists, Lutherans, and Mormons. Less prevalent are a handful of Jews, Muslims, Rastafarians, and Jehovah's Witnesses.

Bermuda today boasts more than 110 churches, an average of five per square mile. They range from the moss-encrusted parish churches established in the earliest days of the colony to modest structures with only a handful of members.

4 History 101

THE EARLY YEARS The discovery of the Bermuda islands is attributed to the Spanish, probably the navigator Juan Bermúdez, sometime before 1511, for in that year a map was published in the *Legatio Babylonica* that included "La Bermuda" among the Atlantic islands. A little more than a century later, the British staked a claim and began colonization.

In 1609 the flagship of Admiral Sir George Somers, the *Sea Venture*, while en route to Jamestown, Virginia, was wrecked on Bermuda's reefs. The dauntless crew built two pinnaces (small sailing ships) and headed on to the American colony, but three sailors hid out and remained on the island. They were the first settlers of Bermuda.

Just three years after the wreck of the *Sea Venture*, the Bermuda islands were included in the charter of the Virginia Company; 60 colonists were sent there from England, and St. George's Town was founded soon after.

Bermuda's status as a colony dates from 1620, when the first parliament convened (it is thus the oldest parliament in continuous existence in the British Empire, now the British Commonwealth). In 1684, Bermuda became a British Crown Colony under King Charles II. Sir Robert Robinson was appointed the Crown's first governor.

Slavery became a part of life in Bermuda shortly after the official settlement. Although the majority of slaves came from Africa, a few were Native Americans. Later, Scots imprisoned for fighting against Cromwell were sent to the islands, followed in 1651 by Irish slaves. The fate of these bond servants, however, was not as cruel as that of plantation slaves in America and the West Indies. All slaves were freed by the British Emancipation Act of 1834.

RELATIONS WITH AMERICA Bermuda established close links with the American colonies. The islanders set up a thriving mercantile trade on the eastern seaboard, especially with southern ports. The major commodity sold by Bermuda's merchant ships was salt from Turks Island.

During the American Revolution, trade with loyalist Bermuda was cut off by the rebellious colonies, despite the network of family connections and close friendships that bound them. The cutoff in trade proved a great hardship for the islanders, who, having chosen seafaring to farming, depended

Dateline

- **ca. 1511** Juan Bermúdez discovers Bermuda while sailing aboard the Spanish ship *La Garza*.
- **1609** The British ship *Sea Venture* is wrecked upon the reefs of Bermuda; all on board make it to shore safely and the settlement of Bermuda begins.
- **1612** The Virginia Company dispatches the *Plough* to Bermuda with 60 colonists on board. Richard Moore is appointed governor of Bermuda.
- **1620** The first Bermuda parliament session is held in St. Peter's Church, St. George's.
- **1684** The Bermuda Company's charter is taken over by the British Crown. Sir Robert Robinson is appointed the Crown's first governor of Bermuda.
- **1775** Gunpowder is stolen in St. George's and is shipped to the American colonies for use against the British.
- **1861** Bermuda becomes involved in the American Civil War when it runs supplies to the South to undermine the Union's blockade.
- **1919–33** Bermudians profit from Prohibition in the United States by engaging in rum-running.
- **1940–45** Bermuda plays an important role in World War II counterespionage for the Allies.
- **1946** The automobile is introduced into Bermuda.
- **1957** Great Britain withdraws militarily after two centuries of rule.

continues

- 1963 Voter registration is open to all citizens.
- 1973 The governor, Sir Richard Sharples, and an aide are assassinated.
- 1979 Bermudians celebrate their own Gina Swainson as winner of Miss World contest.
- 1987 Hurricane Emily causes millions of dollars' worth of damage; some 70 people are injured.
- 1990 Prime Minister Margaret Thatcher confers with President George Bush.
- 1991 Prime Minister John Major meets with President Bush.

heavily on America for their supply of food. Many of them, now deprived of profitable trade routes, turned to privateering, piracy, and "wrecking" (salvaging goods from wrecked or foundered ships).

Britain's loss of its important American colonial ports led to a naval buildup in Bermuda. It was from there that ships and troops sailed in 1814 to burn Washington, D.C., and the White House.

Bermuda got a new lease on economic life during the American Civil War. The island was sympathetic to the Confederacy and, with approval of the British government, ran the blockade that the Union had placed on exports, especially of cotton, by the southern states. St. George's Harbour was a principal Atlantic base for the lucrative business of smuggling manufactured goods into Confederate ports and bringing out cargoes of cotton and turpentine.

When the Confederacy fell, so did Bermuda's economy. Seeing no immediate source of income from trading with the U.S. East Coast, the islanders turned their attention to agriculture and found that the colony's fertile soil and salubrious climate produced excellent vegetables. Portuguese immigrants were brought in as farmers, and soon celery, potatoes, tomatoes, and especially onions were being shipped to the New York market (indeed, so brisk was the onion trade that Hamilton became known as "Onion Town").

During Prohibition, Bermudians again profited by developments in the United States as they engaged in the lucrative business of rum-running. Although the distance from the island to the East Coast was too great for quick crossings in small booze-laden boats (as could be done from the Bahamas and Cuba), Bermuda nevertheless accounted for a good part of the alcoholic beverages transported illegally to the United States before the repeal of Prohibition in 1933.

A HOTBED OF ESPIONAGE   Bermuda played a key role in World War II counterespionage for the Allies. The story is told dramatically in *A Man Called Intrepid*, by William Stevenson, about the "secret war" with Nazi Germany.

Beneath the Hamilton Princess Hotel, a carefully trained staff worked to decode radio signals to and from German submarines and other vessels operating in the Atlantic, close to the United States and the islands offshore. Unknown to the Germans, the British, early in the war, had broken the Nazi code through use of a captured German coding machine called "Enigma." The British also intercepted and examined mail between Europe and the United States.

Bermuda served as a refueling stop for airplanes flying between the two continents. While pilots were being entertained at the Yacht Club, the mail would be taken off the carriers and examined by experts. An innocent-looking series of letters from Lisbon, for example, often contained messages written in invisible ink. These letters were part of a vast German spy network. The British became skilled at opening sealed envelopes, examining their written contents, and then carefully resealing them.

These surreptitious letter-readers were called "trappers." Many of them were young women without any previous experience in counterespionage work, yet some performed very well. As Stevenson wrote, it was soon discovered that, "by some quirk in the law of averages, the girls who shone in this work had well-turned ankles." A

The Bermuda Triangle

The area known as the Bermuda Triangle encompasses a 1.5-million-square-mile expanse of open sea between Bermuda, Puerto Rico, and the southeastern shoreline of the United States. It is the source of the most famous—and certainly the most baffling—legend associated with Bermuda.

The legend of the Bermuda Triangle persists in many guises, some less credible than others, despite attempts by skeptics to dismiss them as fanciful tales. Can some of them be true? Here are three:

In 1881 a British-registered ship, the *Ellen Austin*, encountered an unnamed vessel in good condition sailing aimlessly without a crew. The *Austin*'s captain ordered a handful of his best seamen to board the mysterious vessel and sail it to Newfoundland. A few days later, the two ships encountered each other again on the high seas— but to everyone's alarm, the crewmen who had transferred from the *Austin* were nowhere to be found on the other ship!

Another often-told tale concerns the later disappearance of a merchant ship called the *Marine Sulphur Queen*. It disappeared suddenly and without warning, and no one could say why. The weather was calm when the ship set sail from Bermuda, and apparently everything on board was fine, too, for no distress signal was received from the crew. In looking for explanations, some have held that the ship probably had a weakened hull that gave way, causing it to descend quickly to the bottom. Others attribute its loss to the mysterious forces that are behind all the Bermuda Triangle stories.

The most famous of all the Bermuda Triangle legends occurred in 1945. On December 5, five U.S. Navy bombers departed from Fort Lauderdale, Florida, on a routine mission. The weather was fine; no storm of any kind threatened. A short time into the flight, however, the leader of the squadron suddenly radioed that they were lost—and then the radio went silent; all efforts by the ground to establish further communication proved fruitless. A rescue plane was quickly dispatched to search for the squadron—but it, too, disappeared. The navy ordered a search, which lasted five days, but there was no evidence of any wreckage. To this day, the disappearance of the squadron and of the rescue plane remains a mystery as deep as the waters of the region.

How do those who believe in the Bermuda Triangle legend explain these phenomena? Some contend that the area is a time warp to another universe; others, that the waters off Bermuda are the site of the lost kingdom of Atlantis, whose power sources still function deep beneath the surface of the water. Still others believe that there exists a perpetual focusing of laser rays upon the region from outer space, or that underwater signaling devices are guiding invaders from other planets, who have chosen the site for the systematic collection of human beings for scientific observation and experimentation.

medical officer involved with the project even reported it as "fairly certain that a girl with unshapely legs would make a bad trapper." So, amazingly, the word went out that women seeking recruitment as trappers would have to display their gams.

During the course of their work, these women (and their colleagues, to be sure) discovered one of the methods by which the Germans were transmitting secret messages: They would shrink a whole page of regularly typed text down to the size of a tiny dot and then conceal the dot under an innocuous-looking punctuation mark, such as a comma or period! The staff likened these messages with their secret-bearing dots to plum duff, a popular English dessert. For these "punctuation dots [were] scattered through a letter like raisins in the suet puddings." The term "duff method" then came to be applied to the manner in which the Germans were sending military and other messages through the mail.

When the United States entered the war, it assigned Federal Bureau of Investigation agents to Bermuda. There, they joined the British in their intelligence operations.

BERMUDA COMES INTO ITS OWN   In 1953, British prime minister Winston Churchill chose Bermuda, which he had visited during the war, as the site for a conference with U.S. president Dwight D. Eisenhower and the French premier. Several such high-level gatherings have followed in the decades since; the most recent one, between British prime minister John Major and U.S. president George Bush, took place in 1991.

Bermuda's increasing prominence led to changes in its relationship with Great Britain and the United States as well as significant developments on the island itself. In 1957, after nearly two centuries of occupation, Britain withdrew its military forces, having decided to grant self-government to its oldest colony. The United States, however, under the Lend-Lease Agreement signed in 1941 and due to expire in 2040, continues to maintain a naval air station at Kindley Field, in St. George's Parish. Nearby, on Cooper's Island, the U.S. National Aeronautics and Space Administration operates a space-tracking system.

As Bermudians assumed greater control over their own affairs, they began to adopt significant social changes, but at a pace that did not satisfy some critics. Although racial segregation in hotels and restaurants ceased in 1959, schools were not integrated until 1971. Women received the right to vote in 1944, but the law still restricted suffrage only to property holders. However, this was rescinded in 1963, when voter registration was opened to all citizens.

During the rocky road to self-government, Bermuda was not without its share of problems. Serious rioting broke out in 1968, and British troops were called back to restore order. Then, in 1973, Sir Richard Sharples, the governor, was assassinated; in 1977 those believed to have been the assassins were themselves executed. These events, which occurred at a time when several of the islands in the region as well as in the Caribbean were experiencing domestic difficulties, proved to be the exception rather than the rule. For in the years since then, the social and political climate in Bermuda has been markedly calm; this is better for the island's economic well-being, since it encourages the industries on which Bermuda depends, including tourism.

In 1972, the Bermuda dollar gained its independence from the pound sterling; it is now pegged through gold to the U.S. dollar on an equal basis.

During the 1990s Bermudians have once again been discussing the political status of their island. Some people feel it would be advantageous to achieve complete independence from Britain, while others believe it is in Bermuda's best interest to maintain its present ties to the Crown.

Impressions

Bermuda, despite her small size, her isolation and her position among evil reefs and evil Atlantic [hurricane] weather, was [once for imperial Britain] and is [now for superpower America] of considerable military importance.

—Simon Winchester, *The Sun Never Sets:*
Travels to the Remaining Outposts of the British Empire (1985)

5   Local Art

Art in Bermuda today doesn't even pretend to have reached the status enjoyed by such islands as Haiti and Jamaica. A critic once wrote that "Bermuda is the perfect place for the Sunday painter." Some serious art, however, is displayed at such places as the Masterworks Foundation Gallery at Bermuda House in Hamilton (see Chapter 10). But a lot of Bermuda art is still of the watercolor variety, with idyllic landscapes and seascapes sold at various shops around the island.

Bermuda's earliest works of art were portraits painted by itinerant artists for the local gentry. Most of these were by the English-born Joseph Blackburn, whose brief visit to Bermuda in the mid-1700s led to requests by local landowners to have their portraits painted. Many of these portraits can be found today in the Tucker House Museum in St. George's. A handful of portraits from the same period were done by the American-born artist John Green.

Also prized are a series of paintings from the mid-19th century depicting sailing ships. They're signed "Edward James," but the artist's real identity remains unknown.

During the 19th century, the traditions of the English landscape painters, particularly the Romantics, came into vogue in Bermuda. Constable, with his lush and evocative landscapes, became the model for many.

Other than a few naive artists, however, whose works showed great vitality but little sense of perspective, most of Bermuda's landscape paintings were executed by British military officers and their wives. Their body of work includes a blend of true-to-life landscapes with an occasional stylized rendering of the picturesque or Romantic tradition then in vogue in England. Among the most famous of the uniformed artists was Lt. E. G. Hallewell, a member of the Royal Engineers, whose illustrations of the island's topography were used for planning certain naval installations.

Another celebrated landscapist was Thomas Driver, who arrived as a member of the Royal Engineers in 1814 and remained on the island until 1836. Trained to reproduce detailed landscape observations as a means of assisting military and naval strategists, he later modified his style to become more elegant and evocative. He soon abandoned the military and became a full-time painter of Bermuda scenes. Because of Driver's attention to detail, his works are frequently reproduced by scholars and art historians who hope to recapture the aesthetic and architectural elements of the island's earliest buildings.

Later in the 19th century, other artists depicted the flora of Bermuda. Lady Lefroy, whose husband was governor of the island between 1871 and 1877, painted the trees, shrubs, fish, flowers, and animals of the island in much-imitated detail. Later, at scattered intervals during their careers, such internationally known artists as Winslow Homer, Andrew Wyeth, George Ault, and French-born impressionist and cubist Albert Gleizes have all painted Bermudian scenes.

Among today's prominent Bermuda-born artists is Alfred Birdsey. His watercolors represent some of the most elegiac visual odes to Bermuda ever produced. Birdsey's paintings, as well as those of other artists mentioned above, may be viewed in galleries around the island. Protecting these works from climate damage, however, is a constant problem. As the administrator of one major art gallery explained, "Bermuda's climate is unquestionably the worst in the world for the toll it takes on works of art, with three elements—humidity, salt, and ultraviolet light all playing their part." The U.S. Navy uses Bermuda to test the durability of paint; if paint can endure the sun and humidity in Bermuda, it can withstand almost any tropical environment. The island's humidity is especially harmful to a painting; the canvas can absorb moisture, and it will later appear as mildew coming through the oils. Some very valuable paintings have been totally destroyed. As a result, more and more galleries and exhibition rooms on the island have installed air-conditioning.

In addition to painters, Bermuda also boasts several noted sculptors, including Chelsey Trott, who produces cedarwood carvings, and Desmond Hale Fountain, who creates works in bronze. Fountain's life-size statues often show children in the act of reading or snoozing in the shade.

6 Bermuda Style

Today, Bermuda style is best represented by its architecture—those darling little pink cottages that grace postcards. The architecture of Bermuda is considered its only truly indigenous art form—a collection of idiosyncratic building techniques dictated by climate and the types of building materials available on the island. The early settlers quickly recognized the virtues of the island's most visible building material, coral stone. A conglomerate of primeval sand packed beside crushed bits of coral and shells, this stone has been quarried for generations on Bermuda. Cut into oblong building blocks, it is strong yet porous; however, it would be unusable in any area where the climate entails cycles of freezing and thawing (this would cause it to crack). Mortared together with imported cement, the blocks provide solid and durable foundations and walls.

Bermuda's colonial architects ingeniously found a way to deal with a serious problem on the island—the lack of an abundant supply of fresh water. During the construction of a house or any other sort of building, workers excavated a water tank (cistern) first, either as a separate underground cavity away from the house or as a foundation for the building. These cisterns served to collect rainwater funneled from rooftops via specially designed channels and gutters.

The design of these roof-to-cellar water conduits led to the development of what is considered Bermuda's most distinct architectural feature, the gleaming rooftops of its houses. Gently sloping, and invariably painted a dazzling white, they are constructed of quarried limestone slabs sawed into "slates" about an inch thick and between 12 and 18 inches square. Roofs are installed over a framework of cedarwood beams (or, more recently, pitch pine or pressure-treated wood beams), which are interconnected with a series of cedar laths. The slates are joined together with cement-based mortar in overlapping rows, then covered with a cement wash and one or several coats of whitewash or synthetic paint. This process corrects the porosity of the coral limestone slates, rendering them watertight. The result is a layered effect, since each course of limestone appears in high relief atop its neighbor. The angular, step-shaped geometry of Bermudian roofs has inspired watercolorists and painters to emphasize the rhythmically graceful shadows that trace the path of the sun across the rooflines.

Bermudian houses—unlike those in the Caribbean—are designed without amply proportioned hanging eaves. Large eaves may be desirable because of the shade they afford, but smaller ones have proved to be structurally sounder during tropical storms. Wind gathers more lifting power from an overhanging eave than from any other part of a roofline.

No discussion of Bermudian architecture should neglect to mention a garden feature that many visitors consider distinctive of Bermuda—the moon gate. A rounded span of coral blocks arranged in a circular arch above a wooden gate, the moon gate was introduced to Bermuda around 1920 by the Duke of Westminster's landscape architect; the inspiration came from China and Japan.

Impressions

They be so terrible to all that ever touched on them, and such tempests, thunders, and other fearefull objects are seene and heard about them, that they be called commonly, the Devils Ilands, and are feared and avoyded of all sea travellers alive, above any other place in the world.
—William Strachy, *A True Reportory of the Wracke and Redemption of Sir Thomas Gates* (1610), in *Purchas His Pilgrimes* (1625)

The interiors of Bermudian houses are usually graced with large windows, ample doors, and, in the older buildings, floors and moldings crafted from copper-colored planks of the almost extinct Bermuda cedar. Also common is a feature found in colonial buildings in the Caribbean and other western Atlantic islands as well—tray ceilings, so named because of their resemblance to an inverted serving tray. This shape allows ceilings to follow the lines of the inside roof construction into what would otherwise have been unused space. The effect of these ceilings, whether sheathed in plaster or planking, gives Bermudian interiors unusual height and airiness even if the building has relatively low eaves.

Despite the distinctively individualistic nature of Bermuda's architecture, the island's interior decors remain faithfully (some say rigidly) British, and somewhat more formal than you might have expected. Interior designs seem to be a felicitous cross between what you'd expect in a New England seaside cottage and what a nautically minded society hostess might add to her drawing room in London. Bermuda homes usually have ample Chippendale or Queen Anne furniture (sometimes authentic, sometimes reproduction), and decorators love to include—whenever possible—any piece of antique furniture crafted from almost extinct copper-colored Bermuda cedar. Combine these features with the open windows, gentle climate, and carefully tended gardens of a fertile, mid-Atlantic setting, and the result is some very charming and soothing decors.

All of the above-mentioned characteristics are being modified, however, as the offspring of old Bermuda families intermarry with less conservative newcomers from Europe or the East Coast of the United States; many of today's young Bermudian families are being influenced by interior designs as depicted in such publications as *Architectural Digest*. According to one of Bermuda's leading decorators, Richard Klein of Hamma Galleries, color palettes have become more clear and bright in recent years, thanks to the direct influence of the American market, and furniture (especially in second, rather than primary homes) now tends to be more contemporary. Despite these trends, Klein thinks that there are only about five high-tech homes on Bermuda, most of them owned as second or third homes by full-time residents of America's East Coast. And even those high-tech houses are obliged, because of local building codes, to maintain conservative, time-tested exteriors that are generally comparable to those of their neighbors.

7   From Gombey to Calypso: The Rhythms of Bermuda

Modern Bermudian music, which you hear today mainly in hotel lounges, is a blend of native traditions and music from Jamaica, Trinidad, and Puerto Rico, as well as the United States and Britain. As elsewhere, American and British rock, modified by local rhythms, has proved the strongest and most lasting influence.

Yet despite the popular new musical forms, Bermuda is proud of its original musical idioms. *Gombey* dancing, whose roots lie deep within West Africa, is the island's premier folk art. Gombey dancers are almost always male; in accordance with tradition, men pass on the rhythms and dance techniques from generation to generation in their family. Gombey combines Africa's tribal heritage with the Native American and British colonial influences of the New World. Dancers outfit themselves in masquerade costumes, whose outlandish lines and glittering colors evoke the brilliant plumage of tropical birds. The most strenuous dances are usually preformed during the Christmas season.

Gombey (spelled goombay in some other places, such as the Bahamas) signifies a specific type of African drum, as well as the Bantu word for "rhythm." These rhythms escalate into an ever faster and more hypnotic beat as the movements of the dancers become increasingly uninhibited and the response of the spectators grows ever more fervent.

Although gombey dancing, with its local rituals and ceremonies, might be viewed as a major cultural contribution of Bermuda, it is not unique to the island. Variations are found elsewhere in the western Atlantic, as well as in the Caribbean. Indeed, during its development, gombey dancing was significantly influenced by some of these other versions. In colonial times, for example, when African Caribbeans were brought to Bermuda as slaves or convicts to help build the British military installations on the island, they carried with them their own gombey traditions, which eventually combined with those of Bermuda. What is unique about the Bermudian version of gombey, however, is its use of the British snare drum, played with wooden sticks, as an accompaniment to the dancing.

A handful of gombey recordings are available, enabling you to hear the sounds of this African-based music, with its rhythmic chanting and rapid drumbeat. Among the recordings, the album *Strictly Gombey Music* (Edmar 1165), performed by four members of the Pickles Spencer Gombey Group, offers a nice selection of gombey dances.

Aficionados of this art form, however, will argue that gombey's allure lies not so much in the music as in the feverish—almost trancelike—dancing that accompanies it, as well as in the colorful costumes of the dancers. For that reason, they say, audio recordings cannot convey the full mesmerizing power of a gombey dance the way a videotape can. So, while you're in Bermuda, consider taping a gombey dance to show when you get back home and perhaps remind yourself of some of the enchanting sounds and sights of the island.

Bermuda also has a balladeer tradition. Although its exponents are fewer than they used to be, they continue to enjoy considerable popularity among islanders and visitors alike. Reflecting the wry, self-deprecating humor that has always distinguished their compositions, balladeers can strum on the guitar a song for any occasion. Today, many of their songs have to do with Bermuda's changing way of life.

In the past few years, calypso and reggae—the popular sounds of the Caribbean— have become famous in Bermuda. A more recent import to listen for is *soca,* a rock-influenced calypso, and *zouk,* a fusion of various Caribbean rhythms, with French melodies thrown in.

Visitors are often pleased to discover that the island's best-known singers and musicians can be heard at many of the hotels and nightclubs. Inquire what group is performing during the cocktail hour at your hotel; chances are it may be one of the most popular.

By virtually everyone's estimate, the musical patriarch of Bermuda is Hubert Smith, the island's official greeter in song. A balladeer of formidable talent and originality, Smith has composed and performed songs for the visits of nearly all the foreign heads of state who have graced Bermuda's shores in recent memory.

His performances for members of the British royal family include one of the most famous songs ever written about the island, "Bermuda Is Another World." The song is now the island's unofficial national anthem; it's included in the best-selling album *Bermuda Is Another World* (Edmar 1025).

Almost as popular is a five-member calypso band, the Bermuda Strollers, whose lively rhythms can be heard on gala nights at Bermuda's larger hotels. Look for their album *The Best Of* (Edmar 2005) and also a collection of musical odes to the island's natural beauty, *South Shore Bermuda* (Edmar 1156).

One of the island's youngest and most promising talents is Gene Steede, a balladeer and comic who frequently performs at the Southampton Princess. His most popular album is *Bermuda's Natural Resource* (Edmar 2003).

Bermuda ballads, songs of love, and calypsos are also performed by Stan Seymour, a popular soloist who has been compared to Harry Belafonte. Look for *Our Man in Bermuda* (Edmar 1070).

The lively calypsos of Trinidad and the pulsating rhythms of Jamaica have had their influence on musical tastes in Bermuda. Youth Creation, a dreadlock-sporting local reggae group, adopts the Rastafarian style in *Ja's on Our Side* (Edmar 2002).

Dance aficionados will appreciate the five-member Trinidad-born Clay House Steel Band. They can usually be seen at the New Clay House Inn; three months each year they perform aboard various cruise ships. Their most popular album is *The Real Thing* (Edmar 1111).

A Bermuda-born trio, Steel Groove, performs only instrumentals in the Trinidadian style. Their trademark adaptations use the calypso-derived steel pan combined with a keyboard, an electric guitar, and occasionally a bass guitar. Their most popular album is *Calypso Hits* (produced by Danny Garcia).

A slightly older calypso group (one of the first on the island) is the Esso Steel Band. Their popular albums, among them *The Esso Steel Band* (Sunshine 1003) and *It's a Beautiful World* (produced by Rudy Commissiong), are widely hummed and whistled throughout the islands.

8   Bermudian Cuisine

For years Bermuda was not considered an island of grand cuisine; the food was too often bland, lacking in flavor. However, since the 1970s there has been a notable change. Bermuda has shared in the revived interest in fine cuisine that has swept across America. Chefs seem better trained than ever, and many top-notch—albeit expensive—restaurants dot the archipelago, from Sandys Parish in the west to St. George's Parish in the east.

Italian food currently enjoys much vogue. The Chinese have also landed. And the inevitable fast food is available, including Kentucky Fried Chicken.

In recent years, some Bermudians have shown an increased interest in their heritage, and many traditional dishes and recipes have been revived and published in books devoted to Bermudian cookery (not a bad idea for a souvenir).

Today, Bermuda imports most of its foodstuffs from the United States. Because of the high population density, much farmland has now given way to the construction of private homes. Nevertheless, private gardens are still cultivated, and at one Bermudian home we were amazed at the variety of vegetables grown on just a small plot of land. These plants included sorrel, from which a good-tasting soup was made, along with oyster plants and Jerusalem artichokes.

As related in any history of Bermuda, Admiral Sir George Somers and his 150 castaways arrived on the shores of Bermuda from their ill-fated *Sea Venture*. Within

30 minutes they set about fishing for food. They named the fish they caught "rockfish," and later wrote about how sweet and fat it was.

These early settlers also found wild hogs roaming the island. The swine were believed to have swum to shore when some ship or ships were wrecked off the coast of Bermuda. The settlers captured the boars and fed them cedar berries. Thus, when they didn't want to go fishing or the weather was too choppy, they could roast a pig.

DINING CUSTOMS

Perhaps the most delightful custom on Bermuda is the English ritual of afternoon tea. Many local homes and hotels have maintained the tradition, and visitors to Bermuda seem to enjoy it.

In hotels, the typical afternoon tea is served daily from 3 to 4pm. Adding a contemporary touch, tea is often served around a swimming pool, the guests partaking of the ritual in their bathing suits—a tolerated lapse from the usual formal code that governs social functions on the island.

In its more formal observance, tea is served at a table well-laid with silver, crisp white linen napery, and fine china, often imported from Britain. Finger sandwiches made with thinly sliced cucumber or watercress, or scones and strawberry jam, usually accompany the tea.

Again, like the British, Bermudians enjoy a good sociable pub lunch. There are several pubs in Hamilton, St. George's, and elsewhere on the island. For further information, see Chapter 6, "Dining." For the visitor, a pub lunch—consisting of a healthy serving of fish and chips or some other "pub grub," a pint or two of ale (preferably English), and much animated discussion about politics, sports, or the most recent royal visit—is an experience to be cherished, here as much as in any city or town in Britain.

In many resort hotels, guests are booked in high season (April through November) on the modified American plan (MAP) or half-board arrangement. To escape the routine of eating in the same dining room every night, some hotels offer a "dine around" program, allowing you to dine at other hotels either on your MAP plan or else at somewhat reduced prices. You should inquire about such arrangements when booking a room.

Most of the upscale Bermuda restaurants request men to wear a jacket and tie for dinner; some restaurants dispense with the tie but require a jacket. When making reservations, it is always wise to ask what the dress code is before showing up.

Perhaps the favorite meal of the typical Bermudian is Sunday brunch. Your hotel is likely to feature a big buffet at that time; otherwise, you could take this opportunity to dine at another establishment. "Casual but elegant" dress is preferred at most Sunday buffets.

Nearly all major restaurants, except fast-food eateries, prefer that you make a reservation; many establishments require that you do so as far in advance as possible. Weekends in summer can be especially crowded. At certain popular restaurants, some travel-wise vacationers make their reservations even before they arrive in Bermuda.

The food of Bermuda is better than ever. When in doubt, however, order seafood. Nearly all meat is imported and may have arrived on the island considerably earlier than you have.

THE CUISINE

SEAFOOD   Around the coastline of Bermuda more species of both shore and ocean fish are found than in any other place—that is, if you can believe what any local fisher is likely to tell you. The fish include grunt, angelfish, yellowtail, gray snapper, and the ubiquitous rockfish.

Rockfish, which is similar to the Bahamian grouper, appears on nearly every menu. It weighs anywhere from 15 to 135 pounds (or even more). Steamed, broiled, baked, fried, or grilled, rockfish is a challenge to any chef. There's even a dish known as "rockfish maw," which we understand only the most old-fashioned cooks (there are still a handful left on St. David's Island) know how to prepare. It's the maw, or stomach, of a rockfish that has been stuffed with a dressing of forcemeat and simmered slowly on the stove. If you view dining as an adventure, you may want to try it.

The most popular dish on the island is Bermuda fish chowder. Waiters usually pass around a bottle of sherry peppers and some black rum with which you lace your own soup. This adds a distinctive Bermudian flavor.

Shark is not as popular as it used to be. Many traditional dishes, however, are still made from shark, including hash. Some people still make use of shark liver oil to forecast the weather; it's said to be more reliable than the weatherperson. The oil is extracted at a specific time, then poured into a small bottle and left in the sun. If the oil lies still, then fair weather can be predicted; if, however, droplets form on the sides of the bottle, foul weather can be expected.

The Bermuda lobster—or "guinea chick," as it is known locally—has been called a first cousin of the Maine lobster and is in season only from September to March. Its high price tag has led to overfishing, forcing the government at times to issue a ban on its harvesting. In that case, lobster is likely to be imported from elsewhere.

Occasionally you can still get a good conch stew in Bermuda at one of the local restaurants. Sea scallops, while still available, have become increasingly rare. Mussels are cherished in Bermuda; one of the most popular and traditional mussel dishes is mussel pie, Bermuda-style.

FRUITS & VEGETABLES In both restaurants and private homes, Portuguese red bean soup, the culinary contribution of the farmers who were brought to the island to till the land, precedes many a meal.

The Bermuda onion (once so common on the island that the people of Bermuda were called "onions") figures in a lot of Bermudian recipes, including onion pie. Bermuda-onion soup, an island favorite, is usually flavored with Outerbridge's Original Sherry Peppers.

Bermudians grow more potatoes than any other vegetable; the principal varieties are the Pontiac red and the Kennebec white potatoes. At some homes, the traditional Sunday breakfast of codfish and banana cooked with potatoes is still served.

"Peas and plenty" is a Bermudian tradition. Black-eyed peas are cooked with onions and salt pork, to which rice is sometimes added. Dumplings or boiled sweet potatoes may also be added at the last minute. Another peas-and-rice dish, called Hoppin' John, is eaten either as a main dish or as a side dish with meat or poultry.

Both Bermudians and Bahamians share the tradition of Johnny Bread, or johnnycake, a simple pan-cooked cornmeal bread. Fishermen on their boats would make it over a fire in a box filled with sand to keep the flames from spreading to the craft itself.

The cassava, once an important food in Bermuda, is now used chiefly at Christmas to make the traditional cassava pie. Another dish with a festive holiday connection is sweet-potato pudding, traditionally eaten on Guy Fawkes Day (first week in November).

Bermuda grows many fresh fruits, including strawberries, Surinam cherries, guavas, avocados, and, of course, bananas. Guavas are made into jelly, which in turn often goes into making the famous Bermuda syllabub, traditionally accompanied by johnnycake.

DRINKS All the name-brand alcoholic beverages are sold in Bermuda, but prices on such drinks as Scotch and soda can run as high as $5. To avoid running up huge bar tabs, it is important to consider what and where you drink.

For some 300 years rum has been considered the national drink of Bermuda. Especially popular is Bacardi rum (their headquarters are in Bermuda) and Demerara rum (also known as black rum). The rum swizzle is perhaps the most famous alcoholic drink in Bermuda.

An interesting drink is loquat liqueur, now exported. It can be made with loquats, rock candy, and gin, or more elaborately with brandy instead of gin and the addition of such spices as cinnamon, nutmeg, cloves, and allspice.

Before the advent of bottled drinks, ginger beer—made with green ginger and lemons—was an island favorite.

Planning a Trip to Bermuda

3

Getting to Bermuda has now become easier than ever, thanks to more frequent flights, often direct ones, from such gateway cities as New York, Boston, and Washington, D.C., among others. For those who'd like to relive the glamorous days of "cruising down to Bermuda," several cruise lines sail there from spring until late autumn.

In this chapter you'll find everything you need to plan your trip—from when to go to what things cost.

1 Visitor Information, Entry Requirements, Customs & Money

VISITOR INFORMATION

To obtain information about Bermuda before your trip, contact the **Bermuda Department of Tourism** office nearest you. In the United States, the Bermuda Department of Tourism has offices in: *New York*, Suite 201, 310 Madison Ave., New York, NY 10017 (☎ 212/818-9800 or 800/223-6106); *Boston*, Suite 1010, 44 School St., Boston, MA 02108 (☎ 617/742-0405); *Chicago*, Suite 1070, Randolph Wacker Building, 150 North Wacker Dr., Chicago, IL 60606 (☎ 312/782-5486); *Atlanta*, Suite 803, 245 Peachtree Center, NE, Atlanta, GA 30303 (☎ 404/524-1541); *Los Angeles,* 3151 Cahueng Blvd. W, Suite 111, Los Angeles, CA 90010, (☎ 213/436-0744 or 800/252-0211). In **Canada,** write to Bermuda Department of Tourism, Suite 1004, 1200 Bay St., Toronto, Ontario, Canada M5R 2A5 (☎ 416/923-9600). In the **United Kingdom,** write to Bermuda Department of Tourism, 1 Battersea Church Road, London SW11 3LY (☎ 0171/734-8813).

You may also want to contact the U.S. State Department for background information; write to Superintendent of Documents, **U.S. Government Printing Office,** Washington, DC 20402 (☎ 202/512-1800).

A good travel agent can be a valuable source of information. Make sure he or she is a member of the American Society of Travel Agents (ASTA), however. If you get poor service from an agent, you can write to the **ASTA Consumer Affairs,** 1101 King St., Alexandria, VA 22314 (☎ 703/706-0387).

And the best source of all may be relatives, friends, or colleagues who have just returned from Bermuda.

ENTRY REQUIREMENTS

A U.S. or Canadian citizen does not need a passport to enter Bermuda, although one might be useful as your required identification. Visitors from Great Britain and Europe do need a passport.

Bermuda Immigration authorities require U.S. visitors to have in their possession any one of the following items: a birth certificate or a certified copy of it, a U.S. naturalization certificate, a valid passport, a U.S. Alien Registration card, a U.S. reentry permit, or a U.S. voter registration card bearing the signature of the holder.

Visitors from Canada must have either a birth certificate (or a certified copy of it), a Canadian certificate of citizenship, or a valid passport plus proof of their Landed Immigrant status.

If you stay longer than three weeks, you must apply to the Chief Immigration Officer for an extended stay. You must have a return or onward ticket.

All travelers must pay a passenger tax under the Passenger Tax Act of 1972; see "Taxes" under "Fast Facts" in Chapter 4, "Getting to Know Bermuda."

It is a good policy before leaving home to make copies of your most valuable documents, including the inside page of your passport that has your photograph. You should also make copies of your driver's license, airline ticket, strategic hotel vouchers, and any other type of identity card that might be pertinent. You should also make copies of any prescriptions you take. Leave one copy at home, place one copy in your luggage, and carry the original with you. The information on these documents would be extremely valuable if you experience a loss or theft abroad.

CUSTOMS

U.S. CUSTOMS   You may take out of Bermuda $400 worth of merchandise duty-free if you've been outside the United States for 48 hours or more and have not claimed a similar exemption within the past 30 days. Articles valued above the $400 duty-free limit (but not over $1,000) will be assessed at a flat duty rate of 10%. Gifts for your personal use, not for business purposes, may be included in the $400 exemption, and unsolicited gifts totaling $50 a day may be sent home duty-free. You are limited to one liter of wine, liqueur, or liquor, and five cartons of cigarettes. U.S. Customs preclearance is available for all scheduled flights. Passengers leaving for the United States must fill out written declaration forms before clearing U.S. Customs in Bermuda. The forms are available at Bermuda hotels, travel agencies, and airlines.

Collect receipts for all your purchases. If a merchant suggests giving you a false receipt, misstating the value of your goods, *beware:* The merchant may be a Customs informer. You must also declare all gifts received during your stay abroad.

Compile a list of expensive carry-on items, and ask a U.S. Customs agent to stamp your list at the airport before your departure. For additional information, write to the **U.S. Customs Service,** 1301 Constitution Avenue, P.O. Box 7407, Washington, DC 20229, for the free pamphlet, *Know Before You Go.*

CANADIAN CUSTOMS   For more information, write for the booklet *I Declare,* issued by Revenue Canada, 875 Heron Rd., Ottawa, ON K1A 0L5. Canada allows its citizens a $300 exemption, and they are allowed to bring back duty-free 200 cigarettes, 2.2 pounds of tobacco, 40 imperial ounces of liquor, and 50 cigars. In addition, they are allowed to mail gifts to Canada from abroad at the rate of Can $60 a day, provided they are unsolicited and aren't alcohol or tobacco (write on the package: "Unsolicited gift, under $60 value"). All valuables should be declared on the Y-38 Form before departure from Canada, including serial numbers, as in the case of, for example, expensive foreign cameras that you already own. *Note:* The $300 exemption can be used only once a year and only after an absence of seven days.

BRITISH CUSTOMS   Citizens can bring in goods valued up to £136; and one must be 17 or older to import liquor or tobacco. Britons are allowed 200 cigarettes or 100 cigarillos, 50 cigars, or 250 grams of tobacco. Two liters of table wine, 1 liter of alcohol greater than 22% by volume, and 2 liters of alcohol equal to or less than 22% by volume may also be brought in. British Customs tends to be strict and complicated in its requirements. For details, get in touch with Her Majesty's Customs and Excise Office, New King's Beam House, 22 Upper Ground, London SE1 9PJ (☎ **0171/382-5468** for more information).

MONEY
CASH/CURRENCY

Legal tender is the Bermuda dollar (BD$), which is divided into 100 cents. Prior to 1972, the Bermuda dollar was pegged to the pound sterling; now it is pegged through gold to the U.S. dollar on an equal basis—BD$1 equals U.S. $1. U.S. currency is generally accepted at par in shops, restaurants, and hotels. Currencies from the United Kingdom and all other foreign countries are not accepted. They can easily be exchanged for Bermuda dollars at banks. Banking and credit-card transactions in all foreign currencies involving currency exchange are subject to exchange rates.

TRAVELER'S CHECKS

Most large banks sell traveler's checks, charging fees that range between 1% and 2% of the value of the checks you buy, although some out-of-the-way banks, in rare instances, have charged as much as 7%. If your bank wants more than a 2% commission, it may be worth your while to call the traveler's check issuer directly for the addresses of outlets where the commission is less.

   American Express (☎ **800/221-7282** in the U.S. and Canada) is one of the largest and most immediately recognized issuers of traveler's checks. No commission is charged to members of the AAA and to holders of certain types of American Express credit cards. The company issues checks denominated in U.S. dollars, Canadian dollars, British pounds sterling, and a variety of other currencies. For questions or problems that arise outside the U.S. or Canada, contact any of the company's many regional representatives.

   Citicorp (☎ **800/645-6556** in the U.S. and Canada, or **813/623-1709** collect from anywhere else in the world) issues checks in U.S. dollars, British pounds, and several other currencies.

   Thomas Cook (☎ **800/223-7373** in the U.S. and Canada; otherwise call **609/987-7300** collect from other parts of the world) issues MasterCard traveler's checks denominated in U.S. dollars, Canadian dollars, British pounds, and several other currencies.

   Interpayment Services (☎ **800/221-2426** in the U.S. or Canada; call **212/858-8500** collect from other parts of the world) sells VISA checks that are issued by a consortium of member banks and the Thomas Cook organization. Traveler's checks are denominated in U.S. or Canadian dollars, British pounds, and German marks.

CREDIT CARDS

Credit cards are accepted at many shops and restaurants, but not at all hotels. Check first; you will find this information for every hotel and restaurant listed in the chapters that follow. VISA and MasterCard are the major cards used, although American Express and, to a lesser extent, Diners Club are also popular.

The British Pound & the U.S. Dollar

Here is how British pounds sterling translate into U.S. dollars. At this writing, £1 = approximately $1.60 U.S. (or $1 = approximately 63 pence), although these equivalents can and will change according to various worldwide political and economic factors. This table should be used, therefore, only as a general guide.

The Bermudian dollar—no longer pegged to the pound sterling—has the same value as the U.S. dollar.

U.S.$	U.K.£	U.S.$	U.K.£
0.25	0.16	15	9.38
0.50	0.31	20	12.50
0.75	0.47	25	15.63
1.00	0.63	50	31.25
2.00	1.25	75	46.88
3.00	1.88	100	62.50
4.00	2.50	150	93.75
5.00	3.13	200	125.00
6.00	3.75	250	156.25
7.00	4.38	300	187.50
8.00	5.00	350	218.75
9.00	5.63	400	250.00
10.00	6.25	500	312.50

ATM NETWORKS

Cirrus and other networks connecting automated teller machines operate in Bermuda. For locations of Cirrus abroad, call **800/424-7787.** In addition, if your credit card has been programmed with a PIN number, you can probably use your card at Bermudian ATMs to withdraw money as a cash advance on your credit card. Make sure you know what the frequency limits for withdrawals and cash advances are on your credit card. Furthermore, before leaving home, check to see if your PIN must be reprogrammed for use in Bermuda. Those who have the Discover card will find that it is acceptable only within the United States.

MONEYGRAM

The nightmare of many travelers is the prospect of running out of money. Assuming that you have friends or relatives who can help out, they can wire you emergency money through a service sponsored by American Express. MoneyGram, based in Englewood, Colo. (☎ **800/ 926-9400**), enables funds to be sent from one individual to another at thousands of locations around the world in less than 10 minutes. The prospective sender should call American Express to learn the address of the closest outlet that handles MoneyGrams. At the designated location, the sender must fill out a form, specifying how much money is to be sent. Payment can be made in cash, by major credit card, or occasionally by personal check (with adequate ID).

AMEX collects a fee for the service—$10 for the first $300 sent, and a sliding scale for larger sums. The fee enables the sender to write a short telex-style message that will accompany the money and also to make a three-minute phone call to the

What Things Cost in Bermuda	U.S. $
15-minute taxi ride	5.00
One-way ride on a bus	2.50–4.00
Local telephone call	.20
Double room at Belmont Hotel (deluxe)	225.00
Double at Rosedown (moderate)	170–235.00
Double at Salt Kettle House (inexpensive)	92.00
Lunch for one at Tio Pepe (moderate)	21–23.00*
Lunch for one at Bombay Bicycle Club (inexpensive)	11.95*
Dinner for one at Romanoff Restaurant (deluxe)	33–39.00*
Dinner for one at Chancery Wine Bar (moderate)	16.50–26.50*
Dinner for one at Chopsticks Restaurant (inexpensive)	10.50–28.00*
Bottle of beer in a bar	4.00
Coca-Cola in a cafe	1.50
Cup of coffee in a cafe	3.00
Glass of planter's punch in a restaurant	5.00
Roll of ASA 100 color film, 36 exposures	7.95
Admission to Elbow Beach	3.50
Movie ticket	7.00
*Includes tax and tip but not wine.	

recipient. MoneyGrams can be received in Bermuda. At the outlet where the money is to be received, the beneficiary must present a photo ID and, in some cases, a security code previously established by the sender.

WHAT WILL IT COST?

Time is money, and since Bermuda is less than a two-hour flight from most cities on the East Coast, the savings begin even before visitors land on the island. A four-day, three-night vacation in Bermuda can actually include four days of vacation for the price of only three nights' accommodation. An 8:30am flight from New York gets travelers to Bermuda in time for lunch, with the whole afternoon to play.

The variety of accommodations allows visitors to indulge their preferences and tastes while keeping their budgets under control. There are luxury resort hotels, small hotels, intimate guesthouses, and cottage colonies. Most large resorts offer money-saving package plans that include meals. If you plan to stay for a week or more, a housekeeping unit or cottage with kitchenette might be a good choice.

No rental cars are available, but Bermuda's local transportation is efficient and inexpensive, saving visitors from $250 to $300 or even more over the cost of one week's car rental. Options include the simple and comprehensive bus system, ferries, and bicycle or moped rentals.

Golfers will find that greens fees are comparable to or less than fees at other destinations. For example, Ocean View Golf and Country Club and St. George's Golf Club charge from $28 for 18 holes of golf. There are eight world-class golf courses with varying fees.

Athletic and cultural activities, such as tennis, riding, guided tours, museums, and attractions are good values in Bermuda.

Hotel costs will depend on what time of year you travel. If you're seeking reductions, perhaps 20% to 40% per person, go to Bermuda during the off-season. In Bermuda, unlike the Caribbean, this is from November or December through March.

On the half-board plan (MAP), many hotels charge $125 to $275 per person per day based on double occupancy, with some of the smaller properties charging from $100 to $180 per person per day, double occupancy. A hotel without meals (EP) charges from about $100 to $150 per person daily.

As an alternative to these high tabs, travel agents sometimes offer special packages, which can represent a substantial savings over regular hotel tariffs for families, golfers, tennis players, honeymooners, and some others.

To cut costs even more, families can rent housekeeping efficiencies, apartments, cottages, or even condominiums (some condos are rented like time-share units when the owners aren't in residence).

In figuring your budget, think about transportation. Getting around the island isn't always easy since visitors aren't allowed to rent cars. Therefore, you'll have to rely on public transportation or the very expensive taxis. The more agile can rent bicycles or mopeds. (See "Getting Around," in Chapter 4, for more information.) Fortunately, once you reach a particular parish, many attractions can be covered on foot, and Bermuda becomes almost one vast walking tour.

Dining out is an expensive undertaking in Bermuda. If you patronize the very expensive establishments, you can end up spending as much as $60 to $80 per person, excluding wine. Even moderate to expensive restaurants charge $25 to $50 per person. Any dinner under $25 per person is considered inexpensive. To reduce dining costs, plan to have a picnic lunch or else enjoy pub grub at noon.

If all these hidden or extra costs are intimidating, consider a package tour in which everything will be arranged for you. You'll know the exact cost of your vacation before you leave home.

2 When to Go

Bermuda enjoys a mild climate, and the term "Bermuda high" has come to mean sunny days and clear skies. Bermuda, being farther north in the Atlantic than the Bahamas, is much cooler in winter. Its off-season begins in December and lasts generally until the first of March. Many hotels, therefore, quote their low-season rates—discounts of from 20% to 60%—in winter. During autumn and winter, many hotels also offer discounted package deals, and some hotels even close for a couple of weeks or months in winter.

The off-season rates, which are also listed in this guide, are a bonanza for cost-conscious travelers who are free to travel to Bermuda during the period November (or December) to March.

CLIMATE

Bermuda is a semitropical island, and the Gulf Stream, flowing between it and North America, keeps the climate temperate. There is no rainy season, and no typical month of excess rain. Showers may be heavy at times, but the skies clear quickly. In summer temperatures rarely rise above 85° Fahrenheit. There's nearly always a cool breeze in the evening, but some accommodations have taken the precaution of installing air-conditioning. Springlike temperatures prevail from mid-December to late March, with the average ranging from the low 60s to 70°F. From

Impressions

[Above all the attributes of Bermuda is] that uninterrupted health and alacrity of spirit, which is the result of the finest weather and gentlest climate in the world.

—George Berkeley, in letter to Lord Percival (1722)

mid-November to mid-December and from late March through April, be prepared for either spring or summer weather.

A look at the official chart on temperature and rainfall will give you a general idea of what to expect during your visit.

Bermuda's Average Daytime Temperatures & Rainfall

	Jan	Feb	Mar	Apr	May	June	July	Aug	Sept	Oct	Nov	Dec
Temp. °F	65	64	64	65	70	75	79	80	79	75	69	65
Temp. °C	19	18	18	19	21	24	30	27	30	24	21	19
Rainfall (in.)	4	5	4.6	3	3.9	5.2	4	5.3	5.3	6	4.5	3.9

THE HURRICANE SEASON

The hurricane season—the curse of the Caribbean and Bermuda—lasts officially from June through November. But don't panic. More tropical storms pound the U.S. mainland than hurricanes devastate Bermuda. And islands in the Caribbean are much more likely to be hit by a hurricane than is Bermuda. Satellite forecasts are generally able to give adequate warning of any really dangerous weather so that precautions can be taken in time.

However, if you are unduly concerned, you can call the nearest branch of the National Weather Service (in the phone book it's listed under the U.S. Department of Commerce). Radio and TV weather reports from the **National Hurricane Center** in Coral Gables, Fla., can also keep you posted.

HOLIDAYS

The following public holidays are observed in Bermuda (those without a date change from year to year): New Year's Day (January 1), Good Friday, Easter, Bermuda Day (May 24), the Queen's Birthday (first or second Monday in June), Cup Match Days (cricket; Thursday and Friday preceding first Monday in August), Labour Day (first Monday in September), Christmas Day (December 25), and Boxing Day (December 26). Public holidays that fall on a Saturday or Sunday are usually celebrated the following Monday.

BERMUDA CALENDAR OF EVENTS

January

✪ **Bermuda Festival.** During the winter months, the Bermuda calendar is jam-packed with such events as golf and tennis invitationals, an international marathon race, a dog show, open house and garden tours, and, of course, the **Bermuda Festival,** the six-week International Festival of the Performing Arts, held in Hamilton, featuring drama, dance, jazz, classical and popular music, and other entertainment by the best international artists.

Where: Islandwide. **When:** January and February. **How:** Some tickets are reserved until 48 hours before curtain time for visitors. For details, write the

Bermuda Festival, Box HM 297, Hamilton HM AX, Bermuda (☎ **441/295-1291**).

- **The Bermuda International Marathon,** with international and local runners, takes place January 13-15. For further information and entry forms, contact the International Race Weekend Committee, Bermuda Track and Field Association, P.O. Box DV 397, Devonshire, Bermuda DV BX. (☎ **441/238-2333**).

March

✪ **Bermuda College Weeks.** This is an annual spring odyssey for at least 10,000 students who flock here every year. These weeks began as Rugby Weeks in 1933. Rugby teams from Ivy League schools came to compete against British or Bermudian teams. "Where the boys are," to borrow the popular song title, led to "where the girls are." A tradition was born. The Department of Tourism issues a College Week Courtesy Card to those who have a valid college identification card. This becomes a passport to a week of free—courtesy of the Bermudian government—beach parties, lunches, boat cruises, dances, and entertainment.

    Where: Islandwide. **When:** Dates arranged to coincide with U.S. college spring vacations. **How:** Obtain a list of events from the tourist office.

- **Home & Garden Tours.** Each spring the **Garden Club of Bermuda** lays out the welcome mat at a number of private homes and gardens that are open to view. A different set of houses, all conveniently located in the same parish, is open every Wednesday during this springtime viewing. Normally a total of 20 homes participate in the program, many of them dating back to the 17th and 18th centuries.

    Where: Islandwide. **When:** End of March to mid-May. **How:** The tourist office provides a complete listing of homes and viewing schedules.

April

- **Beat Retreat Ceremony.** Ceremony of the Bermuda regiment and massed pipes and drums, on Front Street in Hamilton at 9pm. Held on the last Wednesday in every month from April through October, except August. (Periodically held in Somerset and St. George's.)
- **Peppercorn Ceremony.** His Excellency the governor collects the annual rent of one peppercorn for use of the island's Old State House in St. George's. April 21 (dates may vary).
- **An agriculture show.** A three-day exhibit of Bermuda's best fruits, flowers, vegetables, and livestock; also equestrian and other ring events. Dates vary.
- **Invitational International Week.** Yachtspeople from the United States, the United Kingdom, Canada, and other countries compete with Bermudians. (Other boat-racing events take place in alternate years.)

May

- **Bermuda Game Fishing Tournament.** Special prizes for top catches of 17 species of game fish. All amateur anglers are eligible. Held from May 1 to November 30.
- **Bermuda Heritage Month.** Culminates in **Bermuda Day,** May 24, a public holiday.

June

- **Queen's Birthday** (first or second Monday in June) is celebrated by a parade on Front Street in Hamilton.
- **The Blue Water Cruising Race.** A race from Marion, Massachusetts, to Bermuda is held in June in odd-numbered years, as is the **MultiHull Ocean Yacht**

Race from Newport, Rhode Island, to Bermuda. In June of even-numbered years, some 180 of the world's finest yachts compete in the **Bermuda Race,** from Newport to Bermuda.

July
- **Marine Science Day.** Lectures, hands-on demonstrations, and displays for adults and children, by Bermuda Biological Station. Call **441/297-1880** for more information. Different date each year, usually mid-month.

August
- **Cup Match and Somers Days.** This spectacular cricket match pits the east against the west end of the island. Held on Thursday and Friday before the first Monday in August.

September
- **Labour Day.** This public holiday features a host of activities (ideal time for a picnic). Climax of the day is a parade from Union Square in Hamilton Bernard Park. Held the first Monday in September.

October
- **Omega Gold Cup International Match Race Tournament.** Top-ranking Match Racing skippers compete with Bermudians. Hosted by the Royal Bermuda Yacht Club. October 18–25.

November
- **The Opening of Parliament.** Traditional ceremony and military guard of honor connected with the **Opening of Parliament** by His Excellency the governor as the queen's personal representative. November 6.
- **World Rugby Classic.** Former international rugby players compete with Bermudians at Bermuda National Sports Club. November 6–12.
- **Guy Fawkes Day.** Annual celebration with a minifair starts with the traditional burning of the Guy Fawkes effigy at the Keepyard of the Bermuda Maritime Museum, Royal Naval Dockyard, beginning at 4:30pm. November 7.
- **Remembrance Day.** A gala parade is held, with Bermudian police, British and U.S. military units, Bermudians, and veterans' organizations taking part. November 11.
- **Bermuda Equestrian Festival.** International Show Jumping Competition at the Botanical Gardens. November 28 and 29.
- **Invitation Tennis Weeks.** More than 100 visiting players vie with Bermudians during two weeks of matches.

December
- **Bermuda Goodwill Tournament.** Pro/amateur foursomes from international golf clubs play over 72 holes on four of Bermuda's eight courses during golfing activity. December 5–9.

3 Weddings & Honeymoons in Bermuda

There are good reasons why Bermuda hosts more than 23,000 honeymooners and second honeymooners each year. It offers an ideal environment, whether couples prefer an active or a relaxing schedule. For those who choose, there are opportunities for scuba diving and swimming, whereas others might prefer such leisure activities as strolling along the beach at sunset or reading poetry to each other while snuggling in a secluded cove. Many of Bermuda's hotels, from luxurious resorts to intimate

Wedding Cake Traditions

Custom dictates that Bermudians have two wedding cakes—a plain pound cake covered with gold leaf for the groom, and a tiered fruit cake covered with silver leaf and topped off with a mini–cedar tree for the bride. The tiny tree is planted on the day of the wedding to symbolize the hope that the marriage will grow and mature like the tree. The rest of the first tier of the bride's cake is frozen until the christening of the first child.

cottage colonies, offer special honeymoon packages. Typically these include airfare, accommodations, meal plans, champagne upon arrival, flowers in the room, and special discounts at local attractions and restaurants. Call **800/BERMUDA** (**800/237-6832**) for details. See "The Best Honeymoon Resorts" in Chapter 1.

GETTING MARRIED IN BERMUDA

Couples who would like to get married in Bermuda must file a "Notice of Intended Marriage" with the Registry General, accompanied by a fee of $150 (in the form of a bank draft, not a personal check). The draft should be made out to "The Accountant General." The draft should be mailed or delivered personally to the Registry General at the Government Administration Building, 30 Parliament St., Hamilton HM 12 (☎ **441/295-5151,** fax 441/292-4568). "Notice of Intended Marriage" forms can be obtained from the Bermuda Department of Tourism offices in Atlanta, Boston, Chicago, Los Angeles, and New York. Since airmail letters from the United States to Bermuda can take 6 to 10 days, make your plans accordingly.

Once the "Notice of Intended Marriage" is received, it will be published—including names and addresses—once in any two of the island's newspapers. Assuming that there is no formal objection, the registry will issue the license 15 days after receiving the notice. It will be valid for three months.

CIVIL CEREMONIES Weddings are performed at the registry by appointment only Monday through Friday, 10am to 4pm, and Saturdays between 10am and noon. The fee is $153, which includes the cost of the ceremony and certificate. Copies of the marriage certificate are available for $17 each. If either of the prospective marriage partners has been married before, that person will need to attach a photocopy of the final decree to the "Notice of Intended Marriage."

WEDDING ARRANGEMENTS Many hotels can help make wedding arrangements, from reserving the church and clergy, to hiring a horse and buggy, ordering the wedding cake, or securing a photographer. **Bermuda Travel Planners,** 350 Fifth Ave., Suite 2718, New York, NY 10018 (☎ **212/564-9502** or **800/323-2020;** fax 212/268-9456), offers popular wedding packages at many of the island's hotels. In addition, the following on-island wedding consultants can assist with these and other details: The Wedding Salon, 51 Reid St., P.O. Box HM 2085, Hamilton HM HX, Bermuda (☎ **441/292-5677,** fax 441/292-2955); and The Bridal Suite, Parkside Building, 3 Park Rd., Suite 7, Hamilton HM 09, Bermuda (☎ **441/292-2025;** fax 441/296-2050).

4 Spa Vacations

Full-fledged spa facilities are available at the **Sonesta Beach Hotel & Spa,** Southampton (☎ **441/238-8122** or **800/766-3782** in the U.S.), considered one of the top 10 health-and-beauty spas of the world. Designed in the European style, it offers the same health-and-fitness regimens that are popular at American spas. Some of the exotic and beneficial treatments offered include: Ionithermie, the inch-reducing treatment from Europe; deluxe facial care from Paris; ancient forms of therapeutic and relaxing massage such as aromatherapy and reflexology; and Swedish massage. Some people check into the hotel on calorie-controlled four-, five-, or seven-day programs. Clients are usually kept busy every day from 8:30am to 7pm with such activities as aerobics, skin and body care, supervised indoor and outdoor stretching exercises, massages, facials, and beauty regimens.

The facilities are also available to hotel guests or outsiders who would like only selected treatments rather than the full spa experience. The up-to-date accoutrements include Universal gym equipment, saunas, steambaths, and massage rooms. The staff conducts daily exercise classes, which outsiders can join for a fee. Each procedure is priced separately for nonpackage participants. For after-workout pick-me-ups, there's a beauty salon adjacent to the health spa. Half- or full-day packages are sold to non-residents of the hotel.

5 Travel Insurance

STAYING HEALTHY

If you need medical attention while in Bermuda, finding a good doctor is no real problem. See Fast Facts, in Chapter 4, for specific locations and addresses.

It's a good idea to carry all your vital medicines and drugs (the legal kind) with you in your carry-on luggage, in case your checked luggage is lost.

If your medical condition is chronic, always speak to your doctor before leaving home. He or she may have some specific advice for you, depending on your problem. For conditions such as epilepsy, a heart problem, or diabetes, wear a Medic Alert identification tag. This tag provides Medic Alert's 24-hour hotline number, so a foreign doctor can obtain medical records for you. For a lifetime membership, the cost is a well-spent $35 for a stainless steel ID bracelet (a silver-plated tag costs $45, and a gold-plated one $60). In addition, there is a $15 annual fee. Contact the **Medic Alert Foundation,** P.O. Box 1009, Turlock, CA 95381 (☎ **800/432-5378**).

INSURANCE

Insurance needs for the traveler abroad can be grouped as follows: health and accident, trip cancellation, and lost luggage.

First, review your present policies before traveling abroad—you may already have adequate coverage on those policies plus what is offered by your credit-card company if your trip tickets were purchased with that card. Fraternal organizations can sometimes provide policies that protect members in case of sickness or accident abroad.

Many homeowners' insurance policies cover theft of luggage and loss of documents (such as your airline ticket) during foreign travel, although coverage is usually limited to about $500. To submit a claim on your insurance, remember that you'll

Impressions

I find Bermuda is a place where physicians order their patients when no other air will keep them alive.

—Thomas Moore, in a letter to his mother (1803)

need police reports concerning the loss (or a statement from a medical authority about the health problem) for which you are seeking compensation. Such claims, by their very nature, can be filed only when you return from Bermuda.

Some policies (and this is the type you should have) provide cash advances or else transferal of funds so that you won't have to dip into your precious travel money to settle medical bills.

If you've booked a charter flight, you'll probably have to pay a cancellation fee if you cancel a trip suddenly, even if you do so because of an unforeseen crisis. It's possible to get insurance that will cover such a fee, either through a travel agency or through a credit-card company (such as VISA or American Express) when such insurance is written into tickets paid for with a credit card.

Companies offering special travel insurance policies include the following: **Travel Guard International,** 1145 Clark St., Stevens Point, WI 54481 (☎ **800/826-1300** outside Wisconsin, **715/345-0505** in Wisconsin), offers a comprehensive seven-day policy that covers lost luggage, emergency assistance, accidental death, trip cancellation, and medical coverage abroad. The cost of the package is $62, but there are restrictions that you should understand before you accept the coverage.

Travelers Insurance PAK, Travel Insured International, Inc., P.O. Box 280568, East Hartford, CT 06128 (☎ **800/243-3174** or **860/528-7663**), offers illness and accident coverage costing from $10 for 6 to 10 days. For lost or damaged luggage, $500 worth of coverage costs $20 for 6 to 10 days. You can also purchase trip-cancellation insurance for $5.50 per $100 of coverage to a limit of $10,000 per person.

Access America, 6600 W. Broad St., P.O. Box 11188, Richmond, VA 23230 (☎ 800/284-8300), offers travel insurance and 24-hour emergency travel, medical, and legal assistance for the traveler. One call to their hotline center, staffed by multilingual coordinators, connects travelers to a worldwide network of professionals who can offer specialized help in reaching the nearest physician, hospital, or legal adviser, and in obtaining emergency cash or the replacement of lost travel documents. Varying coverage levels are available.

Mutual of Omaha (Tele-Trip Company, Inc.), Mutual of Omaha Plaza, Omaha, NE 68175, offers cruise and tour insurance packages priced from $49 to $57 per person for a cruise or tour valued at $1,000. Included in these packages are travel assistance services and financial protection against trip cancellation, trip interruption, bankruptcy, flight and baggage delays, accident and sickness, accidental death and dismemberment, missed connections, trip delays, and medical evacuation. Both cruise and tour packages enable you to waive preexisting condition limitations. Application for insurance can be made over the phone by major credit-card holders (☎ **800/ 228-9792**).

6 Tips for Travelers with Special Needs

FOR TRAVELERS WITH DISABILITIES

Hotels rarely publicize what facilities, if any, they offer those with disabilities, so it's always better to contact a hotel directly. A number of agencies can also provide information to help you plan your trip.

"Air Transportation of Handicapped Persons," published by the U.S. Department of Transportation, is free. Write to Distribution Unit, U.S. Department of Transportation, Publications Division, 3341Q 75 Avenue, Landover, MD 20785 (☎ **301/322-4961;** fax 301/386-5394). Only written requests are accepted.

For information regarding travel facilities and tour operators, contact the **Society for the Advancement of Travel for the Handicapped,** 347 Fifth Ave., Suite 610,

New York, NY 10016 (☎ **212/447-7284**). Yearly membership dues are $45 for senior citizens, $25 for students.

The **Information Center for Individuals with Disabilities,** 29 Stanhope Street, 4th Floor, Boston, MA 02116 (☎ **617/450-9888,** or 800/462-5015 in Mass.) is another good source. It has lists of travel agents who specialize in tours for the disabled, and provides travel tip fact sheets.

For the blind or visually impaired, the best source is the **American Foundation for the Blind,** 11 Penn Plaza, Suite 300, New York, NY 10001 (☎ **212/502-7600** or 800/232-5463 to order information kits and supplies). It acts as a referral source for travelers and can offer advice on various requirements for the transport and border formalities for seeing-eye dogs.

For a $25 annual fee, consider joining **Mobility International USA,** P.O. Box 10767, Eugene, OR 97440 (☎ **503/343-1284;** fax 503/343-6812). It answers questions on various destinations and also offers discounts on videos, publications, and programs it sponsors.

Finally, a bimonthly publication, "Handicapped Travel Newsletter," keeps you current on accessible sights worldwide for the disabled. To order an annual subscription for $15 call **903/677-1260.**

TIPS FOR BRITISH TRAVELERS WITH DISABILITIES

The **Royal Association for Disability and Rehabilitation (RADAR),** Unit 12, City Forum, 250 City Rd., London EC1V 8AF (☎ **0171/250-3222**), publishes annual holiday guides for the disabled. "Holidays and Travel Abroad," covers European destinations and costs £5, whereas "Holidays in the British Isles" sells for £7. RADAR (whose patroness is Elizabeth, the Queen Mother), also provides a number of fact sheets on such subjects as sports and outdoor holidays, insurance, financial arrangements for the disabled, and accommodations in nursing-care units for groups or for the elderly. Each of these fact sheets is available for 75p, or £2 for three. Fact sheets or the above-mentioned holiday guides can be mailed outside the U.K. for a £13 mailing fee.

FOR GAY & LESBIAN TRAVELERS

Think twice before planning a gay holiday in Bermuda. Although many gays live in and visit Bermuda, the colony has rather repressive antihomosexual laws. Relations between homosexuals, even between consenting adults, are subject to criminal sanctions, carrying a maximum sentence of 10 years in prison. Even *attempted* contacts among homosexuals—at least according to the law—can be punished with up to five years in prison.

If your dream vacation includes such activities as visiting gay beaches, gay bars, or gay clubs, it would be better for you to consider such fun-in-the-sun destinations as South Miami Beach, Key West, or Puerto Rico.

FOR SENIORS

Many discounts are available for seniors, but be advised that you must be a member of an organization (such as the AARP) to obtain some of them.

Since 1987 **Golden Companions** has been helping people 45 years and older find compatible traveling companions. It is the only travel companion network to offer personal voicebox mail service enabling members to connect instantly 24 hours a day. Membership services also include free mail exchange, a bimonthly newsletter, "Golden Gateways," get-togethers, and tours. Annual membership is $85, and a newsletter-only subscription is $17.95 for 12 months ($26.95 for 24 months). For a free brochure, write Golden Companions, P.O. Box 5249, Reno, NV 89513 (☎ 702/324-2227; fax 702/324-2236). A sample newsletter is $2.

Grand Circle Travel, 347 Congress St., Boston, MA 02210 (☎ **617/350-7500,** or 800/221-2610), offers extended vacations, escorted programs, and cruises that feature unique learning experiences for seniors at competitive prices. Contact them for a free booklet called *101 Tips for the Mature Traveler.*

Mature Outlook, P.O. Box 10448, Des Moines, IA 50306 (☎ **800/336-6330),** is a membership program for people over 50 years of age. Membership, which costs $14.95 a year, includes the following: a bimonthly magazine, discounts at ITC-member hotels, free coupons for discounts at Sears & Roebuck Co., and savings on selected auto rentals and restaurants.

SAGA International Holidays is well known for its all-inclusive tours for seniors (those 50 years old or older). Both medical and trip cancellation insurance are included in the net price of any of their tours except cruises. Contact SAGA International Holidays, 222 Berkeley St., Boston, MA 02115 (☎ **800/343-0273**).

Information is also available from the **National Council of Senior Citizens,** 1331 F St. NW, Washington, D.C. 20004 (☎ **202/347-8800**). A nonprofit organization, the council has a yearly membership charge of $12 per person or couple; members receive the following: 11 issues each year of a newsletter that includes travel tips; discounts on hotels, motels, and auto rentals; prescription drug services; long-term care options; and insurance programs.

FOR STUDENTS

Students are eligible for a number of travel discounts. The most wide-ranging travel service for students is **Council Travel,** a subsidiary of the **Council on International Educational Exchange (CIEE)**, 205 E. 42nd St., New York, NY 10017 (☎ **212/661-1450**), which provides details about budget travel, study abroad, working permits, and insurance. It also issues a number of helpful publications as well as an International Student Identity Card (ISIC) for $18 to bona fide students. Its free copy of *Student Travels* magazine provides information on all of the council's services and CIEE's programs and publications.

FOR FAMILIES

Bermuda is one of the best vacation destinations for the entire family. The smallest toddlers can spend blissful hours in shallow seawater or pools constructed for them, while older children can enjoy boat rides, horseback riding, hiking, discoing, or even snorkeling.

Most resort hotels will advise you what there is in the way of fun for all, and many have play directors and supervised activities for various age groups.

Impressions

. . . Bermuda is, without doubt, a success. It is, generally speaking, a peaceful place—more so than many Caribbean islands nearby. [Still, there are critics, from whom] you hear complaints about the Americanization of the place, the suggestion that Bermudianism is merely an anomalous cultural hybrid, a mule of a culture, attractive in its own way but of no lasting value or use. And yet it does seem to work; it is rich, it is as content as any place I know, and it is stable.

—Simon Winchester, *The Sun Never Sets:*
Travels to the Remaining Outposts of the British Empire (1985)

Family Travel Times, which is published quarterly by **Travel With Your Children (TWYCH),** includes a weekly call-in service for subscribers. Subscriptions cost $40 a year and can be ordered by writing to TWYCH, 40 Fifth Ave., New York, NY 10011 (☎ **212/477-5524**).

TWYCH also publishes two nitty-gritty information guides, *Skiing with Children* and *Cruising with Children;* they sell for $29 and $22, respectively, but are discounted to newsletter subscribers. An information packet, which describes TWYCH's publications and includes a recent sample issue, can be purchased by sending $3.50 to the above address.

Most hotels will help you find a babysitter.

7 Flying to Bermuda

From North America's East Coast, you can be in Bermuda in approximately two hours by plane.

THE MAJOR AIRLINES

American Airlines (☎ **800/433-7300**) flies to Bermuda nonstop every day from New York's JFK Airport. Departures are timed to coincide with dozens of connecting flights from elsewhere throughout North America. There are also connections via Raleigh/Durham.

Delta (☎ **800/241-4141**) offers daily nonstop service to Bermuda from both Boston and Atlanta. The Boston flight departs in the morning (around 9am), whereas the Atlanta flight leaves around noon, late enough to allow connections from most of the other cities within Delta's vast network.

Continental Airlines (☎ **800/231-0856**) offers daily nonstop service to Bermuda from New Jersey's Newark Airport during spring, summer, and fall, and about five times a week between mid-December and mid-March.

USAir (☎ **800/428-4322**) has daily nonstop flights year-round to Bermuda from Philadelphia, Boston, Baltimore-Washington, and New York's La Guardia Airport.

Air Canada (☎ **800/776-3000** in the U.S., **800/268-7240** in Canada) offers daily nonstop flights from Toronto to Bermuda, with frequent connections into Toronto from virtually every other city in Canada. The flight departs around 9:30am, permitting convenient connections from both Montréal and Québec City. The airline also offers Saturday nonstop flights to Bermuda from Halifax.

The airline of choice for visitors from the United Kingdom is **British Airways** (☎ **0345-222111** in Britain); it flies between London's Gatwick Airport and Bermuda about three times a week year-round. One offbeat but attractive option offered by this airline to U.S. visitors is a package that combines a trip to Bermuda followed by an excursion to London, and then a nonstop return flight from London to the United States. British Airways offers schedules and discounted APEX fares for midwinter pilgrimages to London's West End theater district and the city's countless shops and museums.

REGULAR FARES

The best strategy for obtaining the lowest airfare is to call the various airlines, keeping in mind the bonus miles and frequent flyer programs that many of them offer. Most airlines offer the best deals on tickets ordered at least 14 days in advance, and that includes stopovers in Bermuda of at least three days. Airfares fluctuate according to the season, but tend to remain competitive among the companies vying for shares of the lucrative Bermuda run.

Peak season—summer in Bermuda—is the most expensive time to go; low season—usually mid-September or early November until mid-March—offers less expensive fares. The airlines that fly to Bermuda seldom offer a shoulder (intermediate) season. Because most aircraft flying from North America to Bermuda are medium-sized, there is space for only two classes of service: first class and economy. Economy class is the lowest-priced regular airfare that imposes no special restrictions or requirements.

OTHER GOOD-VALUE CHOICES

Bear in mind that in the airline industry what constitutes good value is always changing. What was the lowest possible fare one day may not be lowest the next day when a new promotional fare is offered.

BUCKET SHOPS   A bucket shop (or consolidator) acts as a clearinghouse for blocks of tickets that airlines discount and consign during normally slow periods of air travel. For Bermuda, that usually means November through March. Charter operators (see below) and bucket shops used to perform separate functions, but many outfits now perform both functions.

Tickets are sometimes discounted up to 35%. The time of payment can vary from 45 days prior to departure to the last minute. Such discount tickets may be purchased through regular travel agents who usually mark them up at least 8% to 10%, thereby reducing your discount.

Many people who use consolidators complain that since they do not qualify for advanced seat assignments, they are likely to be assigned a "poor seat" on the plane at the last minute. In a recent survey many passengers reported no savings at all, since airlines sometimes match the consolidator's ticket when they announce a promotional fare. So, carefully investigate all options to make sure that you will actually be saving money.

Bucket shops abound; look for their ads in your local newspaper's travel section. Although it may be difficult to get a bucket shop fare to Bermuda, you may succeed if you're willing to spend a lot of time and effort. In New York, try **TFI Tours International,** 34 W. 32nd St., 12th Floor, New York, NY 10001 (☎ **212/736-1140** in New York State or **800/745-8000** elsewhere in the United States).

CHARTER FLIGHTS   Charter flights to Bermuda have significant restrictions. Generally, these flights are not allowed to use "gateway" cities such as New York or Boston. This is a complicated situation that changes yearly (sometimes even monthly); it's best to enlist the services of a good travel agent, who should know the least expensive and most direct route for you.

Essentially, charter flights allow visitors to Bermuda to fly at a less expensive fare than on a regularly scheduled flight, in some cases at least 30% less. However, there are a number of drawbacks. One is the typical requirement that tickets be purchased quite far in advance (sometimes at least 45 days or more before the actual trip). Should you be forced by unforeseen circumstances to cancel your flight, you could lose most of the money that you have paid for the ticket. To avoid this disaster, it is best to take out cancellation insurance; ask your travel agent about it.

A charter flight requires you to go to Bermuda and return on specified dates. Again, this allows you no flexibility in scheduling. Some charters also oblige you to prebook hotel rooms and pay for certain "ground arrangements."

If you would like to take a charter flight, work through a travel agent, who will be aware of the business reputation of a packager. If you're a do-it-yourselfer, you can always check the Sunday travel section of your local or a big-city newspaper, looking for the announcements of any charter operators advertising flights to Bermuda.

STANDBY FARES   Courier services no longer operate to Bermuda, but there is another cheap alternative. **Air-Tech Ltd.,** 584 Broadway, Suite 1007, New York, NY 10012 (☎ **212/219-7000**), is a "space-available" travel service, offering standby fares mainly to the Caribbean, Mexico, and Europe. Although your chances of getting a standby fare to Bermuda are not too great, why not give it a try? Air-Tech is also a full travel service.

Space-available travel with Air-Tech is easy. All you need to do is: register with Air-Tech, specify your preferred destination (in this case, Bermuda), indicate a two- to five-day period (the travel window) when you wish to fly, and call Air-Tech the Wednesday before your travel window begins. You will then be informed of whatever flights and seating are available for your specified window period. After that, all you have to do is simply go to the airport and catch your flight. It's that easy.

Passengers who cannot get a flight within their chosen travel window have the opportunity to either reschedule or receive a full refund. Air-Tech's guarantee is to get you on board a flight within your designated travel window or refund your money.

TRAVEL CLUBS   Yet another possibility for low-cost air travel is the travel club; Bermuda is heavily featured in the discounted offerings. A club supplies an unsold inventory of tickets discounted in the usual 20% to 60% range. Some deals involve cruise ships and complete tour packages.

After you pay an annual fee to join, you are given a hotline number to call when you're planning a trip. Many discounts become available several days before an actual departure, although some give you at least a week's (sometimes even a month's) notice. Because you're limited to what's available, however, you need to be fairly flexible. The following are some of the best travel clubs:

Moment's Notice, 7301 New Utrecht Ave., Brooklyn, NY 11204 (☎ **212/ 486-0500**), with an annual membership charge of $25, allows spur-of-the-moment participation in dozens of tours to sunny climes. Each is geared to impulse purchases and last-minute getaways, and each offers air and land packages that may provide substantial savings over what you'd have paid through more conventional channels. Although membership is required to participate in the tours, anyone can call the company's hotline (☎ **212/750-9111**) to learn what options are available. The company's best-value tours generally depart from New Jersey's Newark Airport.

Sears Discount Travel Club, 3033 S. Parker Rd., Suite 900, Aurora, CO 80014 (☎ **800/433-9383** in the U.S.), offers a three-month trial membership for $1 (yearly membership $49), which includes a catalog (issued four times a year), maps, discounts at select hotels, and a limited guarantee that equivalent packages will not be undersold by any other travel organization. It also offers a 5% rebate on the value of all airline tickets, tours, hotels, and car rentals that are purchased through them. (To collect this rebate, participants must complete some questionnaire forms and submit photocopies of their receipts and itineraries.) For actual Travel Membership call **800/255-1487.**

Vacations to Go, 1502 Augusta Dr., Suite 415, Houston, TX 77057 (☎ **800/ 338-4962**), established in 1984, specializes in bringing prospective cruise participants together with cruise lines at discounted prices. The annual membership cost of $5.95 per family, provides access to catalogs and news briefs about cost-conscious cruises of the Atlantic, the Caribbean, and the Mediterranean.

8 Cruises

Conditions have improved remarkably since that innocent abroad, Mark Twain, made his rough sea trips to Bermuda. He considered the place "hell to get to," but thought the charms of Bermuda worth the tough sea voyage. He would surely be amazed at the luxurious way today's seagoing passengers travel to sunny Bermuda.

Cruise ships aren't for everyone, but if you'd like to try this method of travel, Bermuda is a good choice for a first-timer. Since you can sail from the East Coast of the United States to Bermuda and back in just a few days, you aren't committed to an extended time at sea (as you might be on a Caribbean cruise).

Unfortunately, cruise-ship trips to Bermuda are limited, mostly because Bermuda lacks the facilities to handle large cruise ships. Cruise ships tie up at three harbors in Bermuda: St. George's in the East End, the Royal Naval Dockyard in the West End, and the most visited port of call on the island, Hamilton Harbour (the city of Hamilton).

The cruise-ship season is from April to November. Once upon a time, only the wealthy could afford such a trip, but package deals and other cost-saving arrangements devised by the travel industry have opened up the cruise ship to today's middle-income traveler.

Once you've decided to go by cruise ship, you need to choose your cruise line. Some lines want their passengers to have a total vacation—one filled with activities from "sunup to sundown." Others see time at sea as a period of tranquillity and relaxation, with less emphasis on organized activities.

To keep costs down, ask for an inside cabin, which is usually quite small and thus less desirable and cheaper. If you plan to be participating in many of the ship's activities during the day, you won't be spending much time in your cabin, anyway. Cabins are equipped with a private shower and toilet. Many readers have reported that with a midship cabin you are less likely to experience severe rolling and pitching. Cabins on older vessels come in widely different sizes, beginning with deluxe stateroom suites, a throwback to the old days of transatlantic voyages. Modern vessels have more standardized accommodations.

Although white tie and tails are no longer the norm, it's still a good idea for men to bring a dark suit, and for women to bring at least one cocktail dress. Most of the time more casual wear is appropriate for evening: sports coats, slacks, and open shirts for men and sports dresses and pants suits for women.

Unfortunately (considering the investment), one of the most important ingredients for a successful cruise is nearly impossible to know in advance—your fellow passengers. The right crowd can be a lot of fun, while an incompatible group can leave you sulking in your cabin.

A money-saving tip: You can often receive considerable savings on a seven-day cruise by booking early. See a travel agent or call the cruise line.

Celebrity Cruises, 5200 Blue Lagoon Dr., Miami, FL 33126 (☎ **305/262-8322** or **800/437-3111**), offers cruises to Bermuda from New York and other East Coast cities in spring and summer. Celebrity ships are stylish and sleek, a kind of moderate level first-class passage. The ships are strong on cuisine, but lack wraparound promenade decks. The line emphasizes entertainment and recreation, although many readers complain that their shore excursions in Bermuda are dull. Seven-night cruises usually leave New York on Saturday, heading for Bermuda, with two nights each at St. George's and Hamilton. The 30,400-ton, 553-cabin SS *Meridian,* dating from 1967, carries 1,106 passengers, with an international crew of 580, and mainly Greek officers. More than half of its cabins are outside. This is a family favorite, with a children's program offered. Older people seem to like it too, but singles and young couples might prefer other vessels.

Celebrity Cruises also sails the MV *Horizon* to Bermuda. A 46,811-ton vessel with 677 cabins, about 85% of which are outside, this 1990 ship carries 1,354 passengers with an international crew of 642. The passenger/crew ratio is two to one. The ship offers nine passenger decks, filled with entertainment lounges, bars, and other facilities. Cabins are up-to-date and generally quite spacious. On the *Meridian* many outside cabins on the Atlantic Deck have partially obstructed or fully obstructed views; on the *Horizon,* the outside cabins on the Bermuda Deck also have views partially obstructed.

Cunard Line, 555 Fifth Ave., New York, NY 10017 (☎ **212/880-7500** or **800/ 5-CUNARD**), sails RMS *Queen Elizabeth 2* to Bermuda on five-day cruises.

Built in 1969, this 70,327-ton vessel is the most famous cruise ship in the world, carrying 1,810 passengers, with a crew of 1,000 men and women. In November and December of 1994, the ship underwent a $45 million refurbishment. The flagship of the Cunard fleet, the *QE2* sails the British flag to every corner of the globe. But, like English royalty, age is taking its toll; in spite of many face-lifts, the *QE2* is approaching the end of three decades of distinguished service.

The Golden Lion Pub, in traditional British style, is a social hub. On the Upper Deck near the theater and the casino, it offers a variety of draft beers and other drinks, even pub games, an upright piano, and a karaoke center. The Grand Lounge is the venue for big name entertainment, with a new dance floor. The Lido is an informal buffet-style restaurant, offering breakfast, lunch, and a traditional midnight buffet. The atmosphere is that of an informal winter garden. The Mauretania Restaurant on the Quarter Deck has been completely refurbished, and the Caronia Restaurant on the Upper Deck was renamed to honor the Cunard ship of legendary opulence. All of the restaurants have been refurbished, including the Queens Grill, which has been compared to the top dining choices of Paris, London, and New York. The Princess Grill and the Britannia Grill are other dining choices.

You can get lost on the *QE2* since it rises 13 stories high and is three football fields long. The vessel features the QE2 Spa, the most luxurious spa afloat, with a rejuvenating sea-water massage jet and whirlpool treatments, three French hydrotherapy baths, and saunas for men and women. Beauty therapists are also on hand. Among its many other features is a sports center, a jogging track, a library, a club casino, and a shopping promenade with a branch of Harrod's.

The *QE2* usually has three cruises a year from New York to Bermuda, beginning about the last week in April and ending around early September. Because the cabins aboard the *QE2* are so wide-ranging, from sumptuous suites to small inner cabins, the price range also varies, from a low of $820 per person all the way up to $4,040.

Two other Cunard vessels have earmarked Bermuda as a target for cruises, including MS *Sagafjord,* christened in 1965 and last refurbished in 1993, with a gross tonnage of 25,147, a passenger capacity of 589, and a crew of 352. Attracting older, more mature passengers (who comprise a devoted following with a history of repeats), the *Sagafjord* is known for its cuisine and its white-glove service. Entertainment is low key aboard this vessel, although there is sometimes a Broadway-style revue, but more often there is a concert pianist or a jazz band. Most staterooms have large picture windows, and the best open onto private verandas. Some 90% of the cabins have a bathtub as well as a shower, and most cabins are outside. The ship also offers the

Golden Door Spa at Sea. Its schedule calls for November sailings from Fort Lauderdale and Philadelphia, with calls at Charleston, Savannah, and both St. George's and Hamilton in Bermuda. These sailings range from 6 to 13 days.

The *Royal Viking Sun* also calls at Bermuda (Hamilton), after world cruises that include Naples, Puerto Banús, Casablanca, and Funchal (Madeira). An 11-day cruise that begins at the end of April leaves Fort Lauderdale and calls at Savannah before continuing on to St. George's and Hamilton. On the return trip, the ship calls at Charleston before reaching Fort Lauderdale. One of the world's most highly rated cruise ships, the *Royal Viking Sun* was purchased by Cunard in 1994 for $170 million. With a gross tonnage of 38,000, this 1988 vessel carries 756 passengers and a crew—mainly European—of 460. Its officers are mainly Norwegian, and about 95% of its cabins are outside. With one of the most loyal followings in the cruise industry, *Royal Viking Sun* offers handsomely appointed, oversize cabins. It also has a Golden Door Spa at Sea and its cuisine is among the best of any vessel afloat. Sailing to Bermuda aboard the *Royal Viking Sun* is going in style, and virtually every night is formal. It is neither cheap nor corny (as are many Carnival vessels), but attracts more affluent passengers who are seeking a touch of class before it's gone forever.

Majesty Cruise Line, 901 South America Way, Miami, FL 33132 (☎ 305/530-8900 or 800/532-7788), formed in 1991 as a companion company to the Dolphin Cruise Line (but now independent), offers the $220 million MV *Royal Majesty,* sailing to Bermuda. With a tonnage of 32,396, it carries 1,056 passengers overseen by a crew of 525. It features 343 outside staterooms and 185 inside staterooms. It's the first ship to offer a totally smoke-free dining room, and 25% of its cabins are smoke-free. Built in 1992, it provides more amenities and refinement than most vessels used for three- to four-day cruises (such as those to Bermuda). The line offers bountiful buffets and meals, and food is served almost continuously. Unfortunately, the cuisine is not exceptional. The *Royal Majesty* kitchen staff will cater to special diets. You can stay in shape at the Bodywaves Spa, with computerized weight machines and aerobics. This is not a glitzy vessel, and deck space is limited.

The **Norwegian Cruise Line,** 95 Merrick Way, Coral Gables, FL 33134 (☎ 305/445-0866 or 800/327-7030), offers the 1,242-passenger MS *Dreamward* weighing 41,000 tons. Built in 1992, it sails the high seas with a crew of 483. The passenger/crew ratio is 2.5 to 1. With 10 passenger decks, the vessel has 623 cabins, 85% of which are outside.

On Saturdays from April through October (dates subject to change), the *Dreamward* makes seven-day, round-trip cruises from New York to St. George's or Hamilton. For a quality midsize ship at moderate cost, the *Dreamward* is the market leader in cruises to Bermuda. It's known for its innovative design. Both forward and aft, the upper decks of the ship cascade down, thereby creating panoramic seascapes. The service is the best in the Norwegian Cruise Line fleet. The vessel is good for families with children who are seeking an activity-filled schedule.

Instead of one large traditional dining room, this ship has four formal dining rooms: the Four Seasons Dining Room, the Sun Terrace Dining Room, the Terraces Dining Room (the largest dining facility), and Le Bistro (the smallest dining room). Hot dogs, hamburgers, and other fast foods are available at the Sports Bar and Grill on the Sports Deck.

Eight bars and lounges are available, including the Stardust Lounge, where full-length Broadway-type revues can be presented. The lounge also serves as a late-night disco. The Casino Royale provides seven blackjack tables, one roulette, one dice, two Caribbean stud poker games, and 99 slot machines.

The Fitness Center and Spa features a variety of exercise equipment, an aerobics area, Lifecycles, and Lifesteps. There is also a jogging track, a children's playground, two swimming pools with Jacuzzis, a medical center, a duty-free shop, a video arcade for playing video games and watching TV broadcasts of sports events.

Royal Caribbean Cruises Ltd., 1050 Caribbean Way, Miami, FL 33132 (☎ **800/327-6700**), offers MS *Song of America,* weighing 37,584 tons and carrying 1,402 passengers with an international crew (the officers are Norwegian). Built in 1982, the ship has 702 cabins, more than half of which are outside. The cabins are compact and well designed. Despite its size, the *Song of America* is often compared to an ocean-going yacht. A 1994 face-lift has kept the *Song of America* still singing in tune. From May 7 through October 22, it makes seven-night cruises from New York to Bermuda. The suites are situated on the Promenade Deck, but all cabins are above the waterline.

Single passengers typically pay 150% of the double rate, but if you're a flexible single and can wait until embarkation time for your room assignment, you can probably get a discount.

Half a dozen bars, including the Schooner and the Viking Crown Lounge, assure that you will have plenty to drink, and, later, there is the Casino Royale for gambling, a disco, and a piano bar. Entertainment is provided, ranging from a masquerade parade to a country-and-western jamboree. In all, four lounges are devoted to entertainment. The kitchen serves bountiful meals and will accommodate special requests. There are occasional theme dinners.

Both the Sun Deck and Promenade Deck offer walking "trails," while the health club features massages, saunas, treadmills, stationary bicycles, and rowing machines. During the summer and holiday periods, there are special programs for children. For the disabled, wheelchair access is limited.

9 Package Tours

The major advantages of a package tour are economy and convenience. The costs of transportation (usually airfare), hotel, food (sometimes), and sightseeing (sometimes) are combined in one package, neatly tied up with a single price tag.

If you booked your flight and hotel separately, you might pay more than a package tour—hence their immense and increasing appeal. Also, because tour operators can mass-book hotels and make volume purchases, transfers between your hotel and the airport are often included. Of course, there are disadvantages: You might find yourself in a hotel you disliked immensely, yet you are virtually trapped there because you've already paid for it. The single traveler, regrettably, usually suffers too, since nearly all tour packages are based on double occupancy.

Choosing the right package tour can be a problem, but your travel agent might be able to offer one, and certainly all the major airline carriers offer them.

Some companies specialize in package tours. One company that has been marketing travel to Bermuda since 1978 is the **Bermuda Travel Planners,** 350 Fifth Ave., Suite 2718, New York, NY 10018 (☎ **212/564-9502** or **800/323-2020**). It represents almost 50 of the island's hotels, ranging from modest and out-of-the-way guesthouses to deluxe hotels. Particularly popular are the company's wedding packages. Bermuda Travel Planners also arranges vacation packages for horseback riders, scuba enthusiasts, golf and tennis players, and honeymooners. It is open 9am to 6pm Monday through Friday.

Other well-recommended tour operators include those endorsed and approved by two of North America's largest airlines: **Delta Dream Vacations,** 110 E. Broward

Blvd., Fort Lauderdale, FL 33301 (☎ **205/522-1440** or **800/872-7786**), and **American Airlines Flyaway Vacations** (☎ **800/433-7300**). Both groups combine inexpensive airfare with land (that is, hotel) packages, which can save substantial amounts of money over what you'd probably have paid if you'd made the arrangements yourself.

You might also want to contact one of the world's largest travel organizers, **American Express.** Favored treatment and special discounts are sometimes offered to holders of gold or platinum American Express cards (if you have one of these, call **800/525-3355**); but a wide array of interesting and unusual tours are available to members of the general public as well. Call **800/937-2639** and your call will be routed to the closest regional American Express representative.

Shopping around for the right package can be time-consuming and a bore. To speed up the process, call **Tourscan Inc.,** P.O. Box 2367, Darien, CT 06820 (☎ **203/655-8091** or **800/962-2080**). Its computerized list provides both hotel and air package deals not only to Bermuda, but also to The Bahamas and the Caribbean. This organization usually has a whole range of offerings so you can pick and choose from what's out there. Its *Island Vacation Catalog,* which costs $4 and is issued twice yearly, contains complete details. Your $4 will be refunded if you book a tour. If you decide to take a tour, you can either book it directly through Tourscan, or use any travel agent.

Getting to Know Bermuda

Once you've learned to get around without a car, you'll find settling into Bermuda relatively easy. The first-timer soon learns that Bermuda isn't one island, as is commonly thought, but a string of islands linked by causeways and bridges—at least the 20 or so that are inhabited. The other islands can be reached by boat.

Unlike many islands in the Caribbean (including the Dominican Republic) that look rather junky, Bermuda is characterized by neat, trim houses which are a source of great pride to their owners. There won't be a casino at your megaresort—in fact, no casinos at all— and you'd better have your fill of Big Macs before you leave home. There are some fast-food eateries in Bermuda but they are nothing in comparison with those on the U.S. mainland or even those on the Bahama islands. There's a sense of order in Bermuda, and everything seems to work efficiently, even when the weather's hot.

As you become oriented to Bermuda, you'll quickly find that the island offers you two basic choices—a lazy life on the beach with everything done for you when you return to your hotel, or else an activity-filled agenda for the most energetic vacationer.

1 Orientation

ARRIVING
BY PLANE

Chances are, you'll arrive by air, as most visitors do. Planes arrive at the **Civil Air Terminal** at Kindley Field Rd., St. George's, 9 miles east of Hamilton and about 17 miles east of Somerset at the far western end of Bermuda.

The flight from most East Coast destinations, including New York, Raleigh/Durham, Baltimore, and Boston takes about two hours, so you won't have jet lag when you arrive. Even flights from Atlanta take only $2^1/_2$ hours; from Toronto it's nearly three hours.

After clearing Customs, you can pick up tourist information at the airport before heading out to your hotel. Since you aren't allowed to rent a car in Bermuda, you must rely on a bus, taxi, or limousine to reach your hotel.

More than 600 taxis are available in Bermuda, and cabbies meet all arriving flights. Taxis, which are regulated by meter, are allowed to carry a maximum of four passengers. If you and your companion/ spouse have a lot of luggage, you will need the taxi all to yourselves, of course. Including a tip of 10% to 15%, it costs about $22 to reach a destination in Hamilton. Since you're already near St. George's, the fare there is about $11, or $14 to Tucker's Town. To the south shore hotels, the charge is likely to be $25.

To the West End, site of many more resorts, the charge is more than $40. Fares go up 25% between 10pm and 6am as well as all day on Sundays and holidays. Luggage carries a surcharge of 25¢ per piece. Expect to pay about $4 for the first mile and $1.40 for each additional mile. There are several authorized taxi companies on the island, including **Radio Cab** (☎ 441/295-4141), **C.O.O.P.**(☎ 441/292-4476), **B.T.O.C.** (☎ 441/292-5600), **B.T.S.L.** (☎ 441/295-8294), and **Sandy's** (☎ 441/234-2344).

It would be cheaper for a party of four to call a minivan and split the cost among them. This can be done before you arrive in Bermuda by contacting **Bermuda Hosts Ltd.** at 441/293-1334. This outfit can arrange to have a minivan waiting for your flight. Even if you're only two people (rather than four), you can ask a waiting minivan at the airport if it has room to take on two extra passengers. That way, you can lower the cost you'd incur by having a taxi all to yourself. Bermuda Hosts can provide transportation for golfers and can also arrange sightseeing tours.

BY CRUISE SHIP

This is perhaps the easiest way to arrive in Bermuda. The cruise ship staff presents you with a list of tour options long before you arrive in port; almost everything is done for you, unless you opt to make your own arrangements. If you take an independent taxi tour, it will be far more expensive than an organized tour. Most passengers book shore excursions at the same time they reserve the cruise.

Seven-day cruises out of New York spend four days at sea, with three days in port. Most cruise ships arrive in the traditional port of Hamilton, the capital of Bermuda and its chief commercial and shopping center. If shopping is more important to you than sightseeing, be sure that your cruise ship docks here.

If you're more interested in historic Bermuda, make sure that your ship is scheduled to anchor at St. George's, at the eastern tip of the island. With its narrow lanes and old buildings and streets, St. George's has been called the island's equivalent of Colonial Williamsburg in Virginia. Although St. George's has a few shops and boutiques, this is not the primary place to come for shopping. Depending on the cruise line, its schedules, and the current tides, some cruise ships will dock at both St. George's and Hamilton while in Bermuda. Ships often plan to dock at St. George's, but find that they cannot do so because of the tides.

It is not too likely that you'll disembark at Somerset, which is at the western end of the island and farthest away from Bermuda's major attractions. The West End has its own charm and sightseeing appeal; it is, after all, home of the Royal Naval Dockyard, one of the major attractions in Bermuda. In a shopping mall at the dockyard, craft stores and museums exist side by side.

During your stay in port, you can avail yourself of the waiting taxis near your ship, or you could rent a moped or bicycle (see "Getting Around," below) and do some touring and shopping on your own.

VISITOR INFORMATION

You can get answers to most of your questions at the **Visitors Service Bureau** at the Ferry Terminal, Hamilton (☎ 441/295-1480); King's Square, St. George's (☎ 441/297-1642); or in Somerset (☎ 441/234-1388). During the summer the Visitors Service Bureau is open Monday through Saturday from 9am to 4pm; off-season it is open Monday through Saturday from 9:30am to 2pm.

ISLAND LAYOUT

THE CITY OF HAMILTON AND ENVIRONS   With Hamilton at the center, Bermuda can be divided into the West End and the East End; the airport is situated in the East End. At Hamilton Harbour, as you leave the Ferry Terminal you'll see the Visitors Service Bureau and the birdcage police officer.

To your right (east) lies the main shopping artery of Hamilton—Front Street—and to your left (west) is Pitts Bay Road leading to the Princess, Hamilton's leading hotel.

Front Street, which follows the line of the harbor, boasts many of the stores for which Bermuda is famous, including Trimingham's, established in 1844, and Smith's, established in 1889.

Moving away from the harbor, you will encounter other streets with interesting shops—including Reid Street, Church Street, and Victoria Street, all of which are parallel with Front Street. Par-La-Ville Park, which lies directly north of the Ferry Terminal, is the city's largest and most central public garden.

North Hamilton is in Pembroke Parish, as is the city of Hamilton. Hamilton Parish, which begins at Victoria Park, is a largely residential (working-class) district, with relatively neat small houses.

East of Hamilton, Fort Hamilton is one of the original 55 forts that formerly protected Bermuda. Sitting alone in the Atlantic, Bermuda was vulnerable to attack before the installation of these forts. Nearby is the 20-acre arboretum.

THE EAST END   Continuing east from Hamilton, the parish of Devonshire is named after the famous shire in England's West Country, with its rolling hills and "green lungs." The present name—Devonshire—is quite an improvement on its former name: Brackish Pond. One of the major landmarks here is Old Devonshire Church, which is situated south of Middle Road.

From Hamilton you can take Middle Road all the way to Flatts Village, which opens onto the landlocked Harrington Sound. You can also take South Shore Road (also called South Road), which leads eventually to Tucker's Town, an exclusive residential area of multimillion-dollar properties.

The area of Harrington Sound is filled with attractions, and if you're in Bermuda for a few days, you'll probably spend some time here, seeing the Bermuda Aquarium, the Bermuda Glass Blowing Studio, Crystal Caves, Leamington Caves, Bermuda Perfumery, Spittal Pond, Verdmont, and other sights.

Continuing east, follow Blue Hole Hill until you reach the causeway, which takes you to St. David's Island and then on to St. George's, Bermuda's old historic city and its former capital. St. George's is on an island (also named St. George's). To explore the town, it's best to take a walking tour (see Chapter 8, "Bermuda Strolls").

The eastern end of Bermuda was forever changed when the United States used landfill to create a military base during World War II. The present-day Bermuda

Impressions

[As you approach Bermuda by air, you'll notice] dozens of small houses, their roofs pyramid-shaped, and whitewashed, their walls picked out in a variety of soft pastels—lemon, bluebell, lilac, primrose. It all looks very prim and ordered: the lawns look neat, the swimming pools glitter in the late morning sun, the sea is the palest of greens and splashes softly against low cliffs of pink and well-washed orange.
—Simon Winchester, *The Sun Never Sets: Travels to the Remaining Outposts of the British Empire* (1985)

airport emerged from that base. What remains of the American base is today used mainly for routine antisubmarine surveillance flights and as a tracking station for the National Aeronautics and Space Administration. American rights to the base—part of a 99-year lend-lease agreement between the United States and Britain signed in 1941, under which the British received American submarines and other needed war matériel in exchange for use of the base—terminate in the year 2040. Bermuda's only McDonald's is on the base; it can be visited only on Wednesdays, when the base is open to the public.

The base is situated on St. David's Island, the most rustic spot in Bermuda. The island lighthouse, dating from 1879, occupies the loftiest point on Bermuda's East End. Some St. David's islanders, the most provincial of whom may never have traveled as far as Hamilton, refused to be relocated when the naval base was under construction, preferring instead to remain on their homeland. There is a section called "Texas," where the U.S. government built cottages for these islanders, and they and their families remain there today.

THE WEST END   To the west of Hamilton, a different world unfolds, as visitors explore, in this order, the parishes of Paget, Warwick, Southampton, and Sandys, the last of which lies in the far western corner. The landmass of Sandys along Great Sound juts eastward as if it were trying to reconnect with the city of Hamilton.

South of Hamilton and heading west is Harbour Road, which borders the harbor of Hamilton for several miles until it reaches the vicinity of Darrell Island, a tiny green islet that was the site of Bermuda's first airport. You can take a ferry from the city of Hamilton across the harbor to the north coast of Paget and Warwick parishes.

Alternatively, you could take Middle Road, which goes through Paget and Warwick parishes. Continue west through Southampton until you reach Somerset Bridge, which crosses into Sandys Parish.

Many of the best hotels and beaches, including the Elbow Beach Hotel, Warwick Long Bay, and Horseshoe Bay, lie along the southern coast of the western peninsula, reached by going along South Shore Road. If you continue west far enough, South Shore Road merges with Middle Road as it pushes through the parish of Southampton.

Middle Road continues to Somerset Bridge, which leads into Sandys Parish. This parish consists of Somerset Island, the Royal Naval Dockyard, and Ireland, Watford, and Boaz Islands. Although facing the Atlantic on their northern shorelines, these islands and settlements open onto the more protected Great Sound.

Somerset Bridge is best reached by taking the ferry from Hamilton. From the ferry dock at the bridge, you can continue by ferry to Ireland Island and the dockyard, or you could take the ferry directly from Hamilton to the dockyard. Sandys Parish is bisected by Somerset Road.

Many visitors come here to visit Mangrove Bay, an idyllic beach strip lying directly east of Somerset Village, the tiny hamlet that is dominated by Sandys Boat Club.

Somerset Village is where Bermuda's Railway Trail begins, and it's a good place to start if you want to take this walk through the island.

FINDING AN ADDRESS

The island chain of Bermuda isn't the center of Manhattan and, thus, doesn't follow a system of street addresses too rigidly. Most hotels, even in official government listings, don't bother to include street addresses, although they do include post-office boxes and ZIP Codes. It's just assumed that everybody knows where everything is, which is fine if you've lived in Bermuda all your life. But if you're a first-time visitor, you should get a good map and some landmark locations before setting out.

Most of the establishments you will be seeking are on some street plan. Some places use numbers in their street addresses, while others, perhaps their neighbors, don't! The actual building number is not always important, since a building such as a resort hotel is likely to be set back so far from the main road that you couldn't see its number anyway. It's far better to look for a sign indicating, for example, the Sonesta Beach Hotel than for a street number. Cross streets will also aid you in finding an address.

Plot your itinerary carefully and ask questions. If you get lost, be aware that some well-traveled people believe that one of the charms of a visit to Bermuda is to get lost along an unmarked country lane. Many interesting discoveries have been made that way.

MAPS

Check out the free full-color fold-out map we've included for you at the back of this book. More detailed maps are sold in bookstores on the island, and the Bermuda Department of Tourism publishes a free *Bermuda Handy Reference Map*. This tiny pocket map, distributed by the tourist office and available at most hotels, has on one side an overview and orientation map (with key) of Bermuda, highlighting and numbering its major attractions, golf courses, public beaches, and hotels. It does not, however, pinpoint individual restaurants unless they are attached to hotels.

On the other side of the map is a detailed street plan of the city of Hamilton, indicating all its major landmarks and service facilities, such as the Ferry Terminal and the Post Office.

There is also a detailed map of the Royal Naval Dockyard, the West End, and the East End, plus tips on transportation—ferries, taxis, buses—and other helpful hints, such as a depiction of various traffic signs.

2 Getting Around

Driving is on the left, and the national speed limit is 20 mph in the Bermuda countryside, 15 mph in busier areas. Cars are limited to one per family—and none at all for visitors. In such a far-off Eden, the most popular form of transportation is the motorized bicycle, called a "putt-putt," and the most romantic means of transport is the colorful fringe-topped surrey.

BY BUS You can't rent a car. Taxis are expensive. You may not want or be able to ride a bicycle or a motorbike. What's left for getting around Bermuda? Buses, of course. All major routes are covered by the bus network, but be prepared for waits. There's even a do-it-yourself sightseeing tour by bus and ferry, and regularly scheduled buses go to most of the destinations that interest tourists in Bermuda. However, some buses do not run on Sunday and holidays, so be sure to find out about bus schedules for the trip you want to make.

Bermuda is divided into 14 zones of about 2 miles each. The regular cash fare for up to three zones is $2.50, or $4 for more than three zones. Using tokens the fare is $2 for up to three zones, or $3.50 for more than three zones. Children 3 to 13 years pay $1 for all zones. Those 2 and under go free. *Note:* You must have the exact change or tokens ready to deposit in the fare box as you board the bus. Drivers do not make change.

You can also purchase tokens at sub–post offices or at the Central Bus Terminal on Washington Street in Hamilton, where all routes except Route 6 begin and end. The terminal is just off Church Street a few steps east of City Hall. You can get there from Front Street or Reid Street by going up Queen Street or through Walker

Arcade and Washington Mall. If you plan to travel a lot around Bermuda, you might want to purchase a booklet of 15 14-zone tickets (for $22) or 15 3-zone tickets (for $13). For children 15 tickets cost $6, regardless of the number of zones. For more information on bus service, telephone 441/292-3854. Nearly all hotels, guesthouses, and restaurants have bus stops close by.

In the east, **St. George's Mini-Bus Service** (☎ **441/297-8199**) operates a mini-bus service around St. George's Parish and St. David's Island. The basic fare is $1.75 for adults or $1 for children. Senior citizens also ride for $1. Although buses depart from King's Square in the center of St. George's, they can also be flagged down along the road. Service is year-round daily from 7am to 10pm.

The **West End Mini-Bus Service** (☎ **441/234-2344**) runs a minibus service that departs from Somerset Bridge and goes all the way to the Royal Naval Dockyard on Ireland Island. Fares depend on how far you go, but they're never more than $2.50 for the entire run. Children and senior citizens go for half price. Passengers can be dropped off wherever they want, providing it is on the regular bus route. With slight variations, hours are Monday from 8:30am to 1pm, Tuesday through Saturday from 8:30am to 4:30pm, and Saturday and Sunday from 10am to 1pm.

BY TAXI   Although taxis can be an expensive means of getting around, sharing a taxi is reasonable. The hourly charge for taxis is $20 for one to four passengers. A luxury tour van accommodating up to six passengers is $30 an hour. If you want to use one for a sightseeing tour, the minimum is three hours. When a taxi has a blue flag on its hood (locals call it the "bonnet"), the driver is qualified to serve as a tour guide. Because these drivers are checked out and tested by the government, you should use this type of driver if you plan to tour Bermuda by taxi. "Blue-bonnet" drivers charge no more than regular taxi drivers.

For more information, call **Bermuda Taxi Operators** (☎ **441/292-5600**). For radio-dispatched cabs, call **Radio Cabs Bermuda** (☎ **441/295-4141**).

BY CYCLE & SCOOTER   If you're looking for a lot of exercise, you may want to rent a pedal bicycle to travel around the island in the traditional Bermuda fashion, although some of the hills may be a real challenge to your stamina. See Chapter 9.

A number of people prefer a motor-assisted cycle—moped, motor scooter, whatever—which you can rent on an hourly, daily, or weekly basis. To operate such a vehicle, you must be at least 16 years of age, although younger persons may ride as passengers. Some of these vehicles are large enough for two adults. Both driver and passenger are required by law to wear a helmet, which will be furnished by the rental establishment. The chin straps must be securely fastened. *Warning:* Visitors on mopeds have a high accident rate. Exercise extreme caution. Also, you must, as mentioned, *drive on the left,* as in England.

Among the rental establishments listed below, there is a tendency toward price-fixing, so at the present time it's not worthwhile to shop around for a better deal.

Mopeds for one rider rent for $32 for the first day, $55 for two days, and $71 for three days. Scooters for two riders cost $42 for one day, $75 for two days, $103 for three days, $120 for four days, and $135 for five days. For the rental of either mopeds or scooters, a fully refundable $20 deposit is required, plus the purchase of

Impressions

Bermuda is essentially a small town in a glamorous setting.
— David Shelley Nicholl, letter to the (London) *Times* (1978)

Island-Hopping on Your Own

Most first-time visitors think of Bermuda as one island when in fact it is a small archipelago. Many of the islands are uninhabited. If you're a bit of a skipper, you can explore them. With the guidance of the marina from which you've rented a small vessel, and armed with the proper maps, you can discover not only these islands (isles, really), but visit the coral reefs and hidden coves, many evocative of an old Brooke Shields movie.

For this boating adventure, rent a Boston whaler with an outboard engine. The romantic-sounding name of these small but sturdy boats reveals their origins—such boats were once used by New Englanders, such as seafarers from Fall River, Mass., in their pursuit of Moby-Dick. Of course, it's important to exercise caution, remembering that Bermuda itself was founded in 1612 only after the *Sea Venture,* en route to the Jamestown Colony, was wrecked off the Bermuda coast.

In the East End, explore protected Castle Harbour, which is almost completely surrounded by islands that form a protected lake. You can stop somewhere and go fishing. Snapper is your likely catch. Visitors who rent condos or apartments often take their catch of the day back to their kitchenette to prepare for dinner.

To avoid an often powerful swell, drop anchor on the west side of Castle Harbour, near Castle Harbour Golf Club and Tucker's Town. Then, head across Tucker's Town Bay to Castle Island, with its Castle Islands Nature Reserve. In earlier days Castle Island was fortified to protect Castle Harbour from enemy attack. In 1612 Governor Moore ordered a fort to be built here, the ruins of which remain today.

In the West End, it's best to begin your water wonderland exploration by going under Somerset Bridge into well-protected Ely's Harbour. To the north you can visit Cathedral Rocks before making a half-circle to Somerset Village, from which you can explore the uninhabited islands off of Mangrove Bay.

Boston whalers can be rented from the following places: **Mangrove Marina Ltd.,** end of Cambridge Rd., Mangrove Bay, Somerset (☎ **441/234-0914**); **South Side Scuba Water Sports,** at Grotto Bay Beach Hotel, Hamilton Parish (☎ **441/ 293-2915**), with another location at Marriott's Castle Harbour Resort, also in Hamilton Parish (☎ **441/293-2543**); and **Rance's Boatyard,** Crow Lane, in Paget Parish (☎ **441/292-1843**).

Most Boston whalers are 13 to 15 feet in length. For two hours, charges begin at $60. Half-day rentals go from $85, and full-day rentals cost from $135.

---

a one-time insurance policy priced at $10. The insurance is valid for the entire length of the rental. You can rent bikes at most cycle liveries.

Astwood Cycles Ltd. (☎ **441/292-2245**) has shops where you can rent either mopeds or 50-cc scooters: there are two convenient locations along Front Street in Hamilton; at Flatts Village; at the Princess, Sonesta Beach, and Coral Beach Cottages; Stonington, White Sands Hotel and Cottages, and at Horizons and Cottages.

Charging comparable prices and renting out either type of vehicle is **Wheels Ltd.,** Don Donald Street, Hamilton (☎ **441/295-0112**), Marriott's Castle Harbour Resort (☎ **441/293-0007**), Devil's Hill (☎ **441/293-1280**), or at the Southampton Princess (☎ **441/238-3336**).

One of the best rental deals on the island is offered by **Eve's Cycle Livery,** 114 Middle Rd., Paget Parish (☎ **441/236-6247**). Named after a now-legendary matriarch who founded the company more than 40 years ago, it rents men's and women's pedal bicycles (usually 10- to 12-speed mountain bikes, well suited to the island's hilly terrain) for $15 for the first day, $10 for the second day, and $5 for each additional day. A $10 deposit is required. This shop is within a 10-minute drive (or a 20-minute leisurely cycle) west of Hamilton. The company also rents a variety of motorized pedal bikes or scooters for between $22 and $42 for the first day, depending on the model, with successively lower prices for each additional day.

At **Oleander Cycles Ltd.,** Valley Road, P.O. Box 114, Paget Parish (☎ 441/ 236-5235), scooters and mopeds tend to be reliable and well maintained. There is another location on Gorham Road in Hamilton (☎ 441/295-0919) and Middle Road in Southampton (☎ 441/234-0629). Both locations are open daily from 8am to 5pm. Rentals require a $20 deposit and a supplemental charge of $12 for an insurance policy effective for the duration of your rental, or until you cause any damage to your rented vehicle.

BY FERRY   One of the most interesting means of getting around is the government-operated ferry service. Ferries crisscross Great Sound between Hamilton and Somerset, charging $3.50 fare one way; they also take the harbor route, going from Hamilton to the parishes of Paget and Warwick, where so many hotels are concentrated. The ride from Hamilton to Paget costs only $2; children pay half fare. Motorcycles are allowed on the Hamilton to Somerset run (you must pay $3.50 for your cycle, however). Bicycles are carried free. For ferry service information, call **441/ 295-4506** in Hamilton. Ferry schedules are posted at each landing. They are also available at the Ferry Terminal or the Central Bus Terminal in Hamilton. Actually, most hotels will give you a timetable if you ask.

BY HORSE-DRAWN CARRIAGE   Being romantics, Bermudians have kept at least some of their horse-drawn carriages. Although once plentiful, there are now only about a dozen left. Drivers congregate on Front Street in Hamilton, adjacent to the No. 1 passenger terminal near the cruise-ship docks. Before 1946 (when automobiles first came to the island), horses were the principal means of transportation. You can book one of these four-wheeled rigs for a chauffeured tour of the island's midriff. A single carriage (accommodating one to four passengers) drawn by one horse costs $20 for 30 minutes. An additional 30 minutes cost an additional $20. If you want to take a ride lasting more than three hours, the fee is negotiable. Unless you make special arrangements for a night ride, you aren't likely to find any carriages after 4:30pm. Contact **Bermuda Carriages** at **441/238-2640.**

FAST FACTS: Bermuda

American Express   Its representative in Hamilton, Meyer Agencies, 35 Church St. (P.O. Box 510), Hamilton, HM 12 (☎ 441/295-4176), provides complete travel service, traveler's checks, and emergency check cashing.

Area Code   Beginning in 1995, Bermuda broke away from the traditional area code for the Caribbean (809) and began using the area code 441.

Banks   There are three banks, all with their main offices in Hamilton: The **Bank of Bermuda Ltd.,** 6 Front St., Hamilton (☎ 441/295-4000), has branches on Church Street, Hamilton; Par-la-Ville Road, Hamilton; King's Square, St. George's; and in Somerset.

The **Bank of N.T. Butterfield & Son, Ltd.,** 65 Front St., Hamilton (☎ 441/ 295-1111), is one of the major banks of Bermuda, with several branches throughout the island, including one at St. George's and another at Somerset.

The **Bermuda Commercial Bank Ltd.** is at 44 Church St., Hamilton (☎ **441/295-5678**).

All banks and their branches are open Monday through Thursday from 9:30am to 3pm, and on Friday from 9:30am to 4:30pm. All banks are closed Saturday, Sunday, and public holidays. Many of the big hotels will cash traveler's checks, and there are ATM machines all around the island.

Bookstores **Bermuda Book Store (Baxters) Ltd.,** Queen St. (☎ **441/295-3698**), stocks everything that is in print about Bermuda. Some books are available only through this store. There are books on gardening, flowers, local characters, and poets, among other topics. There are also many English publications not easily obtainable in the United States, as well as a fine selection of children's books. You can also buy maps and prints here. Open Monday through Saturday 8:45am to 5pm.

Business Hours Most businesses are open Monday through Friday from 9am to 5:30pm. Stores are generally open Monday through Saturday from 9am to 5:30pm. Several shops open at 9:15am and close at 5pm. A few shops are also open in the evening, but usually only when big cruise ships are in port.

Car Rentals There are no car-rental agencies in Bermuda.

Cigarettes Tobacconists and other stores carry a wide array of tobacco products, generally from either the United States or England. Prices vary but tend to be high. At most tobacconists you can buy classic cigars from Havana, but you must enjoy them on the island, since they can't be taken back to the United States. Smoking in public places (such as restaurants) is generally permitted, but check first before lighting up. Movie theaters set aside a section for nonsmokers.

Climate See "When to Go," in Chapter 3, "Planning a Trip to Bermuda."

Crime See "Safety" below.

Currency See "Visitor Information, Entry Requirements, Customs & Money" in Chapter 3, "Planning a Trip to Bermuda."

Currency Exchange Because the U.S. dollar and the Bermudian dollar are on par, both currencies can be used (it's not necessary to convert U.S. dollars into Bermudian dollars). However, Canadian dollars must be converted into local currency because of their differing valuations.

Customs Visitors going through Bermudian Customs may bring into Bermuda duty-free apparel and articles for their personal use, including sports equipment, cameras, 200 cigarettes, one quart of liquor, one quart of wine, and approximately 20 pounds of meat. Other foodstuffs may be dutiable. All imports may be inspected on arrival. Visitors entering Bermuda may claim a duty-free gift allowance. For details on what you can bring home, see "Visitor Information, Entry Requirements, Customs & Money" in Chapter 3, "Planning a Trip to Bermuda."

Dentists For dental emergencies, call **King Edward VII Hospital,** 7 Point Finger Rd., Paget Parish (☎ **441/236-2345**), and ask for the emergency department. They maintain lists of dentists on call for dental emergencies. One well-recommended dentist you might consider calling directly is Dr. David Roblin, Outerbridge Building, Pitts Bay Road, Pembroke Parish (☎ **441/292-7676**).

Doctors For an emergency, call **King Edward VII Hospital,** 7 Point Finger Rd., Paget Parish (☎ **441/236-2345**), and ask for the emergency department. A private doctor, Dr. Gordon Campbell, Sea Venture Building, Parliament Street,

Hamilton (☎ **441/295-8106**), will treat colds, the flu, and other medical problems.

Documents Required   See "Visitor Information, Entry Requirements, Customs & Money" in Chapter 3, "Planning a Trip to Bermuda."

Driving Rules   Visitors cannot rent cars. In the case of motor-assisted cycles, you must be age 16 or over to operate such vehicles. All cycle drivers and passengers must wear safety helmets that are securely fastened. *Driving is on the left side of the road.* The speed limit is 20 mph, 15 mph in busy areas.

Drug Laws   Importation of, possession of, or dealing with unlawful drugs (including marijuana) is illegal in Bermuda; there are heavy penalties for infractions. Customs officers, at their discretion, may conduct body searches for drugs or other contraband goods.

Drugstores   In Hamilton, try **Bermuda Pharmacy,** Church Street W (☎ **441/ 295-5815**). It's in the Russell Eve Building and is open Monday through Saturday from 8am to 6pm. Under the same ownership is the **Phoenix Drugstore,** 3 Reid St. (☎ **441/295-3838**), open Monday through Saturday from 8am to 6pm.

In Paget Parish, you can go to **Paget Pharmacy,** 130 South Rd. (☎ **441/ 236-7275**), open Monday through Saturday from 8am to 8pm and on Sunday from 2 to 6pm. At 49 Mangrove Bay, the **Somerset Pharmacy** in Somerset Village (☎ **441/234-2484**) is open Monday through Saturday from 8am to 6pm.

Electricity   Electricity is 110 volts, 60 cycles, AC. American appliances are compatible without converters or adapters.

Embassies and Consulates   The **American Consulate General** is at Crown Hill, 16 Middle Rd., Devonshire (☎ **441/295-1342**). Hours are Monday through Friday from 8:30am to 4:30pm. Canadians can refer to the **Canadian Consulate General** (Commission to Bermuda) at 1251 Avenue of the Americas, New York, NY 10020 (☎ **212/596-1600**). Britain doesn't have an embassy or consulate in Bermuda.

Emergencies   To call the police in an emergency, dial **911;** if you need to reach the police, but it's not an emergency, dial **295-0011.** To report a fire, dial **911;** to summon an ambulance, call **911.** For Air-Sea Rescue, dial **297-1010.**

Etiquette   Well-tailored Bermuda shorts are acceptable on almost any occasion, and many men wear them with jackets and ties at rather formal gatherings. Aside from that, Bermudians are rather conservative in their attitude toward dress— bikinis, for example, are banned more than 25 feet from the water.

Eyeglass Repair   **Argus Optical Company** (Henry Simmons, O.D.), Melbourne House, Parliament Street, Hamilton (☎ **441/292-5452**), works with both prescription glasses and contact lenses. Hours are 9am to noon and 1pm to 4:45pm Monday through Friday.

Gasoline   Mopeds take a mixture of oil and gas, and there's always a separate pump at gasoline stations for these vehicles. Honda scooters require regular unleaded gasoline, which costs about $1.15 per liter. The typical touring biker needs about one refill per week. Both Honda scooters and mopeds are rented with full tanks. Gasoline stations are conveniently situated around the island.

Holidays   See "When to Go" in Chapter 3, "Planning a Trip to Bermuda."

Hospital   **King Edward VII Memorial Hospital,** 7 Point Finger Rd., Paget Parish (☎ **441/236-2345**), has a highly qualified staff and Canadian accreditation. Take bus no. 1 to reach the hospital.

Hotline Call **441/236-0224,** ext. 226 or 227 for a consultation on psychiatric problems, but only from 8:45am to 5pm Monday through Friday. After 5pm, call **441/236-3770;** you'll be connected to one of two island hospitals, either the Bermuda Psychiatric Hospital's outpatient clinic, or (in the evening) St. Brendan's Hospital. Either can help with life-threatening problems, personal crises, or referral to a proper medical specialist.

Information For information before you go, see "Visitor Information, Entry Requirements, Customs & Money" in Chapter 3, "Planning a Trip to Bermuda." Once on the island, see "Orientation" earlier in this chapter.

Legal Aid If you should become ill or injured in Bermuda, American citizens may need the services of the U.S. consulate (see "Embassies and Consulates" above). The staff there can suggest where to get medical help and will notify close relatives. If your problem is a legal one (such as a drug arrest), the consulate will inform you of your rights (limited) and offer a list of attorneys. However, the consulate's office cannot interfere with Bermuda's law-enforcement officers.

A hotline in an emergency—useful for questions about U.S. citizens arrested abroad—is the Citizens' Emergency Center of the Office of Special Consular Services in Washington, D.C. (☎ **202/647-5225**). They'll also tell you how to send money to U.S. citizens arrested abroad.

Liquor Laws Bermuda sternly regulates the sale of alcoholic beverages. The legal drinking age is 18, and most bars close at 1am. Some nightclubs and hotel bars can serve liquor until 3am. Many places are closed on Sunday.

Mail Regular mail can be deposited in the red pillar boxes on the streets. You'll recognize them by the monogram of Queen Elizabeth II. The postage rates for air-mail letters up to 10 grams and for postcards is 60¢ to the United States and Canada, 75¢ to the United Kingdom. Airmail letters and postcards to the North American mainland can take five to seven days, and to Britain possibly a little longer. Often visitors have returned home before their postcards arrive.

Newspapers/Magazines One daily newspaper is published in Bermuda, the *Royal Gazette.* Three weekly papers, the *Bermuda Sun,* the *Bermuda Times,* and the *Mid-Ocean News,* are issued on Friday. Major U.S. newspapers, including the *New York Times* and *USA Today,* and magazines (such as *Time* and *Newsweek*) are delivered to Bermuda on the day of their publication on the mainland. *This Week in Bermuda* is a weekly guide published for tourists.

Passports See "Visitor Information, Entry Requirements, Customs & Money" in Chapter 3, "Planning a Trip to Bermuda."

Pets If you want to take your pet with you to Bermuda, you'll need a special permit issued by the director of the Department of Agriculture, Fisheries & Parks, P.O. Box HM 834, Hamilton HM CX, Bermuda (☎ **441/236-4201**). Animals arriving without proper documents will be refused entry and will be returned to the point of origin, since there are no quarantine facilities in Bermuda. Some guesthouses and hotels will allow you to bring in small animals, but others will not, so be sure to inquire about this in advance. You should always check to see what the latest regulations are before attempting to bring a dog or other pet into Bermuda, including seeing-eye dogs.

Photographic Needs If you want to buy a camera or film, or develop either Kodak or Fuji film, try **Stuart's,** 5 Reid St., near the corner of Queen St. (☎ **441/295-0303**), Hamilton's leading camera store. Film can be developed in-house in about three hours (sometimes within one hour for a surcharge). Open Monday through Saturday 9am to 5pm.

Police   In an emergency, call **911;** otherwise, call **295-0011.**

Post Offices   The General Post Office, at 56 Church St., Hamilton (☎ **441/ 295-5151**), is open Monday through Friday from 8am to 5pm and on Saturday from 8am to noon. Post office branches and the Perot Post Office, Queen Street, Hamilton, are open Monday through Friday from 8am to 5pm. Some post offices are closed for lunch from 11:30am to 1pm. Airmail service for the United States and Canada closes at 9:30am in Hamilton, leaving daily. See also "Mail" above.

Radio and TV   News is broadcast on the hour and half-hour over AM stations 1340 (ZBM), 1230 (ZFB), and 1450 (VSB). The FM stations are 89 (ZBM) and 95 (ZFB). Tourist-oriented programming, island music, and information on activities and special events are aired over AM station 1160 (VSB) daily from 7am to noon.

The television channel, 10 (ZBM), is affiliated with America's Columbia Broadcasting System (CBS).

Restrooms   Hamilton and St. George's provide public facilities, but only during business hours. In Hamilton, toilets are located at City Hall, in Par-la-Ville Gardens, and at Albouy's Point. In St. George's, they are at Town Hall, Somers Gardens, and Market Wharf. Outside of these towns, you'll find restrooms at the public beaches, the Botanical Gardens, in several of the forts, at the airport, and at service stations; but, often you'll have to use the facilities in hotels, restaurants, and whatever else you can find.

Safety   In the case of Bermuda, there is no particular need for a crime alert. Bermudians are generally peaceful people, not given to the expression of violence. To be sure, the island has experienced racial tensions in the past, but right now relations between its white and black residents seem to be harmonious, as blacks assume a greater role in Bermuda's affairs.

Crimes, violent or otherwise, against tourists are rare, but don't be lulled into a false sense of security, either. Crime does exist, as in any society. Take care to protect your valuables, especially when you're at the beach. Lock your moped each time you leave it. If you bring very valuable items with you to Bermuda (this is not advisable), place them in your hotel safe (if your hotel has one) and never leave them carelessly in your room.

It is generally safe to go anywhere in Bermuda, but, here again, caution should be exercised, particularly late at night and if you're a woman traveling alone.

Taxes   Visitors to Bermuda are levied a tax before departing from the island. For those who leave by air, the tax, collected at the airport, is $20 for adults or children. (Children under 2 are exempt.) For those who leave by ship, the tax, collected in advance from the cruise ship company, is $60 (children under 2 are exempt).

All room rates, regardless of the category of accommodation or the plan under which you stay, are subject to a 7.5% Bermuda government tax, to be paid when you check out of your hotel.

Taxis   See "Getting Around" earlier in this chapter.

Telegrams/Telexes/Faxes   Worldwide phone and cable service is available, and the charges may be reversed. Direct dialing is possible from Bermuda to the United States and Canada. To send telegrams, telexes, or faxes, go to **Cable & Wireless**

Office, 20 Church St., Hamilton (opposite the City Hall). Hours are Monday through Saturday from 9am to 5pm. For information, call **441/297-7000.**

Telephone   Cable & Wireless (see above), in conjunction with the **Bermuda Telephone Co., Ltd.,** provides international direct dialing (IDD) to more than 150 countries. Country codes and calling charges may be found in the latest edition of the Bermuda telephone directory. Telephone booths are available at the Cable & Wireless office, and customers can either prepay for their calls or purchase cash cards in $10, $20, and $50 denominations. Cash cards may also be purchased at the Visitors Service Bureau in Hamilton, St. George's, or the dockyard. Cash card phone booths are also available at numerous locations around the island. Making international calls with cash cards can be a lot cheaper than using the phone at your hotel, which might impose stiff surcharges. To make a local call, deposit 20¢, either Bermudian or U.S. Hotels often charge from 20¢ to $1 for local calls.

Special phones have also been installed at passenger piers in Hamilton, St. George's, and the dockyard that will connect you directly with an AT&T, US Sprint, or MCI operator in the United States, thus permitting you to make collect or calling card calls.

Telephone Directory   All Bermuda telephone numbers appear in one phone book, revised annually. The helpful **Yellow Pages** in the back list all the goods and services you are likely to need.

Time   Bermuda is one hour ahead of Eastern Standard Time. Daylight Saving Time is in effect from the first Sunday in April until the last Sunday in October, as it is in the United States.

Tipping   In most cases, a service charge is added to your hotel and/or restaurant bill. In hotels, this is in lieu of tipping the various individuals such as the bellman, maids, and restaurant staff (for meals included in a package or in the daily rate). Otherwise, a 15% tip for service is customary.

Tourist Offices   See "Visitor Information" in Chapter 3.

Transit Information   For information about ferry service, call **441/295-4506.** For bus information, call **441/292-3854.**

Useful Telephone Numbers   For time and temperature, call **977-1.** To learn "What's On in Bermuda," dial **974.** For medical emergencies or the police, dial **911.** If in doubt during any other emergency, dial **0** (zero), which will connect you with either your hotel's switchboard or the Bermuda telephone operator.

Water   Tap water is generally considered safe to drink.

Weather   This might be an all-important consideration for your Bermuda plans. In addition to the newspaper and the radio, you can call **977** at any time of the day or night for a forecast covering the next 24-hour period.

5 Accommodations

Bermuda offers a wide choice of lodgings, ranging from small guesthouses to large luxury hotels. You'll find a variety of sizes and facilities in each category. Members of the Bermuda Hotel Association require two nights' deposit within 14 days of confirming a reservation; full payment 30 days prior to arrival; and notice of cancellation 15 days prior to scheduled arrival, or your deposit will be forfeited. Since some smaller hotels and other accommodations levy an energy surcharge, you should inquire about this when you make your travel arrangements.

All room rates, regardless of what eating plan you have chosen, are subject to a 7.5% Bermuda tax, which is added to your bill. A service charge (ranging from 10% to 15%) is also added to your room rate in lieu of tips. Service charges do not cover bar tabs. Third-person rates (for those occupying a room with two other people) are lower, and children's tariffs vary according to their age.

Generally, there are two major seasons in Bermuda, winter and summer. Bermuda has the reverse of the Bahamian or Caribbean high season, with its major season in spring and summer. Most establishments start to charge their high-season tariffs in March (Easter is the peak period) and lower their rates again around mid-November. A few hotels have year-round rates, and others charge in-between, or "shoulder," prices in spring and autumn. If business is slow, many smaller places will shut down in winter.

What follows is only a rough guideline to price ranges. In several large old resorts, because of the wide range of accommodations, prices are not uniform. Thus, one guest at the Elbow Beach Hotel might be paying a "moderate" cost, while another might be booked at a "very expensive" rate. It all depends on your room assignment.

In general, **Very Expensive** hotels in Bermuda offer double rooms for around $275 and up—and we do mean **up.** These rates are on the Modified American Plan (MAP) or half board.

Hotels considered **Expensive** offer MAP doubles for anywhere from $200 to $275. Hotels classified as **Moderate** charge from $125 to $200 for a double, but are likely to include only breakfast. Hotels or guesthouses classified as **Inexpensive** ask around $125 for a double room, usually including breakfast. Of course, these prices are only rough guidelines.

In many of the cottage colonies, breakfast is not available. You can either go out for breakfast or buy supplies the night before and prepare your own morning meal.

Rate Plans

AP (American Plan)   Includes three meals a day (sometimes called full board or full pension).

BP (Bermuda Plan)   Popularized first in Bermuda, this option includes a full American breakfast (sometimes called an English breakfast).

CP (Continental Plan)   A continental breakfast (that is, bread, jam, and coffee) is included in the room rate.

EP (European Plan)   This rate is always cheapest, as it offers only the room—no meals.

MAP (Modified American Plan)   Sometimes called half board or half pension, this room rate includes breakfast and dinner (or lunch, if you prefer).

EMERGENCY ACCOMMODATIONS

If you didn't have time to reserve rooms before going to Bermuda, you might want to go to the **Visitors Service Bureau** at the airport (☎ **441/293-0030**). Located near Customs clearance and open from 11am to 4pm, it can help you make a reservation. Unless you have a specific hotel reservation and a return airplane ticket, you will not be allowed to proceed beyond this point.

TIPS ON ACCOMMODATIONS

Accommodations in Bermuda basically fall into five major categories, as follows:

RESORT HOTELS   These generally large properties are Bermuda's best, offering many facilities, services, and luxuries—but also charging the highest prices, especially in summer. It's usually cheaper to choose the MAP rates (breakfast and dinner) than to order all your meals à la carte. The lowest rates are in effect from mid-November to March, usually about 20% less. The large resorts usually have their own beaches or beach clubs, along with swimming pools; some even have their own golf courses.

COTTAGE COLONIES   A uniquely Bermudian offering, colonies typically consist of a series of bungalows constructed around a clubhouse, which is the center of social life, drinking, and dining. The cottages, usually scenically arranged on landscaped grounds, are designed to provide maximum privacy, and are typically equipped with kitchenettes (for preparing light meals). Most of the colonies have either their own beaches or swimming pools.

HOUSEKEEPING COTTAGES & APARTMENTS   These accommodations (often called efficiencies in the United States) are generally situated on landscaped estates, with a main clubhouse. All of them offer kitchen facilities, and some are designed as wings or modern apartment-style units surrounding a pool or opening onto a beach. Most of them offer minimal daily maid service.

GUESTHOUSES   These are the cheapest accommodations in Bermuda. The large ones are old Bermuda homes, with garden settings. Generally, they have been modernized, with comfortable guest rooms. Some of them have their own swimming pools. A number of these guesthouses are small, modest places, offering breakfast only; the bath may be shared with other guests. If you stay in one of these places, you may have to "commute" to the beach.

RENTAL VILLAS & VACATION HOMES   You could rent a big villa, a nice-sized apartment in someone's condo building, or even a small beach cottage (more accurately called a cabaña).

Private apartments are also available with or without maid service. These provide fewer frills than either villas or condos. The buildings housing the apartments may not have swimming pools or even a front desk to help you.

Cottages, or cabañas, offer the most freewheeling life-style in this category of vacation accommodations. Some open onto a beach, while others are clustered around a communal swimming pool. Most of them are fairly basic, consisting of just a simple bedroom plus a small kitchen and bath. For the peak summer season, you should make your reservations at least five or six months in advance.

Several U.S. and Canadian agents can arrange these types of rentals. You might try **Rent-a-Home International,** 7200 34th Ave. NW, Seattle, WA 98117 (☎ **206/789-9377;** fax 206/789-9379), which specializes in condos and villas. It can arrange bookings for a week or longer.

1 Resort Hotels

The big resort hotels can provide enough amenities so that guests do not have to leave the premises, but of course visitors generally want to see what's going on outside. The large hotels typically have their own beaches or beach clubs and swimming pools, and some even have their own golf courses. Most of these hotels boast such luxury facilities as porter and room service, planned activities, sports facilities, shops (including a cycle shop), beauty salons, bars, nightclubs, entertainment, and taxi stands.

VERY EXPENSIVE

Belmont Hotel Golf & Country Club

Middle Road (P.O. Box WK 251), Warwick WK BX, Bermuda. ☎ **809/236-1301** or 800/225-5843 in the U.S. and Canada. Fax 809/236-6867. 151 rms. A/C MINIBAR TV TEL. Apr–Oct $225–$250 double; Nov–Mar $210–$235 double. Rates include MAP (breakfast and dinner). AE, DC, MC, V. Ferry from Hamilton.

Overlooking Hamilton Harbour with views over Great Sound, this British-inspired country-club resort is situated on 110 acres of manicured grounds that include an outstanding golf course. If you like a British aura and are sports oriented, this hotel is for you. Refurbished in 1994, it retains an old-fashioned atmosphere, in contrast to the stark modernity of the Sonesta Beach. For value, its rival, Harmony Club, offers a better deal—unless you're a dedicated golfer.

The hotel's exterior is a modern interpretation of a Bermuda colonial building. The rooms feature designer decor and Queen Anne–style furniture. Bathrooms tend to be small. The garden has a limestone moon gate, and there are summer-only outdoor bars.

Dining/Entertainment: The main dining room, called the **Tree Frogs,** with a view of the golf course, offers continental cuisine and Bermudian specialties. **Kiskadee's,** named in honor of a local bird, features Caribbean food. Our favorite place for a drink is the **Harbour Sights Bar,** off the main lobby; it's one of the most elegant modern bars in Bermuda, with finished hardwoods and panoramic views of the Great Sound.

Services: Complimentary taxi to nearby Horseshoe Bay Beach in summer. Laundry, babysitting, room service (breakfast and dinner only), children's program.

Facilities: An 18-hole championship golf course, designed by Robert Trent Jones; a miniature golf course; three tennis courts; outdoor swimming pool.

○ Elbow Beach Hotel/A Wyndham Resort

60 South Shore Rd. (P.O. Box HM 455), Hamilton HM BX, Bermuda. ☎ **441/236-3535** or 800/996-3426 in the U.S. Fax 441/236-8043. 220 rms, 70 suites. A/C MINIBAR TV TEL. Apr 1–Nov 15, $305–$450 double, from $475 suite for two. Off-season, $225–$295 double, from $320 suite for two. Rates include MAP (breakfast and dinner). Packages available. Children 12 and under stay and eat free when sharing rooms with adults and using existing beds. AE, DC, MC, V. Bus: 1, 2, or 7 from Hamilton.

This is the best full-service resort on the island, far exceeding the Hamilton Princess or the Belmont Hotel Golf & Country Club. Its appeal is basically to the vacationer who likes everything under one roof (or at least on site). Another advantage is its proximity to Hamilton, 10 minutes away by taxi. It's set in 50 acres of gardens with its own quarter-mile pink-sand beach on the south shore. During College Weeks, more students congregate here than at any other property on Bermuda. What it lacks is true charm and a Bermudian character, such as that found at Pompano Beach Club. The hotel could be virtually anywhere—definitely, Hilton Head, S.C.

The resort has been given a $20 million restoration. Guests can choose from a wide array of rooms or suites—everything from bedrooms with balconies overlooking the water to duplex cottages. Some lanai rooms overlook the pool and the Atlantic, while others are surfside. Many bedroom walls are draped in silk, and Italian marble baths and up-to-date plumbing have been installed. The most spacious units are situated in low-rise buildings on terraces leading to the sands, whereas the least desirable rooms open onto a heavily trafficked corridor on the lobby floor.

Dining/Entertainment: All guests, including those on MAP, may choose dinner at any of the hotel's three restaurants, all with ocean views, or from one outdoor theme party nightly. The main dining room, **Ondine's,** is the most formal of the restaurants. At **Café Lido,** the resort's beachfront restaurant, seafood with a Mediterranean accent is the focus. After dinner festivities continue with "bamboo dancing" or limbo. Every Sunday a lively Elbow Beach Party and barbecue is held on the resort's pink sand beach, featuring music and entertainment.

Services: Room service, babysitting, laundry, beauty salon, moped rental.

Facilities: Private beach, five all-weather tennis courts (two lit), large swimming pool, children's program, game room, health club with exercise room and whirlpool. Water sports include deep-sea fishing and windsurfing.

Grotto Bay Beach Hotel

11 Blue Hole Hill, Hamilton Parish CR 04, Bermuda. ☎ **441/293-8333** or 800/582-3190 in the U.S., 800/463-0851 in Canada. Fax 441/293-2306. 198 rms, 3 suites. A/C MINIBAR TV TEL. Apr–Oct $185–$198 double; Nov–Mar $115–$135 double. Suites from $350 year-round. MAP $48 per person extra. AE, MC, V. Bus: 1, 3, 10, or 11.

This resort, unattractively located across from the airport, appeals to young couples and families who don't check in here expecting all the activities of an Elbow Beach. This sprawling, 21-acre resort is made up of 11 three-story balconied buildings that provide sea views but no elevators. If you're assigned a room far from the main building, you may think you've been sentenced to Siberia. All accommodations, which were renovated in 1995, are equipped with safes and hairdryers. The best accommodations are at the beach if you don't mind a steep climb to reach them. The resort, although named after its subterranean caves, is lushly planted with tropical fruit trees, including one called "locust and wild honey."

The swimming pool, which has been blasted out of natural rock, is ringed with serpentine edges, much like a grotto. A sandy but mediocre beach nearby offers a view of an unused series of railroad pylons, leading onto forested Coney Island across the bay.

⊕ Family-Friendly Hotels

Belmont Hotel Golf & Country Club *(see p. 70)* Its "Kee Kee Club" allows visitors to enroll their kids (ages 2–12) in a package plan that features day-care services and free meals.

Elbow Beach Hotel/A Wyndham Resort *(see p. 71)* Children stay free in parents' room. Ask, however, about the "Family Value Package," which includes accommodations, transfers, daily breakfast buffet, and a host of activities and extras.

Grotto Bay Beach Hotel *(see p. 71)* A longtime family favorite, this hotel features a "Family Special" (two adults and two children under 16), requiring a minimum stay of four nights. Rates are heavily discounted.

Southampton Princess *(see p. 76)* This pocket of posh offers the best children's program on the island, including parties and reliable babysitting services. Furthermore, children 16 and under stay free in a room with one or two adults and receive a complimentary breakfast and dinner daily.

From the sea side, the airy public areas look like a modernized version of a mogul's palace, with big windows, thick white walls, and three peaked roofs with curved eaves.

Dining/Entertainment: The restaurant serves a fair continental cuisine, enlivened with fresh seafood; there's also a poolside restaurant that serves lunch and theme barbecues. Nightly live entertainment is provided in the **Rum House Lounge,** and there are a handful of other bars on the property. Afternoon tea is served every day, and there is also a daily happy hour.

Services: Nature walks, twice-weekly "cave crawls," daily cave swims, complete program for children, frequent tennis clinics, daily Jazzercise in the Rum House Lounge before breakfast, scavenger hunts, communal croquet near the bar, fish feeding, bridge competitions, organized activities for teenagers. Also laundry, room service, babysitting.

Facilities: Excursion boat, small health club, scuba diving, snorkeling, swimming pool with swim-up bar, Jacuzzi, four tennis courts (two lit), and nearby golf course.

✪ Marriott's Castle Harbour Resort

2 South Rd. (P.O. Box HM 841), Hamilton HM CX, Bermuda. ☎ **441/293-2040** or 800/223-6388 in the U.S. and Canada. Fax 809/293-8288. 402 rms, 18 suites. A/C TV TEL. Apr–Oct $240–$375 double; Nov–Mar $130–$185 double. Suites $450–$985 year-round. MAP $45 per person extra. AE, DC, MC, V. Bus: 1 from St. George's.

All the conventions and groups that book in here find a completely self-contained resort, rivaling the Southampton Princess or Elbow Beach, except that Castle Harbour has more tradition. It is also the best hotel for sports on the island. It has access to two small nearby beaches, plus a private beach on the south shore. Originally built of coral blocks on a hilltop overlooking Castle Harbour and Harrington Sound in the 1920s, this property had fallen into disrepair before Marriott undertook a $60 million renovation late in 1986. Thanks to the renovation, more than 100 bedrooms were added, the gardens were landscaped, and the public rooms became the most elegant hotel interiors on the island. The 250 acres of prime real estate surrounding the property are maintained by at least 50 gardeners.

The most glamorous room in Bermuda is an 18th-century salon, which somewhat resembles a room in an English country house. Filled with copies of Chippendale and Queen Anne furniture and sheathed with mahogany paneling, it's a showplace. Adjacent to this salon is an elegant dining room, whose chinaware duplicates the original 1920s Castle Harbour china.

There are several different buildings on the property. The accommodations, most recently renovated in 1992, are typically furnished with good replicas of traditional English furniture.

Dining/Entertainment: The hotel has a disco called **Blossoms** and five restaurants: the **Windsor Room,** the **Golf Club Grill, Cafe Cascade, Terrace Cafe,** and the **Mikado** (reviewed separately).

Services: Massages, laundry, babysitting, room service.

Facilities: Well-equipped and upgraded health club free to guests, 18-hole Castle Harbour Golf Course, six tennis courts, three pools (one Olympic size), full water sports complex.

✪ The Princess

76 Pitts Bay Rd. (P.O. Box HM 837), Hamilton HM CX, Bermuda. ☎ **441/295-3000** or 800/ 223-1818 in the U.S., or 800/268-7176 in Canada. Fax 441/295-1914. 447 rms, 27 suites. A/C TV TEL. Apr 2–Nov 25 $205–$295 double, $350–$1,150 suite; off-season $150–$185 double, $220–$845 suite. MAP $42 per person per day. AE, DC, MC, V. Bus: 7 or 8.

In its latest reincarnation, the "wedding cake" of Hamilton sits on the edge of Hamilton Harbour (without a beach, unfortunately). Unlike all other Bermuda properties, it's hosted a roster of visitors that range from Mark Twain to Michael Jackson (what a stretch!). Often called the Hamilton Princess, it's the hotel of choice for Hollywood and European movie stars as well as the yachting set. Opened in 1887 and named for Princess Louise (Queen Victoria's daughter), it is far more staid than its cousin, the Southampton Princess (see below) and doesn't even attempt to offer the activities of Elbow Beach. The young and the restless might want to book elsewhere. This is the flagship of the Princess Hotel chain, and it is certainly the one with the most history—British intelligence officers stationed here during World War II worked to crack secret Nazi codes.

The colonial core is flanked by modern wings, each of which is pierced with row upon row of balconied loggias. The property, just a short stroll from downtown Hamilton, was designed around a concrete pier that extends into the harbor, near which lies a Japanese-style floating garden. The botanical theme is repeated in the lobby.

In 1992 management renovated the well-decorated bedrooms and public salons, continuing a program of making a good property even better. Many of the guest rooms offer private balconies; each room was designed "to create the feeling that you'd choose the same kind of bedroom if you owned a home here." Some 40% of the guests are repeat visitors.

Dining/Entertainment: The hotel has a wide array of bars and restaurants; for more details, see Chapter 6, "Dining," and Chapter 11, "Bermuda After Dark."

Services: Frequent ferryboat service (weather permitting) between the Hamilton Princess and the Southampton Princess, laundry, room service, babysitting.

Facilities: Heated freshwater swimming pool; unheated saltwater swimming pool; water aerobics classes; dive shop (independent concessionaire); moped rental; access to tennis, sailing, white-sand beaches, and golf at the Southampton Princess. The hotel's fitness center, usually open daily from 6am to 9pm, features an exercise room, massage area, saunas, showers, and advanced exercise equipment (Quinton Club Trac Treadmill, Stairmasters, Life Fitness Cycles, Badger/Magnum Nine Station Circuit Strength Machine).

Bermuda Accommodations

Atlantic Ocean

Ireland Island N.

Ireland Island S.

Mangrove Bay

Somerset Village

1

SANDYS

Ely's Harbour

Great Sound

Two Rock Passage

Bay Rd.

PEMBROKE

North Shore

37
36
35 **33** **32**
34 **31**

Hamilton

Middle Rd.

Ferry

Hawkins Island

Long Island

Ports Island Hinson Island

Darrell Island

Hamilton Harbour

22

Botanic Garden

19 **20** **21**

2

18

17

PAGET

30

28 **29** **26**

27

23 **24** **25**

Little Sound

Harbour Rd.

15

Middle Rd.

16

3

4

WARWICK

11 **13**

14

SOUTHAMPTON

7 **8**

South Shore Rd.

9 **10** **12**

5

6

Angel's Grotto **40**
Ariel Sands Beach Club **38**
Astwood Cove **11**
Belmont Hotel
Golf & Country Club **15**
Cambridge Beaches **1**
Edgehill Manor **36**
Elbow Beach Hotel **24**
Fourways Inn **16**
Greenbank Guest House **19**
Greene's Guest House **4**
Grotto Bay Beach Hotel **43**

Harmony Club **30**
Hill Crest Guest House **45**
Horizons and Cottages **23**
Lantana **2**
Little Pomander Guest House **22**
Longtail Cliffs **10**
Loughlands **29**
Marley Beach Cottages **12**
Marriott's Castle Harbour Resort **42**
Mermaid Beach Club **9**
Newstead **21**

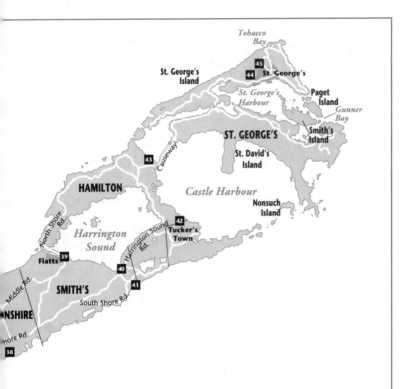

Tobacco Bay

St. George's
Island

45

44 St. George's

St. George's
Harbour

Paget
Island

Gunner
Bay

Smith's
Island

ST. GEORGE'S

St. David's
Island

43 Causeway

HAMILTON

Castle Harbour

Nonsuch
Island

Harrington
Sound

42
Tucker's
Town

North Shore Rd.

Harrington Sound Rd.

39 Flatts

40

41

Middle Rd.

SMITH'S

South Shore Rd.

...nore Rd.

38

...NSHIRE

Atlantic Ocean

0   2 km
       1.5 m

N

Oxford House **32**	Royal Palms Hotel **37**
Palm Reef Hotel **18**	Salt Kettle House **20**
Palmetto Hotel & Cottages **39**	Sandpiper Apartments **13**
Parquet Guest Apartments **27**	Sky-Top Cottages **28**
Pink Beach Club & Cottages **41**	Sonesta Beach Resort **6**
Pompano Beach Club **3**	Southampton Princess **8**
Pretty Penny **17**	St. George's Club **44**
The Princess **34**	Stonington Beach Hotel **25**
The Reefs **5**	Surf Side Beach Club **14**
Rosedon **33**	Waterloo House **31**
Rosemont **35**	White Sands Hotel & Cottages **26**
Royal Heights Guest House **7**	

Sonesta Beach Resort

South Shore Road, Southampton Parish (P.O. Box HM 1070), Hamilton HM EX, Bermuda. ☎ **441/238-8122** or 800/766-3782 in the U.S. Fax 441/238-8463. 373 rms, 34 suites. A/C TV TEL. Apr 1–Nov 15 $250–$370 double, $410–$1,050 suite; off-season $130–$168 double, $188–$380 suite. MAP $50 per person per day. Discounted honeymoon and family packages available. AE, DC, MC, V. Bus: 7.

Completely renovated in 1994 and 1995, and now better than ever, this is Bermuda's only major luxury resort boasting access to three beaches. As a full-service hotel, it is outclassed only by Elbow Beach. As a spa, it's considered one of the best in the world. Built in the shape of a crescent, the resort is located on 25 acres of prime seafront property, curving along the spine of a rocky peninsula whose jagged edges provide views of the coastline. It boasts ample lengths of oceanside walkways. Those who are seeking Bermudian charm and character would probably prefer Cambridge Beaches or Lantana Colony Club, but spa devotees, honeymooners, and water sports and beach buffs like this resort a lot.

Shaped like a circle and flanked by limestone cliffs and sandy beaches, the bay fronting the Sonesta was used long ago by gunpowder smugglers (and later by rum-runners) because of its well-camouflaged entrance. With the encircling palm-covered cabañas and bars and the soft sandy bottom, the bay looks like a small corner of Polynesia transported onto the sands of Bermuda.

Each room, equipped with a private terrace, offers a flowery kind of charm. The rates are based solely on the view.

Dining/Entertainment: The hotel features five restaurants, including **Lillian's,** an elegant restaurant offering northern Italian cuisine. The **Boat Bay Club** is a bistro-type eatery, and the **Sea Grape Island Grill** provides al fresco dining overlooking Boat Bay. MAP guests can dine in each of these restaurants as well as at **Henry VIII.** (See Chapter 6, "Dining.") For nightlife, there's the **Palm Court Club.**

Services: Room service, laundry, babysitting.

Facilities: Beach, spa facilities (see "Spa Vacations" in Chapter 3), outdoor swimming pool, indoor swimming pool, complete center for snorkelers and scuba divers, children's program, six tennis courts (two illuminated for night play), and full-time tennis pro.

✪ Southampton Princess

101 South Shore Road (P.O. Box HM 1379), Hamilton HM FX, Bermuda. ☎ **441/238-8000** or 800/223-1818 in the U.S. or 800/268-7176 in Canada. Fax 441/238-8968. 600 rms, 36 suites. A/C TV TEL. Apr 2–Nov 25 $389–$519 double, $590–$1,259 suite (these seasonal rates include MAP—breakfast and lunch); off-season $150–$185 double, $295–$1,000 suite (meals not included). AE, DC, MC, V. Ferryboat from Hamilton.

This Princess, even more than the Hamilton Princess, deserves to be called royal, especially after its $2.5 million renovation. It is the largest and most luxurious property on the island, having surpassed even Elbow Beach. Its biggest drawback is the large number of conventions and groups that book in here. Yet it justifies its membership in "The Leading Hotels of the World," sitting atop Bermuda's highest point, overlooking the ocean and bay. As Bermuda's premier luxury resort, this is not the place for those who want an intimate romantic hideaway. Several of its restaurants serve the best food of any Bermuda hotel, and its sports and facilities are among the island's finest.

Guests who never want to leave enjoy a self-contained village of bars, restaurants, shops, and athletic facilities. These public rooms, situated on three floors, are connected by baronial staircases. All of the hotel's furnishings are well-upholstered,

Hamilton Accommodations & Dining

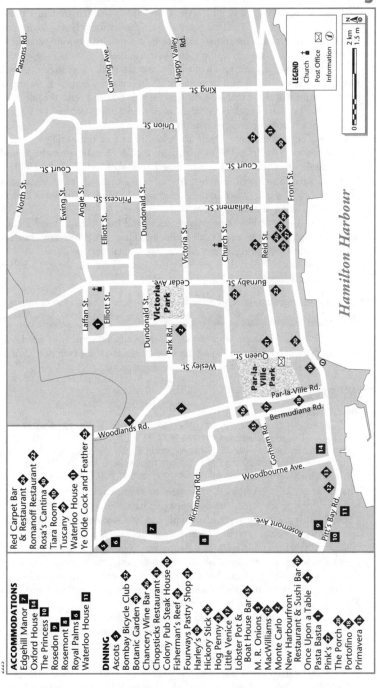

LEGEND
- † Church
- ⊠ Post Office
- ⓘ Information

2 km
1.5 m

Hamilton Harbour

ACCOMMODATIONS
- Edgehill Manor **7**
- Oxford House **14**
- The Princess **10**
- Rosedon **9**
- Rosemont **8**
- Royal Palms **6**
- Waterloo House **11**

DINING
- Ascots **5**
- Bombay Bicycle Club **32**
- Botanic Garden **20**
- Chancery Wine Bar **25**
- Chopsticks Restaurant **31**
- Colony Pub Steak House **30**
- Fisherman's Reef **23**
- Fourways Pastry Shop **21**
- Harley's **19**
- Hickory Stick **16**
- Hog Penny **23**
- Little Venice **17**
- Lobster Pot &
  Boat House Bar **45**
- M. R. Onions **3**
- MacWilliams **12**
- Monte Carlo **4**
- New Harbourfront
  Restaurant & Sushi Bar **19**
- Once Upon a Table **4**
- Pasta Basta **1**
- Pink's **27**
- The Porch **28**
- Portofino **4**
- Primavera **13**

- Red Carpet Bar
  & Restaurant **24**
- Romanoff Restaurant **22**
- Rosa's Cantina **40**
- Tiara Room **29**
- Tuscany **4**
- Waterloo House **11**
- Ye Olde Cock and Feather **23**

77

reflecting an 18th-century English style. Guest rooms—which are rather plush—are arranged in wings that radiate more or less symmetrically from a central core. This design allows each luxurious bedroom to incorporate a private veranda with a sweeping view of the water. Some rooms have a minibar.

The favorite pool is a re-creation of a Polynesian waterfall, where streams of heated water spill from an artificial limestone cliff. You can swim here even during cold weather because of the greenhouse constructed above. If you crave the salty waters of the sea, the hotel beach is sheltered in a jagged cove, flanked by cliffs and studded with rocky outcroppings lashed by the tides.

Dining/Entertainment: Meals are taken in one of the hotel's restaurants (see Chapter 6, "Dining"). The dining rooms include **Windows on the Sound,** a three-tiered palace that seems to combine London's Mayfair of the 1930s and New York's Rainbow Room. Through 20-foot-high arched windows one can see the islands of Great Sound. Other dining choices include **Wickets Brasserie, Newport Room, Rib Room, Whaler Inn,** and **Waterlot Inn.**

Services: A shuttle bus transports guests to and from various hotel facilities; hotel ferryboats make runs along Little Sound into Hamilton. Also available are room service, laundry, babysitting, beauty salon, moped rental, massages.

Facilities: Private beach club; outdoor pool; indoor pool; par three, 18-hole golf course; tennis; fitness center with spa facilities.

2 Small Hotels

In contrast to the big luxury and first-class hotels is the informality of small hotels. Many of them have their own dining rooms and bars, and some even have their own beaches or beach clubs. All of them offer pools and patios.

VERY EXPENSIVE

Harmony Club

South Shore Road (P.O. Box PG 299), Paget PG BX, Bermuda. ☎ **441/236-3500** or 800/225-5843 in the U.S. and Canada. Fax 441/236-2624. 71 rms. A/C TV TEL. Apr 15–Oct 15 $225 per person double; Oct 16–Nov 28 $175 per person double. No one under 18 admitted. 30% discount if you book 30 days or more in advance. Rates include all meals, drinks, activities, taxes, and service. AE, DC, MC, V. Closed off-season. Bus: 7, 8, or 27.

This is the place for vacationers who prefer to stay at a resort where everything is included for one set price (even champagne, bathrobes, and toiletries). This is a couples-only resort; however, the couple can be any combination of gender or age, even two friends traveling together. In the 1830s, this property had been Harmony Hall, the family estate of a Bermudian shipping merchant. It remained a private dwelling until the early 20th century; its most recent renovation was in 1993.

The accommodations, furnished with Queen Anne–style furniture, are located in a series of rambling pink-sided wings, which encircle formal gardens with gazebos. Those near the road tend to be somewhat noisy.

Dining/Entertainment: A full English tea is served every afternoon; evening meals are served by candlelight on fine china and crystal in the Garden Room; there are weekly cocktail parties, and entertainment six nights a week. Harmony Club has a dine-around plan with the Belmont Hotel.

Services: Laundry, moped rental.

Facilities: Freshwater swimming pool; whirlpool; two tennis courts; Jacuzzis; two saunas; complimentary beach club privileges; unlimited use of a double-seat motorscooter (one per couple) during a week's stay; putting green on-site, and free greens fees at nearby Belmont golf course.

Pompano Beach Club

36 Pompano Beach Rd., Southampton SB 03, Bermuda. ☎ **441/234-0222** or 800/343-4155 in the U.S. or Canada. Fax 441/234-1694. 32 rms, 20 suites. A/C TV TEL. May 1–Nov 15 $335–$360 double, from $345 suite. Nov 16–Apr 30 $220–$240 double, $280–$305 suite. Rates include MAP (breakfast and dinner). No credit cards. Hamilton ferry to Somerset.

This accommodation is for those seeking a personal, friendly welcome, which is impossible to come by at such megaresorts as Elbow Beach. Golfers especially like this place, and it attracts both younger and older couples who want privacy and tranquillity. On the southwest shore, the Pompano Beach Club was Bermuda's first fishing club when it opened in 1956. Today, it's one of the most delightful smaller hotels on the island, owned and operated by the Lamb family, who give it lots of Bermudian character. Part of the hotel's allure stems from its setting on the side of a limestone hill, virtually surrounded by the Port Royal Golf Club. Years ago, stair-stepped terraces were cut in the hill to accommodate the "Pompano pink" buildings of this well-maintained property.

From the terraced beach below the clubhouse, water lovers can walk waist-deep along a clean sandy bottom for the length of 2½ football fields before reaching deep water. The renovated accommodations provide great water views; each of the hillside villas scattered over the landscaped property is equipped with either a balcony or terrace.

Dining/Entertainment: The cuisine served in the dining room, the **Cedar Room,** is international; each dish is prepared by a team of five chefs. The hotel maintains a dine-around plan with four other small Bermuda hotels. Mealtime is relatively informal; jackets and ties for men are required only three nights a week. The hotel also has a British-style pub where you can watch the sun set over the ocean.

Services: Laundry, babysitting.

Facilities: Freshwater swimming pool; ocean and poolside Jacuzzi; four all-weather tennis courts (two lit); fitness center; easy access to the government-owned Port Royal Golf Course; sunfish and windsurfer rentals.

The Reefs

56 South Shore Rd., Southampton SN 02, Bermuda. ☎ **441/238-0222** or 800/742-2008 in the U.S. or Canada. Fax 441/238-8372. 67 units, 8 suites. A/C TEL. Apr 14–Nov 10 $336–$396 double, $366–$926 suite; off-season $220–$280 double, $260–$630 suite. Rates include MAP (breakfast and dinner). No credit cards. Bus: 7.

Not as refined—but also not as stuffy—as Horizons, Lantana Colony Club, or Cambridge Beaches, this is one of the most state-of-the-art inns on the island, with top-notch maintenance, first-class personal service, and ocean views unmatched by its rivals. This lanai colony on Christian Bay is arranged along a low coral ridge. The uncrowded cluster of salmon-pink cottages faces a private beach of pink-flecked sand surrounded by palm trees and jutting rocks. Guests can also enjoy a kidney-shaped swimming pool, situated on a ledge with a nice ocean view. The Reefs offers lanais decorated with rattan furniture and island colors, all with private sundecks and ocean views. Bathrooms are small.

Dining/Entertainment: Guests can dine either in the plant-filled **Terrace Dining Room** or al fresco at **Coconuts,** the beach deck between palm trees. Continental and North American cuisine is served. The main clubhouse, with a beam-ceilinged lounge, offers entertainment seven nights a week in summer, ranging from calypso to pub-style sing-along favorites.

Hotels of Bermuda at a Glance

	Access for disabled	Directly beside the beach	On-site swimming pool	Restaurant on premises	Cable TV in bedroom	Fitness facilities	Access to golf nearby	On-site tennis courts	Convention facilities	Welcomes children	Childcare facilities	On-site spa facilities	Access to water sports	Accepts credit cards	Air-conditioned bedrooms	Live on-site entertainment	Wharf or marina facilities
Angel's Grotto	•		•			•			•				•	•	•		
Ariel Sands Beach Club		•	•	•			•	•		•	•		•	•	•	•	
Astwood Cove			•							•					•		
Belmont Hotel Golf & CC	•		•	•	•		•	•	•	•	•		•	•	•	•	•
Cambridge Beaches		•	•	•		•	•	•		•		•	•		•	•	•
Edgehill Manor			•		•					•					•		
Elbow Beach Hotel	•	•	•	•	•	•	•	•	•	•	•		•	•	•	•	
Fourways Inn			•	•	•		•		•					•	•		
Greenbank Guest House										•			•	•	•		•
Greene's Guest House			•		•		•			•					•		
Grotto Bay Beach Hotel	•	•	•	•	•	•	•	•	•	•	•		•	•	•	•	•
Harmony Club		•	•	•			•	•					•	•	•		
Hillcrest Guest House							•			•					•		
Horizons and Cottages			•	•			•	•		•	•				•	•	
Lantana			•	•	•		•	•	•	•			•	•	•	•	•
Little Pomander Guest House	•				•		•			•			•	•	•		
Longtail Cliffs	•		•		•		•			•				•	•		
Loughlands			•				•	•		•					•		
Marley Beach Cottages		•	•		•		•			•			•	•	•		
Marriott's Castle Harbour Resort	•		•	•	•	•		•	•	•	•		•	•	•	•	
Mermaid Beach Club		•	•	•						•			•	•			
Newstead Hotel			•	•			•	•		•	•		•	•	•	•	•
Oxford House, The					•					•				•	•		

	Access for disabled	Directly beside the beach	On-site swimming pool	Restaurant on premises	Cable TV in bedroom	Fitness facilities	Access to golf nearby	On-site tennis courts	Convention facilities	Welcomes children	Childcare facilities	On-site spa facilities	Access to water sports	Accepts credit cards	Air-conditioned bedrooms	Live on-site entertainment	Wharf or marina facilities
Palm Reef Hotel		•	•				•			•	•		•	•	•	•	
Palmetto Hotel & Cottages			•	•			•			•	•	•		•	•	•	•
Paraquet Guest Apartments				•	•		•			•						•	
Pink Beach Club & Cottages		•	•	•			•	•	•	•	•		•	•	•	•	
Pompano Beach Club		•	•	•		•	•	•	•	•	•		•		•	•	
Pretty Penny			•				•			•				•	•	•	
Princess, The (Hamilton)	•		•	•	•	•	•	•	•	•	•	•	•	•	•	•	•
Reefs, The		•	•	•	•		•	•		•	•	•	•	•		•	•
Rosedon			•		•					•				•			
Rosemont			•		•					•	•			•	•		
Royal Heights Guest House			•		•					•				•	•		
Royal Palms Hotel			•	•	•					•				•	•		
St. George's Club	•	•	•	•	•		•	•	•	•	•	•		•	•	•	
Salt Kettle House							•			•			•		•		•
Sandpiper Apartments			•		•					•					•	•	
Sky-Top Cottages							•			•					•	•	
Sonesta Beach Resort	•	•	•	•	•	•	•	•	•	•	•	•	•	•	•	•	
Southampton Princess	•	•	•	•	•	•	•	•	•	•	•	•	•	•	•	•	•
Stonington Beach Hotel		•	•	•			•	•	•	•	•		•	•	•	•	
Surf Side Beach Club		•	•	•	•		•			•	•			•	•	•	
Waterloo House			•	•				•	•			•	•	•	•		
White Sands Hotel & Cottages		•	•	•	•		•			•	•		•	•	•		

Services: Laundry, babysitting.
Facilities: Beach, swimming pool, two all-weather tennis courts, fitness center.

Stonington Beach Hotel

South Shore Road (P.O. Box HM 523), Hamilton, HM CX, Bermuda. ☎ **441/236-5416** or 800/447-7462 in the U.S. or Canada. For reservations and information, contact Prima Hotels, 747 Third Ave., New York, NY 10017 (☎ 212/223-2848, fax 441/236-0371). 64 rms. A/C TEL. Apr–Oct $365–$405 double; Nov–Mar $228–$260 double. Rates include MAP (breakfast and dinner). AE, DC, MC, V. Bus: 7.

Near Elbow Beach, this $6 million structure is operated by the Hospitality and Culinary Institute of Bermuda, whose classrooms and headquarters are located at the top of a nearby knoll. As such, it's a bit of an offbeat choice, but—training ground or not—is still a worthy choice, with a gracious welcome and atmosphere. Some of the employees are students, and they are supervised by a professional international staff. Actually, the students are likely to be more helpful than many battle-trained, jaded personnel in the hotel field, although if you're looking for mistakes you will no doubt find them.

A lamplit drive leads visitors through foliage up to the buff-colored facade. A stucco passageway follows a trail to an inner octagonal courtyard graced by a palm tree. The reception area is high-ceilinged, its dark pine beams alternating with white plaster.

The accommodations are situated in four outlying buildings. The rooms are comfortably spacious, equipped with either a wide balcony or patio offering an ocean view. Decorated in blue and yellow, the rooms have ceiling fans, small refrigerators, and love seats that could serve as an extra folding bed. A complete refurbishing was done in 1994. The hotel's sandy beach is reached via steps cut through foliage and limestone.

Dining/Entertainment: A library with a fireplace is most inviting, as is the restaurant and bar, the **Norwood Room** (see Chapter 6, "Dining"). The hotel has a dinner exchange program with four surrounding properties.

Services: Laundry, babysitting.
Facilities: Beach, freshwater swimming pool, two tennis courts, business center.

Waterloo House

Pitts Bay Road (P.O. Box HM 333), Hamilton HM BX, Bermuda. ☎ **441/295-4480** or 800/468-4100 in the U.S. and Canada. Fax 441/295-2585. 22 rms, 8 suites. Apr–Nov $230–$350 double, $380–$400 suite; Dec–Mar $180–$280 double, $300 suite. Rates include full breakfast. MAP $30 per person extra. AE, MC, V. Bus: 1, 2, 10, or 11.

On the edge of Hamilton Harbour in Pembroke Parish (just on the outskirts of town), this is an enlarged and remodeled private home (ca. 1910). Terraced gardens descend to the water in the Italian Riviera style. Behind salmon-colored walls, the gardens are filled with palms and magnolias, poinsettias, and urns of ivy; a splashing fountain; and white iron garden furniture with fringed parasols. Guests can enjoy afternoon tea on the lawn at the water's edge. There are nooks for drinks and sunbathing. Shade trees stand at the edge of an open-air, freshwater swimming pool. There are also a private dock, a waterside barbecue area, and a terrace for rum-swizzle parties.

Inside, the drawing room is furnished with English antiques and decorative tile floors. The main dining room, overlooking the terrace and harbor, is graced with Queen Anne chairs. On the lower terrace level is a bar lounge with Moorish arches, English armchairs, and hand-woven pillows. The bedrooms vary in size and decoration; each evokes the feeling of a country-house guest room.

EXPENSIVE
Newstead Hotel

27 Harbour Rd. (P.O. Box PG 196), Paget PG BX, Bermuda. ☎ **441/236-6060** or 800/
468-4111 in the U.S. and Canada. Fax 441/236-7454. 48 rms, 2 suites. A/C TEL. Apr 1–Jan 4
$256–$335 double; Jan 5–Mar 31 $230 double. Suites $355–$375 year-round. Rates include
MAP (breakfast and dinner). AE, MC, V. Ferry from Hamilton.

On Harbour Road in Paget Parish, overlooking Hamilton Harbour, Newstead—
owned by a local family—is a Bermudian landmark. The original guesthouse accommodated only 12 guests when it opened in 1923, but today there is room for 107
guests. Part of the property, Lyndham, was the former home of Sir Richard and Lady
Fairey. Long ago it was expanded to include several adjoining properties, comprising what is now a waterfront resort on a flowering hillside overlooking the harbor.
From the estate, it's a 10-minute ferry ride to Hamilton.

The ancestral home has become the hub of social activities. The setting is traditional, with drawing rooms, a library, and lounges, furnished in part with English
antiques, a true country-house flavor, and many informal touches. This is one of the
very best small resorts in Bermuda, as its large number of older repeat guests are only
too willing to tell you. They wouldn't think of staying anywhere else. The place is
dignified and refined—definitely not for hell-raisers.

On the extensive grounds there are well designed and furnished bungalows, offering a view of either the harbor or the garden. Accommodations are also available in
the main house.

Dining/Entertainment: The hotel restaurant is known as **"The Harbour Room."**
MAP guests can either dine here or participate in the dine-around plan (involving
two other hotels). There is an outdoor terrace, where guests can enjoy waterside
barbecue buffets, rum-swizzle parties, calypso music, and dancing, according to the
season. Newstead also operates **Breccas,** a casual dining spot overlooking Hamilton
Harbour.

Services: Laundry, babysitting, room service.

Facilities: Swimming pool (you can also swim from two private docks); sauna
room; two clay tennis courts; guest privileges at the Coral Beach Tennis Club;
on-site putting green; use of the nine-hole mashie golf course at Horizons.

Palmetto Hotel & Cottages

Harrington Sound Road (P.O. Box FL 54), Flatts FL BX, Bermuda. ☎ **441/293-2323** or 800/
982-0026 in the U.S. for reservations. Fax 441/293-8761. 42 units. A/C TEL. Apr–Oct $231–$271
double; off-season $186–$231 double. Rates include MAP (breakfast and dinner). Special
package plans available. AE, MC, V. Bus: 10 or 11.

The rates are fairly high here for what you get, but it is popular among couples and
young families because of its Bermudian character. This had been the ancestral home
of the Bermudian Tucker family, whose offspring, Teddy, became famous in the
1950s for dredging up treasures from 17th-century wrecked ships.

The hotel is located on Harrington Sound, about 4¹/₂ miles east of Hamilton.
There is a raised beach beside the sound, with access for both swimming and
snorkeling to the sandy bottom of the bay. The exterior of the main building, the
cottages, and the outbuildings is pink. The main building's reception area is paneled
in Bermuda cedar.

The main building has 26 double rooms; the remaining units are found in
separate cottages, all providing views of the water. The rooms are attractively
furnished.

Dining/Entertainment: Dinner can be taken on an à la carte basis or booked for your entire stay at the MAP rate. The **Inlet Restaurant** (see Chapter 6, "Dining") overlooks the moon gate, which frames a view of Harrington Sound. The **Ha' Penny Pub** is a darkly intimate hideaway with big windows behind the dark-grained bar. Afternoon tea is served here.

Services: Bus fare is provided to two South Shore beaches that are five minutes away. There is also laundry service, as well as babysitting.

Facilities: Swimming pool that overlooks the water; swimming and snorkeling in bay.

White Sands Hotel & Cottages

55 White Sands Rd., Paget Parish PG BX Bermuda. ☎ **441/236-2023** or 800/548-0547 in the U.S., and 800/228-3196 in Canada. Fax 441/236-2486. 40 rms. A/C TV TEL. Apr 1–Nov 15 $250–$290 double; Nov 16–Mar 31 $175–$205 double. Rates include MAP (breakfast and dinner). AE, MC, V. Bus: 7 or 8.

For years honeymooners and families have sought out this rather British hotel, which still evokes the period when it was built (the 1950s), although it is constantly being upgraded and improved. The original owners, the Browne family, still run the hotel today. Comprising a compound of salmon-colored buildings amid terraced gardens, it is just a short walk downhill to a wide, semiprivate beach at Grape Bay, with exceptionally fine sand. Of all the hotels on Bermuda's south shore, this one is the closest to Hamilton—just a 10-minute ride by taxi or bus.

The rooms are furnished with wall-to-wall carpeting, large closets, small refrigerators, a radio, a coffeemaker and comfortable beds. Each is spacious, airy, and bright, and generally decorated with modern furniture. Especially noteworthy is a tower room (Room 222) whose five oversized windows provide an eagle's-nest view of the surrounding shoreline. In addition to the main building, there are several two- and three-bedroom cottages.

Dining/Entertainment: A formal but relaxed dining room, **The Captain's Table,** outfitted in a colonial English motif; the **Terrace Club** poolside restaurant for lunch; and an English-inspired pub, the **Sandbar.**

Services: Room service (8–8:45am and 7–8:30pm); babysitters available with advance notice.

Facilities: A heated freshwater swimming pool; easy access to tennis, golf, and water sports facilities at nearby south shore hotels; moped rentals.

MODERATE

⑨ Palm Reef Hotel

1 Harbour Rd. (P.O. Box HM 1189), Hamilton HM EX, Bermuda. ☎ **441/236-1000** or 800/221-1294 in the U.S. Fax 441/236-6392. 94 rms. A/C TEL. Apr 1–Nov 15 $120–$190 double; Nov 16–Mar 31 $96–$116 double. Golf, honeymoon, and family packages available. AE, MC, V. Bus: 7 or hotel ferry.

This is something of a sleeper hotel for Bermuda, although it has maintained a devoted following throughout its long history. Dating back to the 17th century, this was Bermuda's first hotel, formerly known as the Inverurie. It's located on Harbour Road at Cobbs Hill Road, where Paget and Warwick Parishes meet. Despite its $1 million massive renovation and refurbishment, which was long overdue, this hotel is not even listed in certain guidebooks. It's ideal for those who want a small hotel without ostentation that offers good value for the money.

The hotel overlooks Hamilton Harbour; Hamilton is only 10 minutes away by ferry. The main buildings, in Bermuda pink, are surrounded by landscaped grounds.

Many of the well-furnished but smallish rooms are equipped with refrigerators, and all have sliding glass doors that open onto private terraces or balconies.

Dining/Entertainment: The hotel has a cocktail lounge, a dining room, **Le Bistro,** and a nightclub called **The Gombey Room.**

Services: The hotel's own ferry takes guests to and from Hamilton. Laundry, babysitting.

Facilities: Large open-air, temperature-controlled swimming pool; scuba diving facilities; tennis court.

Rosedon

Pitts Bay Road (P.O. Box HM 290), Hamilton HM AX, Bermuda. ☎ **441/295-1640.** For information and reservations, contact Island Resorts Reservations, P.O. Box 4477, Lutherville, MD 21094 (☎ **410/628-1718** or 800/742-5008. Fax 441/295-5904). 42 rms. TV TEL. Apr–Nov $170–$235 double; off-season $125–$190 double. Rates include full breakfast. Extra person sharing room $32. MC, V. Bus: 7 or 8.

If you shun megahotels (such as the Hamilton Princess across the street), this hotel may appeal to you. Housed in a stately 1906 mansion, it is big on Bermudian charm and character. Although its rates are rather high for what is, after all, an overblown guesthouse, it has its fans. Business travelers often stay here because of its proximity to Hamilton.

The house is surrounded by extensive gardens and lawns. Look for the loquat tree, a Bermuda trademark. Other shrubs include hibiscus, banana plants, and birds of paradise. Rosedon resembles a colonial-era plantation Great House, with a pristine white exterior and royal blue shutters. Once occupied by an English family, this was the first house in Bermuda with gaslights. The formal entry hall is dominated by an open staircase and a midway landing window. There are two antique-filled lounges. Guests can sit on a flagstone terrace under parasol-shaded tables around a large, temperature-controlled pool. The honor system prevails at Nigel's Bar.

There are individually decorated bedrooms with private baths. The back modern veranda rooms—called lanai suites—open onto a pool, and there are also air-conditioned colonial-style rooms in the main house; each unit has a private refrigerator. The rates also include room service, English afternoon tea, and access to tennis courts and the beach at Elbow Beach, with free round-trip taxi service (10 minutes).

3 Cottage Colonies

These accommodations are considered uniquely Bermudian. Each colony has a main clubhouse with a dining room, lounge, and bar, plus its own beach or pool. The cottage units, spread throughout landscaped grounds, offer privacy and sometimes luxury. Most have kitchenettes suitable for beverages and light snacks, but not for full-time cooking.

VERY EXPENSIVE

Ariel Sands Beach Club

34 South Shore Rd., Devonshire (P.O. Box HM 334), Hamilton HM BX, Bermuda. ☎ **441/ 236-1010** or 800/468-6610 in the U.S.; call collect from Canada. Fax 441/236-0087. 49 rms. TEL. Apr–Oct $288–$370 double; Nov–Mar $204–$280 double. Rates include MAP (breakfast and dinner). AE, MC, V. Bus: 1.

Secluded at the ocean's edge, this has been one of the best cottage colonies in Bermuda since its establishment in 1959. This is a quiet place, much in demand by families that want a summer retreat.

The grounds are well landscaped, with flowering trees and coconut palms. One of the most original sculptures on the island is the stainless-steel statue of Ariel (created by Seward Johnson Jr.), who dances like a water sprite on the surf. The resort has a series of public rooms where, in cold weather, a double-hearth fireplace emits both light and heat into a reception lounge and a conservatively attractive bar area.

The often small accommodations, with private entrances, offer a simple but attractive decor of white walls, Bermudian flower paintings, and bentwood furniture. Most provide private porches as well, although the least expensive rooms do not have sea views. The decor of many of the private and public rooms here are based on themes from Shakespeare's **The Tempest,** including Miranda's Cabana, Sea Nymph, and Prospero.

Dining/Entertainment: International cuisine is served in **Calibans,** and during the season a local calypso band often entertains.

Service: Laundry, room service (at mealtimes only), babysitting.

Facilities: Swimming at an oval freshwater pool, a rectangular saltwater pool whose waters are replenished daily by the tides, or a sandy beach; three tennis courts (two lit for night games).

✪ Cambridge Beaches

30 Kings Point Rd., Sandys MA 02, Bermuda. ☎ **441/234-0331** or 800/468-7300 in the U.S., 800/463-5990 in Canada. Fax 441/234-3352. 58 units, 24 suites. A/C MINIBAR TEL. Mar 1–Apr 9 $270–$370 double, from $400 suite. Apr 10–Nov 15 $325–$450 double, $525–$1,025 suite. Nov 16–Feb 28 $230–$315 double, $370–$720 suite. Rates include MAP (breakfast and dinner). No credit cards. Bus: 7.

On a peninsula overlooking Mangrove Bay in Somerset, Cambridge Beaches has qualities not offered by any other cottage colony, and for that reason it is the most desirable in its category. Its nearest competitor is Horizons (see below). Although each place has its loyal followers, your preference is really a matter of taste. Cambridge Beaches occupies the entire western tip of the island—25 acres of semitropical gardens and green lawns—and its guests have a choice of five palm-fringed private beaches. It also boasts a wealth of water sports programs, equipment, and facilities.

As the 1947 pioneer of Bermudian cottage colonies, Cambridge Beaches is centered around an old sea captain's house. The main lounges are tastefully furnished with antiques; the dominant feeling here is that of a country estate.

Scattered throughout the gardens are nicely furnished, pink-and-white units, some of which are nearly 300 years old and retain their distinct Bermudian architectural features. The conservative furnishings are color- and fabric-coordinated. All cottages, some of which were once private homes, have sun-and-breakfast terraces, generally with unobstructed views of the bay and gardens. Each unit is also equipped with a small refrigerator.

Dining/Entertainment: Informal lounges for drinking include the **Port O' Call Pub** and the piano bar. Calypso and other entertainment are usually provided six nights a week. Dining is in the air-conditioned main dining room—**Pamarisk**—or on the terrace, where barbecues are sometimes held.

Services: Massage facilities, room service, laundry.

Facilities: Three all-weather tennis courts; a golf course—Port Royal—designed by Robert Trent Jones is just seven minutes away; the resort has its own putting green. Guests swim in a temperature-controlled pool or at a nearby beach. A full marina with Boston whalers and various sailboats is on-site. Water sports include windsurfing with instruction, canoeing, kayaking, snorkeling, and fishing (equipment is available). Parasailing, sailing, and snorkeling trips, plus glass-bottom-boat excursions and fishing voyages are available here. Adjacent to the colony are two bone fishing flats. The full-service spa features exercise equipment, whirlpool, steam, sauna, and hair dressing, plus 50-odd types of skin, beauty, and relaxation treatments.

✪ Horizons and Cottages

33 South Shore, Paget PG, Bermuda. ☎ **441/236-0048** or 800/468-0022 in the U.S. and Canada. Fax 441/236-1981. 50 units. A/C TEL. Mar 15–Nov 30 $306–$436 double, $496–$700 suite; off-season $206–$336 double, $400–$600 suite. Rates include MAP (breakfast and dinner). No credit cards. Bus: 7.

For snob appeal and a posh address, Horizons is always in a neck-to-neck race with Cambridge Beaches (with which it is most often compared) and with Lantana Colony Club (over which it has a slight edge). All three are popular with a discerning and well-heeled crowd. Each "colony" is characterized by subdued sophistication. Horizons and Cottages have at their core a converted manor farm (circa 1690), where much of the aura of the past has been retained. A Relais & Châteaux member, Horizons is situated on a 25-acre estate with terraced gardens and lawns, atop a hill overlooking Coral Beach. The reception rooms of the manor house have old Bermudian architectural details, as well as antiques from England and the Continent; several drawing rooms have open fireplaces.

Double accommodations are the norm, whether in the cottages or the main building. All are handsomely furnished—with Italian terra-cotta tile floors, scatter rugs, traditional tray ceilings, and ceiling fans—and all have separate dressing areas as well as private terraces overlooking the ocean. Some units are split-level. Minibars and TVs are available on request.

Dining/Entertainment: The main dining room serves French **cuisine naturelle,** using all fresh products. Lunch can be enjoyed on the terrace. In the evening, the terrace is transformed into an entertainment area, with informal dancing and often calypso music. Lunch and dinner, by reservation, can be exchanged at Newstead and Waterloo House.

Services: Laundry, room service, babysitting.

Facilities: Nine-hole mashie golf course, 18-hole putting green, tennis courts, heated freshwater swimming pool.

✪ Lantana

P.O. Box SB 90, Somerset Bridge SB BX, Bermuda. ☎ **441/234-0141** or 800/468-3733 in the U.S., 800/463-0036 in Canada. Fax 441/234-2562. 58 suites, 6 cottages. A/C MINIBAR TV TEL. May–Oct $310–$460 double suite, $480 cottage for two, $720 two-bedroom cottage for four. Off-season $210–$315 double suite, $380 cottage for two, $580 two-bedroom cottage for four. Rates include MAP (breakfast and dinner). No credit cards. Closed Jan 5–Feb 15. Hamilton ferry to Somerset Bridge.

Overlooking Great Sound, a 25-minute ferry ride from Hamilton, this complex is like a private club. Established in the 1950s and renovated in 1992, it caters to a wealthy clientele who want privacy and are not seeking glitter or nightlife. Its main competitors are Horizons and Cambridge Beaches. It occupies 23 acres of cultivated gardens, offering both poolside and bay swimming, along with tennis courts.

Around the main building are clusters of Bermudian cottages and lanai suites. The accommodations are restrained and traditional in decor, with an emphasis on comfort; they are all equipped with irons and hairdryers. One cottage even has its own private swimming pool. The clubhouse, with its large fireplace, is a popular rendezvous spot.

Dining/Entertainment: The hotel's restaurant is open to the public (see Chapter 6, "Dining"). Amid greenery and flowers, a superb dinner (continental cuisine) is served.

Services: Laundry, room service (breakfast only).

Facilities: Solarium, outdoor patio, freshwater pool, sundeck, two all-weather tennis courts, lawn croquet, putting green, small artificially created beach, and water sports from a private dock.

Pink Beach Club & Cottages

South Shore Road (P.O. Box HM 1017), Hamilton HM DX, Bermuda. ☎ **441/293-1666** or 800/355-6161 in the U.S. Fax 441/293-8935. 81 units. A/C TEL. Apr 15–Oct 31 $335–$385 double; off-season $241–$261 double. Rates include MAP (breakfast and dinner). MC, V. Closed Jan 5–Feb 28. Bus: 1.

In a remote location, this cottage colony doesn't have the posh or flair of Cambridge Beaches, Horizons, or Lantana, but it does attract an affluent international crowd.

This is the largest cottage colony on Bermuda. Its 18-acre garden setting is graced with bay grape trees and hibiscus bushes, and its pink cottages are surrounded by two private south shore beaches. Each cottage has a little kitchenette outside the door, and a maid will come each morning and prepare breakfast for you (just as you requested it the night before). The staff—among the best on the island—includes many people who have been with Pink Beach since it began in 1947. The cottages range from a studio (bed-sitting room, bath, and patio) to a full unit with living room and terrace.

Dining/Entertainment: The heart of the colony is the limestone clubhouse, painted pink, with its natural-wood dining room, where "backyard" vegetables and fresh seafood are used for the international cuisine. Every table provides a view of the ocean and the South Shore breakers.

Services: Laundry, babysitting.

Facilities: A large saltwater pool, sun terrace, and two tennis courts are on the grounds. There are two championship golf courses two minutes away from the hotel.

St. George's Club

Rose Hill (P.O. Box GE 92), St. George's GE, BX, Bermuda. ☎ **441/297-1200.** Fax 441/297-8003. 69 cottages. A/C TV TEL. Year-round $250 cottage for up to four, $450 cottage for up to six. AE, DC, MC, V. Bus: 6, 8, 10, or 11.

Far less snobbish and stuffy than the cottage colonies listed above, this is your best bet if you would like a cottage in the area of St. George's. This resort, encompassing 18 acres atop Rose Hill, off York Street, in St. George's, features clusters of traditionally designed Bermudian one- and two-bedroom cottages. The complex functions primarily as a time-share property, where units are rented to the public when the owners are not using them. The accommodations offer private balconies or patios, comfortable living and dining areas, fully equipped kitchens, and baths with sunken tubs and marble vanities. The units provide views of the ocean, the pool, or the golf course.

Dining/Entertainment: An elegant restaurant on the premises, the **Margaret Rose,** is open to the public (see Chapter 6, "Dining"). The **Sir George Pub** is also a popular rendezvous spot.

Services: Laundry, babysitting.

Facilities: There is a convenience store—the Ample Hamper—in the clubhouse. There are three freshwater swimming pools (one is heated), and three all-weather tennis courts (two can be lit at night). A shuttle bus takes guests to the beach club at Achilles Bay. Golfers receive preferential tee time at reduced rates on the adjacent 18-hole golf course designed by Robert Trent Jones.

4 Housekeeping Units

Housekeeping apartments, Bermuda's efficiency units, vary from modest to superior. Most are equipped with kitchens or kitchenettes and provide minimal daily maid service. The housekeeping cottages, which are all air-conditioned and have fully equipped kitchens, are located either on or close to a beach. The cottages offer privacy and casual living.

EXPENSIVE

Fourways Inn

1 Middle Rd. (P.O. Box PG 294), Paget PG BX, Bermuda. ☎ **441/236-6517** or 800/525-4800 in the U.S. and Canada. Fax 441/236-5528. 5 rms, 5 suites. A/C MINIBAR TV TEL. Apr–Oct $230 double, $325–$555 suite; Nov–Mar $140 double, $180–$320 suite. Rates include continental breakfast. MAP $40 per person extra. AE, MC, V. Bus: 8.

This little pocket of posh is really a secret hideaway, so you shouldn't tell anybody about it. Pink-sided, airy, and stylish, these Bermudian cottages were erected in the garden of one of the best restaurants on the island—the Fourways Inn Restaurant (see Chapter 6, "Dining"). The main building is a former private home dating from 1727. Each of five suites consists of two accommodations, a patio, a private safe, a fully equipped kitchenette, conservatively comfortable furniture, a satellite-connected TV, and lots of extra touches. The cottages ring a communal heated swimming pool and a well-maintained garden. The beaches of the south shore are close by. The management prefers not to accept children under 16, and it wouldn't be their kind of place anyway.

Mermaid Beach Club

South Shore Road (P.O. Box WK 250), Warwick WK BX, Bermuda. ☎ **441/236-5031** or 800/441-7087 in the U.S. and Canada. Fax 441/236-8325. 79 units (44 with kitchens). A/C TEL. Apr 15–Nov 1 $180–$212 double, $260–$370 apartments with kitchens. Off-season $110–$130 double, $160–$270 apartments with kitchens. MAP $35 extra per person per day. AE, MC, V. Bus: 7.

Set beside a curved shoreline that combines both rocky cliffs and sandy beachfront, this complex is made up of two-story cement-sided buildings; the buildings and the amenities have gradually increased since the beach club was founded in the 1940s. Unlike some of Bermuda's snobby and stiff resorts and hotels, this one is decidedly informal, attracting both older and younger couples who want to have a good time without having to dress up too often. The beach is on the premises; there is also a snack bar and a main bar (outfitted in a nautical theme), a bike-rental shop, a restaurant (the **Jolly Lobster**), and a curved-sided swimming pool situated on a terrace above the beach. All units were built with patios or balconies, and the majority of them overlook the sea (the rest look out over a garden). Bedrooms are simple and summery, decorated with pastel colors and rattan furniture, and equipped with refrigerators.

MODERATE

Angel's Grotto

P.O. Box HS 81, Smith's HS BX, Bermuda. ☎ **441/293-1986** or 800/637-4116 in the U.S., 800/267-7600 in Canada. Fax 441/293-4164. 7 apts. (all with kitchenettes). A/C TV TEL. Apr 1–Oct 31 $115–$130 double; off-season $95–$115 double. AE, MC, V. Bus: 3.

These housekeeping cottages, among the best in Bermuda, are generally preferred by couples. Following renovations in 1994, they are now better than ever. Situated on

$1^1/_2$ acres of seafront property overlooking Harrington Sound, this complex consists of three white-sided structures, originally built as a private home in the 1940s. Later, it functioned as a disco and nightclub, as one might surmise from the large seafront terrace, site of long-ago dance parties. Now converted into accommodations consisting of an air-conditioned bedroom, well-equipped kitchen, and combination living room/dining area, the property has been owned by Daisy Hart since 1981. Those units that overlook the water are slightly more expensive. The coastline adjacent to the complex is too rocky for swimming, but a sandy beach lies within a 10-minute walk.

⑤ Astwood Cove

49 South Shore Rd., Warwick WK 07, Bermuda. ☎ **441/236-0984** or 800/637-4116 in the U.S. Fax 441/236-1164. 20 apts. A/C TEL. Apr 1–Nov 15 $108–$138 double; Nov 16–Mar 31 $76–$90 double. No credit cards. Bus: 7 from Hamilton.

Nigel (Nicky) and Gabrielle (Gaby) Lewin own this homestead, which was built in 1720 on a dairy farm. The house bears the name of the three Astwood sisters—Maude, Ada, and Mary—who stipulated in their will that it should always carry their name. The apartment complex enjoys a peaceful setting, overlooking lightly wooded meadows and the south shore; additional features include a sauna, pool, and gas-fired barbecue stations.

Each of the 20 self-contained, air-conditioned units has a private bath with shower (no tubs), a telephone (no charge for local calls), a radio, ceiling fans, and a terrace or porch. Some units have sitting rooms, and all have kitchenettes equipped with English china. Guests prepare their own breakfast. A new building (all apartments) was added in 1985 with a communal terrace and pavilion, TV, and an exercise machine. The closest large beach, Long Bay, is a quarter of a mile away; however, Astwood's Beach and Mermaid Beach are only a three-minute stroll from the compound.

Longtail Cliffs

34 South Shore Rd. (P.O. Box HM 836), Hamilton HM CX, Bermuda. ☎ **441/236-2864** or 800/637-4116 in the U.S., 800/267-7600 in Canada. Fax 441/236-5178. 13 units. A/C TV TEL. Apr 1–Oct 31 $255 two-bedroom apartment for three, $295 two-bedroom apartment for four; $40 per day for each additional person. Off-season $150 two-bedroom apartment for three, $170 two-bedroom apartment for four; $20 per day for each additional person. AE, MC, V. Bus: 7 from Hamilton.

Longtail Cliffs may be short on personality and Bermudian charm—it is, in fact, a bit like a motel—but if you have difficulty or don't want to climb the steep steps of Bermuda, check in here. Longtail Cliffs is relatively flat. The establishment has only limited facilities, but enjoys a reputation as one of the better small apartment hotels.

Bird-watchers will enjoy the dozens of longtails (a form of seagull) that nest in the cliffs below. A swimming pool is set into the lawn, and a row of hedges marks the beginning of a steep drop-off toward the sea. Beachcombers can walk a short distance to one of the neighboring coves.

Longtail's facade (as seen from the road) isn't dramatic, but once you're in one of the rooms, especially those on the upper floor, you'll be rewarded with lots of space, cathedral-like ceilings, and comfortable accommodations. Each unit has a kitchen (where you can prepare your own breakfast or other meals), a radio, and a wall safe. On the premises is a coin-operated laundry.

Marley Beach Cottages

South Shore Road (P.O. Box PG 278), Warwick PG BX, Bermuda. ☎ **441/236-1143** or 800/ 637-4116 in the U.S. Fax 441/236-1984. 14 cottages. A/C TV. Apr 1–Nov 15 $172–$256 double, $281–$320 cottage for four; off-season $138–$216 double, $200 cottage for four. AE, MC, V. Bus: 2 or 7.

If you're part of two couples traveling together (as often happens in Bermuda), this may be your best bargain. These pink-walled cottages were erected on a steep but beautifully landscaped plot of land—on the south shore near Astwood Park—that was used for scenes in **The Deep** and **Chapter Two**. More recently part of another film—**Bermuda Grace**—was shot there. Three narrow beaches lie at the bottom of the slope that leads to the sea, and there is a curved heated freshwater swimming pool as well as a whirlpool on the property. The spacious cottages offer sea views from the patio, and come with fully equipped kitchens and hibachis. Each cottage is made up of both a suite and a studio apartment, which you can rent as one unit or two, depending on your needs. Guests can either prepare their own meals or eat out. These house-keeping cottages have been called complete "do-it-yourself" retreats, with groceries and drinks delivered daily, although there is daily maid service. It's not the most ideal place for children since there is little for them to do, other than enjoy the pool.

Paraquet Guest Apartments

South Shore Road (P.O. Box PG 173), Paget PG BX, Bermuda. ☎ **441/236-5842.** Fax 441/236-1665. 12 apartments. A/C TV. Apr–Oct $120 double without kitchen, $145 double with kitchen. Nov–Mar $105 double without kitchen, $125 double with kitchen. No credit cards. Bus: 7.

Come here if you're looking for a bargain and are happy to settle for clean but rather Spartan accommodations, somewhat motel-like in character. This buff-colored collection of Bermudian houses, landscaped into a gentle knoll, is a five-minute walk from Elbow Beach. Built in the mid-1970s, the complex is owned by the Portuguese-born Correia family. Nine of the units are equipped with kitchenettes, and all have private baths, maid service, and functional modern furniture. The focal point here is the restaurant—**Paraquet Restaurant** (see Chapter 6, "Dining").

Pretty Penny

7 Cobb's Hill Rd. (P.O. Box PG 137), Paget PB BX, Bermuda. ☎ **441/236-1194** or 800/637-4116 in the U.S. Fax 441/236-3290. 7 apartments. A/C TEL. Apr–Nov $140 double; off-season $100 double. AE, MC, V. Ferry from Hamilton or bus: 8.

The owners and managers of this home, located in an excellent neighborhood, are the Bermudians Diana and Stephen Martin. A food market is located close by, so that guests can easily stock up, especially for breakfast. The ferryboat to Hamilton is just a two-minute walk from the front desk. There is a variety of beaches within a 20-minute walk of the premises, and there's a deck-ringed pool on the grounds.

The names of several accommodations may evoke a smile: Tuppence, Thruppence, Sixpence, Playpenny, and Sevenpence. Each consists of a hillside bungalow, with kitchenette and attractive furnishings; one unit has a fireplace. Each unit can accommodate at least two guests.

Ⓢ Rosemont

41 Rosemont Ave. (P.O. Box HM 37), Hamilton HM AX, Bermuda. ☎ **441/292-1055** or 800/367-0040 in the U.S., 800/267-0040 in Canada. Fax 441/295-3913. 34 units, 3 suites. A/C TV TEL. Mid-Mar to mid-Nov $128–$134 double, $240 suite; Mid-Nov to mid-Mar $96–$100 double, $225 suite. MC, V. Bus: 7 or 8.

Rosemont is a cluster of gray-walled cottages, each with a large veranda, set on a flow-ered hillside near the Hamilton Princess Hotel. Two of the cottages had been homes that were built in the 1940s; the rest are more modern structures built within the past 15 years or so. The harbor, with its passing ships, is visible from the raised terrace beside the small L-shaped swimming pool. The policy of the Rosemont is to "keep it quiet," so that business travelers, families, and mature couples who stay here can enjoy peace and quiet. For that reason, the hotel usually doesn't accept college students or large groups. There is a grocery store close by, and downtown Hamilton is just 10 minutes away. Elbow Beach, a 15-minute ride, provides saltwater swimming. Upon request, the hotel will arrange a motor-scooter rental.

Each of the well-furnished rooms is equipped with a kitchen, a radio/alarm clock, and a full bath, although the units may be a little dark. As many as three rooms can be joined together, which some families prefer. In addition to regular rooms, the hotel has three suites with private entrances and better furnishings. The rates do not include service and taxes. Laundry and babysitting can be arranged. There is no restaurant on the premises since everybody cooks in.

Sandpiper Apartments

South Shore Road (P.O. Box HM 685), Hamilton HM CX, Bermuda. ☎ 441/236-7093 or 800/441-7087 in the U.S. Fax 441/236-3898. 9 units, 5 suites. A/C TV TEL. Mar 16–Nov 15 $120 double, $160 suite; off-season $75 double, $120 suite. AE, MC, V. Bus: 7.

Built in 1979 and frequently upgraded, this apartment complex is a suitable choice for a budget-conscious vacation; it is just a short walk to several beaches. This complex is not for those who are seeking glamour, but it provides an outdoor whirlpool and swimming pool for relaxation as well as gardens for lounging. Nine of the units are studios (suitable for one or two persons): each has two double beds in the bedroom, a bathroom, and a fully equipped kitchenette. Five of the units are made up of a bedroom (with king-size or twin beds), a kitchen, a bathroom, and a living/dining area with two double pull-out sofa beds. All the apartments provide radios, balconies, and daily maid service. The Sandpiper is only minutes away from restaurants and the supermarket.

⊖ Sky-Top Cottages

65 South Shore Rd. (P.O. Box PG 227), Paget PG BX, Bermuda. ☎ 441/236-7984. 11 units. A/C TEL. Mar 15–Nov 30 $90–$125 double; Dec 1–Mar 14 $75–$95 double. Extra person $25 in summer, $15 off-season. Off-season weekly and monthly discounts available. MC, V. Bus: 7.

Set on a hilltop above Paget's southern shoreline, opposite the Elbow Beach Hotel, this collection of cottages provides some of the most comfortably isolated accommodations in their price bracket. The units are contained in four cozy, English-style cottages, two of which, dating from early this century, were assembled into a single unit by the English-born wives of two local doctors, Marion Stubbs and Susan Harvey. Each cottage, which is decorated conservatively, has a small private terrace. Nine of the units offer fully equipped kitchenettes.

The units take their names from some of the flowers in the garden; thus, you may find yourself staying in Morning Glory, Pink Corallita, or Allamanda. On all sides of the property, emerald-colored lawns encompass shrubs and trees whose sightlines permit a view of the sea. There are few social activities here, except an occasional rainy-day party to cheer everybody up. Nevertheless, a kind of English-inspired camaraderie is present. It is just a five-minute walk to Elbow Beach, and a 10-minute ride by cab, bus, or moped to Hamilton.

Surf Side Beach Club

South Shore Road (P.O. Box WK 101), Warwick WK BX, Bermuda. ☎ 441/236-7100 or 800/553-9990 in the U.S. Fax 441/236-9765. 36 units. A/C TV TEL. Apr–Oct $185–$215 double, $260–$325 for up to four; off-season $105–$125 double, $170–$200 for up to four. Extra person in any unit $25. Off-season discounts available for extended stays. MC, V. Bus: 2 or 7.

The Surf Side Beach Club was terraced into a steeply sloping hillside that descends, after passing through gardens, to a crescent-shaped sweep of private beachfront. The property was redesigned nearly a quarter of a century ago and still maintains the varied array of flowering trees and panoramic walkways. The stonemasons added several lookout points in the garden, where visitors can see grouper and other fish swimming among the distant rocks of the shallow sea.

Some accommodations consist of one-bedroom apartments near the terrace pool, while other lodgings are in hillside buildings. Each of the units is simple and sunny, furnished in bright colors with comfortable accessories; and each is self-contained, with a fully equipped kitchenette (English china, wine glasses, even salt and pepper shakers). Eleven units are equipped with a shower, and the rest with a tub. Each unit has a private balcony or patio. Some of the accommodations have sitting rooms as well. There's a laundry on the premises.

5 Guesthouses

These are usually comfortable old converted manor houses in garden settings. Some have pools and terraces. The smaller ones offer fewer facilities and are much more casual—often with simple, "lived-in" furniture. Most guesthouses serve only breakfast. Those accommodating fewer than 12 guests are usually small private homes; some have housekeeping units, while others offer shared kitchen facilities for guests to prepare snacks.

Edgehill Manor

Rosemont Avenue (P.O. Box HM 1048), Hamilton HM EX, Bermuda. ☎ **441/295-7124.** Fax 441/295-3850. 9 rms. A/C TV. Mar 16–Nov 15 $108–$124 double; off-season $82–$92 double. Rates include continental breakfast. Children under 12 pay $10 when staying in parents' room. Special honeymoon rates. No credit cards. Bus: 7 or 8.

Just outside the city limits, in a quiet residential area that is nevertheless convenient to restaurants and shopping in Hamilton, Edgehill Manor just might become your "little home in Bermuda." Painted green, it was built around the time of the American Civil War and still exudes an old-fashioned, homelike quality, attracting a rather middle-aged clientele. Your landlady is British-born Bridget Marshall, who continues the tradition of serving English tea in the afternoon. Although each unit has its own style, all come with small balconies or patios; at least two are equipped with kitchenettes. Ms. Marshall's continental breakfast, she is proud to say, is "all home baked."

Greenbank Guest House

17 Salt Kettle Rd. (P.O. Box PG 201), Paget PG BX, Bermuda. ☎ **441/236-3615,** or 800/ 637-4116 in the U.S. Fax 441/236-2427. 11 units. A/C TEL. Apr 1–Nov 14 $95–$125 double; Nov 15–Mar 31 $75–$105 double. AE, MC, V. Ferry from Hamilton.

At the water's edge in Salt Kettle, this guesthouse stands across the bay from Hamilton, a 10-minute ferry ride away. It's an old Bermuda home, hidden under pine and palm trees, with shady lawns and flower gardens. The oldest section dates from the 1700s. The manager welcomes guests to an antiques-filled drawing room with its original floor, a fireplace, and a grand piano. The atmosphere is relaxed and personalized. Greenbank offers accommodations with private entrances and kitchens—either waterside or garden view cottages. There is daily maid service, but guests are responsible for their own breakfast. Greenbank has a private dock for swimming; there is also a charter operation on the property for renting motorboats and sailboats.

Greene's Guest House

71 Middle Rd. (P.O. Box SN 395), Southampton SN BX, Bermuda. ☎ **441/238-0834.** Fax 441/238-8980. 8 rms. A/C TV TEL. Year-round $100 double. Rates include continental breakfast. No credit cards. Bus: 7 or 8.

The exterior of this guesthouse, which overlooks Great Sound, appears well maintained, clean, and unpretentious. A look on the inside reveals pleasant and conservatively furnished rooms, which are more impressive than you might have initially supposed. The entryway is flanked by a pair of lions resting on stone columns. The tables of the dining room, which can be closed off from the adjacent kitchen by a curtain, are set with a full formal dinner service throughout the day. Wall-to-wall carpeting covers the floors of the entrance lobby as well as the spacious and well-furnished living room. Guests are free to use this room, as well as the sun-washed terraces in back. There is a swimming pool is in the back garden. The owners are Walter (Dickie) Greene and his wife, Jane.

Each of the bedrooms is equipped with an ironing board and iron, a coffeemaker, a radio, and a refrigerator. Facing the sea there's a cozy bar, where guests use the honor system to record their drinks. Dinner is available in the dining room if requested in advance. The regular Bermuda bus going to and from Hamilton stops at the front door. The beach and the Port Royal Golf Course are both about five minutes away.

Little Pomander Guest House

16 Pomander Rd. (Paget P.O. Box HM 384), Hamilton HM BX, Bermuda. ☎ **441/236-7635.** Fax 441/236-8332. 6 rms, 3 apts. A/C TV TEL. Apr 1–Oct 31 $115 double, $125–$150 apts. Off-season $80 double, $85–$110 apts. Room rates (but *not* apartment rates) include continental breakfast. AE, MC, V. Bus: 1, 7, 8.

This establishment, which consists of two pink-sided Bermuda houses separated from one another by a nonrelated building, once served as the annex to what is now a privately operated tennis club across the street. (Known as the Pomander Tennis Club, it offers temporary memberships for $10 and free use of its tennis courts to guests of Little Pomander.) Little Pomander's main building, possibly one of the oldest on Bermuda, can trace its history and foundations back to the 1630s. The grassy lawn stretches a short distance down to the rocky shoreline, where one can see the cruise ships anchored in Hamilton Harbour. The bedrooms have been tastefully outfitted with floral prints and alpine-style curtains by the decorator Irene Trott who, along with her daughters, owns the inn. Each of the three apartments has a full kitchenette, but even the conventional bedrooms here are equipped with microwave ovens and small refrigerators.

ⓢ Loughlands

79 South Shore Rd., Paget PG 03, Bermuda. ☎ **441/236-1253.** 25 rms (19 with bath). A/C. Mar 15–Nov 14 $75 single without bath, $118 double with bath; off-season $60 single without bath, $80 double with bath. Rates include continental breakfast. No credit cards. Bus: 2 and 7 stop nearby.

Built in 1920, Loughlands is the stately, former residence of the president of the Staten Island Savings Bank in New York, who bestowed his name, Lough, on the estate. It is now the largest guesthouse in Bermuda. Situated on 9 acres of landscaped grounds in the center of the island, it is plantation chalk-white, and its entry hall bears a large portrait of Queen Victoria. Loughlands was purchased in 1973 by Stanley and Mary Pickles, who sold their large country house in Cornwall, England, and shipped many of their antiques to Bermuda. The bedrooms at Loughlands are handsomely decorated, some with high-post beds and antique chests. At breakfast one may enjoy such Bermudian treats as fresh citrus fruit or bananas and homemade preserves.

On the grounds are a swimming pool and a tennis court. Close by there is bus service to all parts of the island. It is just a short walk to Elbow Beach.

The Oxford House

Woodbourne Avenue (P.O. Box HN 374), Hamilton HM BX, Bermuda. ☎ **441/295-0503** or 800/548-7758 in the U.S., 800/272-2306 in Canada. Fax 441/295-0250. 12 rms. A/C TV TEL. Mar 16–Nov 30 $138 double; off-season $125 double. Rates include full breakfast. MC, V. Bus: 1, 2, 10, or 11.

The Oxford House is one of the best and most centrally located guesthouses in Hamilton. Possibly the only property in Bermuda constructed specifically as a guesthouse, it is located on a side street that leads into Front Street, near the Bermudiana Hotel. It was built in 1938 by a doctor and his French wife, who requested that some of the architectural features follow French designs.

The white- and cream-colored entrance portico is flanked by Doric columns, corner mullions, and urn-shaped balustrades. Inside, a curved stairwell sweeps upward to the spacious, well-furnished bedrooms, each of which is named after one of Bermuda's parishes. There's even an upstairs sitting room, bathed in sunlight. Each bedroom evokes the feeling of a private home—with a private bath, high ceilings, dressing areas, and a coffeemaker. The Bermudian breakfast, in season, might include a fresh fruit salad made with oranges and grapefruit grown in the yard. Your gracious host is Welsh-born Ann Smith.

Royal Heights Guest House

Lighthouse Hill (P.O. Box SN 144), Southampton SN BX, Bermuda. ☎ **441/238-0043.** Fax 441/238-8445. 7 rms. A/C TV. Apr–Nov $125 double, $175 triple; off-season $100 double, $150 triple. Rates include full breakfast. Children under 12 pay $50 when staying in parents' room. MC, V. Bus: 7 or 8.

Set at the top of a steeply inclined driveway near the summit of Lighthouse Hill, this guesthouse is convenient to the Southampton Princess Hotel with its varied nightlife and dining facilities. This is a modern, turquoise-trimmed building, whose two wings embrace the front entryway. Terraced near the foundation, the swimming pool permits bathers to see ships passing by on Great Sound. Guests are welcome to gather in the living room of the owners, Russel Richardson and his wife, Jean, who will suggest activities for you. Each of the spanking-clean bedrooms is equipped with a balcony and comfortable furniture.

Royal Palms Hotel

24 Rosemont Ave. (P.O. Box HM 499), Hamilton, HM CX, Bermuda. ☎ **441/292-1854,** or 800/678-0783 in the U.S., 800/799-0824 in Canada. Fax 441/292-1946. 12 rms, 1 cottage. A/C TV TEL. Apr 1–Oct 31 $150–$160 double; $170 cottage. Off-season $132 double, $150 cottage. Rates include continental breakfast. AE, MC, V. Bus: 1, 2, 10, or 11.

Located just a five-minute walk from Hamilton, the family owned and managed Royal Palms is one of the most sought-after small hotels on the island, thanks to the care and restoration work of the brother-sister team, Richard Smith and Susan Weare. The exact year of the house's construction is not known, but it's definitely a century old.

Nearby residents often walk by the Royal Palms' garden to admire the marigolds and zinnias. The house is a fine example of Bermudian architecture, with coral-colored walls, white shutters, and a white roof, plus a wraparound front porch with rocking chairs and armchairs. Cozy public areas include the **Ascots Restaurant,** which serves both European and Bermudian cuisine, a bar surrounded by a terrace, and a veranda overlooking a freshwater pool.

What had formerly been the living rooms, parlors, and bedrooms of a grand private house were converted into guest rooms. Today, each is spacious, sunny, and comfortably furnished. Rich fabrics have been used throughout, and most units have high ceilings and tall windows. Each accommodation is equipped with a tea kettle or coffeemaker, and many have small refrigerators. In the mews next to the hotel there are four additional units, some with kitchen facilities.

INEXPENSIVE

Hill Crest Guest House

1 Nea's Alley (P.O. Box GE 96), St. George's GE BX, Bermuda. ☎ **441/297-1630.** Fax 441/297-1908. 11 units. A/C. Year-round $72 double, $104.40 triple. No credit cards. Bus: 1, 3, 6, 10, or 11.

Hill Crest is a green-and-white, early-18th-century home spread on the rise of a hill off Old Maid's Lane. With its wide verandas, lawns (with a moon gate), and trees, it has a homelike look. The interior is pleasant and comfortable, filled with clutter and antiques. The small entry hall has Edwardian furnishings, and each of the rather spacious but clean units has a private bathroom and clock radio. There are two small honeymoon cottages on the grounds. From Hill Crest it is about a five-minute walk to several restaurants, where you can have breakfast; also nearby are shops, golfing, regular buses, and the major attractions of the historic town of St. George's. In 1804 the Irish poet Thomas Moore roomed here for several weeks; he developed a fondness for Nea Tucker next door, and wrote some romantic verses for her.

Salt Kettle House

10 Salt Kettle Rd., Paget PG 01, Bermuda. ☎ **441/236-0407.** Fax 441/236-8639. 8 units (four with kitchenettes). A/C. Year-round $46 per person, double. Units with kitchenettes, $50 per person. Rates include full breakfast. No credit cards. Hamilton ferry to Salt Kettle (three-minute walk from ferry stop).

The core of this guesthouse is a 200-year-old cottage that, over the years, was enlarged. Today it is informal and secluded. In the late 1970s, another cottage was custom-built on the lot's only remaining space. Today, the compound is a cheerful architectural hodgepodge situated on a narrow peninsula that juts into Hamilton Harbour. One can see the ships going into and out of the harbor. Four cottages are equipped with kitchens, and the guests staying in the main house also have use of a fully equipped kitchen. The guest lounge has cable TV. The owner-manager is Mrs. Hazel Lowe.

Dining 6

Wahoo steak, shark hash, mussel pie, fish chowder laced with rum and sherry peppers, Hoppin' John (black-eyed peas and rice), and the succulent spiny Bermuda lobster (called guinea-chick) await you in Bermuda. Trouble is, you'll have to search hard to find these offbeat dishes, since many hotels and a large number of restaurants serve typical international resort cuisine. For a more detailed description of Bermudian cookery, see "Bermudian Cuisine" in Chapter 2, "Introducing Bermuda."

Bermudian food has improved in recent years, but dining out is not a major reason people come here. Both American dishes and British dishes (for example, steak-and-kidney pie) are common. Since most of the meat has to be imported, your best bet is to stick to selections from the briny whenever possible. The fish is generally excellent, especially Bermuda rockfish.

Sunday brunch is a Bermuda tradition. Hot and cold dishes are served buffet-style at several restaurants, including our favorite for brunch, the Waterlot Inn in Southampton Parish (see below).

Most restaurants, at least the better ones, insist on a dress code, preferring men to wear a jacket and tie after 6pm. At the better places, women usually wear casual, chic clothing in the evening. During the day, no matter what the establishment, be sure to wear a cover-up—do not arrive for lunch decked out in a bikini.

Restaurants rated **Very Expensive** charge more than $60 per person, excluding drinks and service. Restaurants listed as **Expensive** charge from $38 to $50 per person for dinner; **Moderate,** $25 to $38, and **Inexpensive,** less than $25 per person for dinner.

TIPS ON DINING

In general, it is not a good idea to order meat very often; it has probably been flown in, and one cannot be sure how long it has been held in storage. Whenever possible, it is best to stick to local food; for a main dish, that usually means fish caught in the deep sea. To find the dishes that are truly worthy, you'll have to pick and choose your way carefully through the menu. So-called "gourmet fare" often isn't, although the prices charged would make you think that you're getting something really special.

Dining in Bermuda is generally more expensive than it is in the United States and Canada. Because virtually everything except fish must be imported, restaurant prices are more comparable to those in Europe than to those in America. Although a service charge is usually added to most restaurant bills (typically 10% to 15%), if service has been good, it is customary to leave something extra.

If you're booked into a hotel on MAP rates (half board)—some hotels require this during the peak summer season—you can sample some of the local restaurants at lunch. That way, your stomach won't become completely "hotel bound."

Because of the absence of inexpensive transportation on the island, many travelers on a budget eat at their hotels at night to avoid adding transportation expenses to the high cost of dinner. If you like to dine around, either find a hotel that offers a variety of dining options or stay at one in or near Hamilton so that you can walk to and from restaurants in town.

PICNIC FARE & WHERE TO FIND IT

If you enjoy picknicking and bicycling, you can do both in Sandys Parish. Start by going over Somerset Bridge (heading in the direction of Somerset Village), and continue along Somerset Road to Fort Scaur Park, where you can enjoy a panoramic view of Ely's Harbour.

Another nice location is Spanish Point Park in Pembroke, where you will find a series of little coves and beaches. Here you don't need to go to the trouble of packing a picnic basket, since a lunch wagon rolls around every day at noontime (except in winter). Private picnicking is also possible at one of the island's best beaches, Warwick Long Bay. There are restrooms at the western end if you'd like to wash up beforehand.

The kitchens of many major hotels can prepare a picnic lunch for you, but you need to ask for it at least a day in advance. Or you can walk along Front Street in Hamilton, selecting sandwiches at a cafe plus a bottle of wine or mineral water at a local shop. If it's a weekday, the best place to buy picnic supplies is the Hickory Stick (see below).

AFTERNOON TEA & SUNDAY BRUNCH
AFTERNOON TEA

Bermuda still observes the British tradition of afternoon tea. Many guests prefer to have afternoon tea at their own hotels, which provides a good opportunity to meet fellow guests. Others like to visit a variety of hotels for afternoon tea. Before doing this, however, it would be wise to check whether a given hotel will serve afternoon tea to anyone who is not a registered guest.

Among restaurants and cafes, the two offering the best traditional afternoon tea are the **Botanic Garden** and **Fourways Pastry Shop.** (See Section 1, "City of Hamilton," below).

SUNDAY BRUNCH

Sunday brunch is a real tradition in Bermuda. In Bermudian homes, the traditional "Sabbath fare" consists of new potatoes with boiled salt cod, often accompanied by banana and avocado slices topped with an egg-enriched cream sauce. Many Bermudians also make a codfish dish flavored with tomatoes.

Nearly all hotels serve a traditional Sunday brunch. Although many guests prefer to stay at their hotel and enjoy Sunday brunch there, others want to sample it at one of the popular restaurants, such as **Henry VIII, Loyalty Inn,** or the **Carriage House** (see below). Perhaps the most popular place for Sunday brunch is the **Waterlot Inn** (see below).

1 City of Hamilton

The location of Hamilton restaurants and pubs is shown on the map "Hamilton Accommodations and Dining" (p. 77).

VERY EXPENSIVE

✪ Once Upon a Table

49 Serpentine Rd., west of City Hall. ☎ **441/295-8585.** Reservations required. Jackets required for men. Main courses $32.50–$45; fixed-price menu $36.50. AE, DC, MC, V. Dinner daily 6:30–9 or 9:30pm. Closed Jan. Bus: 1, 2, 10, or 11. FRENCH.

We'd be drawn here just because of the charming name, but fortunately, it has a lot more going for it than that. If Bermuda ever had a belle-époque period, it can be found here in a restored 18th-century island home, furnished in part with antiques. Some dinner guests still arrive by horse and buggy. Inside, you are shown to a table in one of the intimate rooms, with lace curtains at the windows.

This restaurant is run by hospitable Bermudians, who serve superb, candlelit dinners. Not every dish is a masterpiece, but most of them are flavorful and prepared with flair. For example, the fresh Bermuda fish is studded with banana and presented on caramelized red cabbage. If you like nonsweet fish or meat, try the grilled yellowfish tuna presented with a tomato confit or the breast of chicken roasted on a bed of potatoes and foie gras. Among the soup and hors d'oeuvres selections, there's always something interesting, perhaps the sweet Bermuda onion soup finished with apples and Calvados. Desserts are worth saving room for, especially the pecan and amaretto crème brûlée served in a tartlet with a coffee bean sauce.

The restaurant also operates the Buttery in the gardens, serving breakfast and lunch al fresco.

Romanoff Restaurant

34 Church St., just west of Burnaby Street. ☎ **441/295-0333.** Reservations required. Jackets and ties required for men. Main courses $33–$39; business lunch $17.75. AE, DC, MC, V. Mon–Fri noon–2:30pm and Mon–Sat 7–10pm. Bus: 1, 2, 10, or 11. RUSSIAN/CONTINENTAL/FRENCH.

In an atmosphere evoking the theatrical style of Old Vienna, continental cuisine is served. Wedgwood china, damask linen, brass lamps, and crystal accompany your meal in a burgundy-colored room with smoked-glass mirrors. Because of greater competition on the island, this restaurant no longer enjoys the status it once did, but it still adheres to the same classical Russo-European dining traditions as always.

The best appetizers are snails in garlic butter and smoked rainbow trout. The chef prepares crêpes filled with assorted seafood and also makes tempting kettles of soup, including the traditional Russian borscht, lobster bisque, and French onion soup. Dover sole is prepared in classic ways, but if you want something fresh from local waters, try either the excellent broiled wahoo fillet or the Bermuda lobster. Shashlik is served Georgian style (that is, flambéed with vodka), or you might prefer chicken Kiev or duckling à l'orange. However, the chef's pièce de résistance is his tournedos flambé Alexandra, which is beef tenderloin flamed with cognac and served with a sauce made at your table. Each night you can also select the chef's creation of the evening from a silver trolley. For dessert, try one of the marvelous soufflés or crêpes, or perhaps a zabaglione.

EXPENSIVE

Ascots

In the Royal Palms Hotel, 24 Rosemont Ave. ☎ **441/292-1854.** Reservations recommended. Lunch main courses $9.75–$12.50; dinner main courses $22.50–$28.50. AE, MC, V. Daily noon–2:30pm and 6:30–10pm. Closed Sat lunch. Bus: 1, 2, 10, or 11. ITALIAN/FRENCH.

This restaurant, in the Royal Palms Hotel, remains relatively undiscovered in spite of its tempting continental menu; it deserves to be better known. Situated within a spacious house, originally built around 1870, it is located in a residential neighborhood at the end of a Bermuda country lane at the edge of Hamilton. Before-dinner drinks are served from a large bar crafted from Bermuda cedar and brass in a setting of antique porcelain, Queen Anne armchairs, and Welsh pine that somewhat resembles a chintz-filled English country house.

In the summer, candlelit tables are placed on the front porch and sometimes beneath a tent in the garden. Owner Claudio Vigilante, originally from San Remo, Italy, oversees the cuisine, which might include pasta Claudio, prepared at your table by the owner himself using sun-dried tomatoes, black olives, capers, onions, garlic, and "a family secret." The rest of the culinary repertoire is based on classic techniques and first-rate ingredients. The menu has one of the best hot and cold appetizer lists in Hamilton, ranging from a Mediterranean chicken salad with goat cheese to a fresh homemade ravioli filled with crabmeat and served in a smoked salmon and spinach cream sauce. Vegetarian dishes are available. Count on the chef's catch of the day, prepared virtually as you like it, or else a delectable grilled rockfish served with black bean sauce and drizzled with roasted red pepper crème fraîche. If you shun ostentation, you might settle for a plain grilled sirloin, accompanied here by roast garlic sauce and grilled polenta.

Monte Carlo

9 Victoria St. ☎ **441/295-5453.** Reservations recommended. Lunch main courses $8.75–$12.50; dinner main courses $18.50–$23. AE, MC, V. Mon–Fri noon–3pm; Mon–Sat 6–10:30pm. Bus: 1, 2, 10, or 11. CONTINENTAL/ITALIAN.

This cheery restaurant was established in 1991 behind Hamilton's City Hall to celebrate the cuisines of southern France and Italy. Seating is within either of two dining rooms: Booths and banquettes in the outer room are ringed with a local artist's impressions of the countryside around Monaco. Tables and chairs in the main dining room center around a brick-sided fireplace. The chefs prepare the best bouillabaisse in Hamilton; they achieve the savory style that is typical of Marseilles using Atlantic seafish. One of the better dishes is fillet of tuna marinated in oil and herbs and grilled over charcoal. The wahoo might be better left alone instead of "gilding the lily" by serving it with a lobster sauce. The rack of lamb is tender and well seasoned with provençal herbs. Classic lamb chops appear with the flavoring of the Côte d'Azur, and the veal scaloppine is sautéed and served with sun-dried tomatoes and peppers on angel-hair pasta. With a flourish desserts are wheeled on a trolley through the dining room.

New Harbourfront Restaurant & Sushi Bar

Front Street, between Queen Street and Par-la-Ville Road. ☎ **441/295-4207.** Reservations recommended. Lunch main courses $9.75–$19.75; dinner main courses $16–$29.75. AE, DC, MC, V. Mon–Sat 11:30am–6pm and 6:30–10pm. Bus: 1, 2, 10, or 11. ITALIAN/SEAFOOD.

Front Street was once known for establishments selling ale and fish 'n' chips, but this restaurant has challenged its neighbors by offering some innovative continental dishes and even the town's best selection of sushi. No longer does fish have to be deep-fried in oil left over from last week. The cuisine here fairly bursts with flavors and aromas.

If some dishes aren't as successful as others, at least the kitchen should be applauded for trying to wake up the sleepy tastebuds of Hamilton.

Hot appetizers are delectable, especially the juicy tender mussels baked in a spicy Cajun sauce. A special sushi chef also serves a selection as an appetizer. The inevitable Bermuda fish chowder appears, but miso soup is also available. A number of pasta specialties are featured—none better than the large open-faced ravioli topped with lobster meat and rockfish drizzled with a red pepper sauce. Fresh fish from the dock is grilled and served with a lemon-flavored butter sauce, or you might prefer the pan-fried Bermuda wahoo. Here the Bermuda Triangle is a fine offering, since it includes a sample of the three best catches of the day topped with individual sauces, including saffron, basil, and honey-mustard.

The spacious restaurant is on the second floor of an old Hamilton building across from the ferry terminal in the center of town. A balcony, which juts out over the street, has a limited number of tables and is quite popular in nice weather.

Tiara Room

In the (Hamilton) Princess, 76 Pitts Bay Rd. ☎ **441/295-3000.** Reservations required. Jackets and ties required for men. Main courses $15–$25. AE, DC, MC, V. Daily 6:30–9:30pm. Bus: 7 or 8. CONTINENTAL.

The gourmet choice of the Hamilton Princess, this modernized restaurant has tiara-shaped chandeliers and offers a panoramic view of Hamilton Harbour. Dozens of flickering candles seem to set fire to the fine crystal and heavy silver. Flambé dishes are a specialty here, adding a touch of theatricality to the decor.

The cuisine is continental, and the menu often changes. This is elegant hotel dining at its finest in Hamilton. The Tiara is a suitable choice for a regal night on the town. The food here is actually better than it's been in years, if not worthy of a full crown, certainly a tiara. The pastas are delectable, especially the lobster linguini or a seafood casserole with lobster, scallops, shrimp, and mussels in a saffron cream. If that sounds too rich, choose a broiled or pan-fried fresh grouper fillet or even the fresh catch of the day. As in the classic English tradition, there's a roast of the evening—your captain will tell all about it. Some of the main dishes are those allegedly preferred by Queen Elizabeth herself: grilled lamb chops, roast duckling (or chicken), and filet mignon. Specialty flambé desserts include baked Alaska and cherries jubilee for two.

Waterloo House

Pitts Bay Road. ☎ **441/295-4480.** Reservations as well as jacket and tie required at dinner. Main courses $23–$28; lunch from $15. Daily noon–2:30pm and 7–9:30pm. AE, MC, V.

At the edge of Hamilton Harbour, this former private home—now the most famous inn on Bermuda—is a Relaix & Châteaux property, and its dining facilities are open to the public. Terraced gardens descend to the water, and these are often the setting for waterside buffets. Meals are served either outside on the harborfront terrace or in the elegantly appointed, English-style dining room where a fire roars in the fireplace on nippy evenings. Guests dine by candlelight.

Some reports have suggested that the food has declined in quality, but that is not what we found on our recent visit. You might begin with a cedar-smoked duck breast with a dried cherry dressing, or else snails baked in new potatoes with sour cream. The soups served here are often innovative, such as a chilled island pumpkin soup or a wild berry soup. The best main dishes are fish or shellfish, perhaps salmon with crushed mustard seeds and a saffron grapefruit sauce, or else Cajun scallops in a sweet and sour sauce with curried vegetables.

Bermuda Dining

Bailey's Ice Cream
   & Fool D'Lites Restaurant **18**
Black Horse Tavern **16**
Dennis's Hideaway **17**
Fourways Inn **10**
Frog & Onion **1**
Henry VIII **7**
Il Palio **3**
Inlet Restaurant **13**
La Plage **4**

Lantana Restaurant **4**
Lillian's/The Sea Grape **5**
Loyalty Inn **3**
Mikado **15**
Newport Room **6**
Norwood Room **12**
Ondine's **11**
Paraquet Restaurant **11**
PawPaws Restaurant & Bar **9**
Pirates Landing **1**

Atlantic Ocean

Plantation ⑭
Rib Room Steak House ❻
Somerset Country Squire Tavern ❸
Swizzle Inn ⑱
Tamarisk Dining Room ❷
Tio Pepe ❽
Tom Moore's Tavern ⑲
Waterlot Inn ❻
Whaler Inn ❻
Wickets Brasserie & Cricket Club ❻

The classics are still served, ranging from roast rack of lamb to peppered Angus steak, but there's always something unusual on the menu as well—perhaps quail with a honey, apple, and thyme sauce. Lunches include vegetarian specials, soups (such as a green gazpacho), salads, sandwiches, and several items from the grill, such as Bermuda codfish cakes with a tomato and pineapple salsa.

MODERATE

Chancery Wine Bar

Chancery Lane, between Reid and Front Streets. ☎ **441/295-5058.** Reservations recommended. Lunch main courses $7.50–$19.50; dinner main courses $16.50–$26.50. AE, MC, V. Mon–Fri noon–2:30pm; daily 6–10pm; bar daily 6pm–1am. Bus: 1, 2, 10, or 11. CONTINENTAL.

Located in a street-level building whose vaulted ceiling and thick stone walls date from the early 1900s, this cozy wine bar offers a candlelit ambience very much like that of a European wine cellar. There is a trellis-covered courtyard in back with a handful of tables for al fresco dining. Oenophiles will appreciate the tasteful selection of vintages from around the world—more than 160 different wines. Despite the wine bar's European antecedents, the dress code here is casual and the atmosphere relaxed. Since the menu changes monthly, you never know what to expect. There might be an unusual soup—creamy rutabaga with caraway croûtons—or perhaps a salmon, potato, and wild mushroom strudel, with Sevruga caviar, all served as appetizers. Main dishes are likely to include a delicious rack of veal chop stuffed with sun-dried tomatoes, or else médaillons of pork, lamb, and beef tenderloin with a wild mushroom ratatouille, basil, and balsamic vinegar sauce. It's not the best restaurant in Hamilton, but in its limited, unpretentious way it succeeds admirably.

Colony Pub Steak House

In the (Hamilton) Princess, 76 Pitts Bay Rd. ☎ **441/295-3000.** Main courses $14.95–$29.95; lunch buffet $14.25. AE, DC, MC, V. Daily 11:45am–2:30pm and 6:30–10pm. Bus: 7 or 8. AMERICAN/STEAK.

Some dining critics consider this establishment Bermuda's only true steakhouse, modeled after many counterparts in the United States. The restaurant, whose meat is flown in fresh three times a week, serves generous portions. Even if the restaurant's goal—having "the best meat anywhere outside the U.S."—isn't necessarily met, customers are generally satisfied. You might want to start with the garlicky plate of escargots, then move on to a Caesar salad or a beefsteak tomato and Bermuda onion salad. The most popular items on the menu are a 16-ounce New York strip sirloin and the 22-ounce lamb chops. The meat is fork tender, well flavored, and juicy. The huge baked potatoes are flown in from Idaho. For those who aren't meat lovers, there is a selection of fish and chicken, including the catch of the day. In the unlikely event you still have room for dessert, one recommendation is a chocolate brownie with cappuccino ice cream.

Fisherman's Reef

5 Burnaby Hill. ☎ **441/292-1609.** Reservations recommended. Main courses $18–$30; fixed-price lunch $14.95; "early bird" dinner (6–7:30pm) $18.95. AE, DC, MC, V. Mon–Fri noon–2:30pm; daily 6–10:30pm. Bus: 1, 2, 10, or 11. SEAFOOD/BERMUDIAN.

Fisherman's Reef, situated above the Hog Penny Pub in the heart of Hamilton, is a good choice for local seafood and typically Bermudian dishes. Its setting is predictably nautical, with a separate bar and cocktail lounge. You can order wahoo, one of Bermuda's most popular game fish, cut into steaks and topped with banana and bacon strips. Since we have never been fond of wahoo and banana, we usually order the Bermuda rockfish instead. It can be prepared in any of a half-dozen ways.

Our favorite is grilled and served with a sauce of Black Seal rum; other diners prefer it either blackened in the Cajun style or served in the Mediterranean fashion with herbs and shrimp. Also, in season, Bermuda guinea chicks—that is, small lobsters—are broiled on the half-shell, and are they ever good—if only they weren't so expensive. Ask the waiter about the daily catch—snapper, grouper, yellowtail, or shark—which can be pan-fried, broiled, or poached. Although most people come here for fish, the chef also prepares fairly standard meat courses such as peppersteak flambé as well as a number of veal specials, including Oscar, marsala, and français. Banana fritters laced with black rum are a favorite dessert. Dress is "smart casual."

Harley's

In the (Hamilton) Princess, 76 Pitts Bay Rd. ☎ 441/295-3000. Reservations recommended at dinner. Lunch main courses $7.95–$14.95; dinner main courses $16.95–$26.95. AE, DC, MC, V. High season (usually May–Oct) daily noon–4:30pm, Mon–Sat 6–10pm. Closed off-season (usually Nov–Apr). Bus: 7 or 8. MEDITERRANEAN.

The popular Harley's is named after the bearded bon vivant who established the Princess a century ago. In warm weather, outdoor tables are moved closer to the edge of the swimming pool, creating the effect of a flowering terrace on the Italian Riviera.

The food, which used to be merely safe and predictable, has acquired some flair, making this restaurant a worthy choice even if you aren't a hotel guest. Many people who are shopping in Hamilton for the day like to drop by for lunch when there is a large selection of "salad extravaganzas"; our favorite is classic Caesar salad with grilled *goujons* of grouper. The catch of the day can also be grilled for you, and, yes, there are burgers galore, including one served "topless." Pizzas are also featured, and one part of the menu is reserved for kids. The dinner menu is significantly better, with a choice of pastas—the best is grilled salmon fillets on linguini. Many of the main dishes will bring back memories of sunny Italy, especially beef tenderloin with shrimp and chicken suprême served with a trio of sauces; or tender breasts of chicken with tomato, green pepper, olives, red onions, mushrooms, and fresh herbs.

Little Venice

Bermudiana Road, between Par-la-Ville Road and Woodbourne Avenue. ☎ 441/295-3503. Reservations recommended. Two-course fixed-price lunch $13.75; lunch main courses $13–$16; dinner main courses $16–$28. AE, DC, MC, V. Mon–Fri 11:45am–2:30pm; daily 6:30–10:30pm. Bus: 1, 2, 10, or 11. ITALIAN/CONTINENTAL.

This is one of the best-established and most visible Italian restaurants in Bermuda, a staple that has been here as long as anyone can remember. The owner (originally from Capri) is proud of his specialties, one of which is a savory *casseruola di pesce dello chef.* This consists of a medley of Bermuda-derived products, including lobster, shrimp, mussels, clams, and several kinds of fish cooked together with white wine, herbs, and tomatoes. Other choices include a well-flavored fish chowder, a tender tournedos Rossini, several veal dishes, and an array of pastas, including a superb homemade ravioli stuffed with spinach and Ricotta cheese. If you have room for dessert, you might try the smooth zabaglione. Italian wines are featured, either in bottles or (less expensively) in carafes. An abbreviated menu is offered at lunchtime. Dress is "smart casual."

✪ Lobster Pot & Boat House Bar

6 Bermudiana Rd. ☎ 441/292-6898. Reservations recommended. Main courses $22–$25; fixed-price lunch $11.75; fixed-price dinner $25. AE, DC, MC, V. Mon–Sat 11:30am–5pm and 6–10:30pm. Bus: 1, 2, 10, or 11. SEAFOOD.

Many local Bermudian food connoisseurs we know shun all of the places listed above, referring to them as "just for tourists." They prefer to dine at this favorite local eatery, a fixture off Front Street since 1973. It specializes in local seafood cooked just right and with flair. Not surprisingly, the decor is nautical. Although the Bermuda fish chowder, laced with black rum and sherry peppers, is very good, you can get that elsewhere. A unique appetizer here is curried Bermuda rockfish (delicately seasoned and rolled in a thin crêpe). Fresh oysters are available all year and are priced according to the season. We suggest the baked Bermuda fish for two—fresh fish that has been seasoned and stuffed. You can also try the lobster potpourri, the deep-fried tiger shrimp and scallops, or a perfectly cooked wahoo steak (a game fish). Bermuda lobster (the so-called guinea chick) is available in season (that is, from mid-September until the end of March). The Bermuda banana fritter is a popular dessert. Dress is casual.

ⓢ MacWilliams

75 Pitts Bay Rd. ☎ **441/295-5759.** Reservations not required. Main courses $9.50–$18. AE, MC, V. Daily 8am–10pm. Bus: 1, 2, 10, or 11. INTERNATIONAL.

Even in the high-rent area of downtown Hamilton, there is a down-home place serving the type of unpretentious and inexpensive cuisine that Bermudians enjoyed for decades—"before all those foreign chefs arrived." Situated on the western waterfront road leading to the most congested part of Hamilton, this informal coffee shop is sheathed in light-colored brick and neutral-colored paneling. Often patronized by guests from the upscale, nearby Hamilton Princess, the restaurant does a thriving lunchtime business. It serves breakfast, lunch, and dinner, as well as coffee and snacks. The lunch menu includes an array of sandwiches, hamburgers, soups, and salads. The evening meal may offer a Bermuda fish dinner, a fisher's platter, sirloin steak, liver with onions, spaghetti with meatballs, and barbecued ribs. The most popular appetizer is fish chowder.

The Porch

93 Front St., between Burnaby and Parliament Streets. ☎ **441/292-4737.** Reservations recommended. Lunch main courses $7.75–$14.25; dinner main courses $15.75–$22.50. AE, MC, V. Bus: 1, 2, 10, or 11. INTERNATIONAL.

Lined with bricks and aged paneling, this warmly decorated restaurant is housed in a century-old building that served for many years as a private apartment building and the island headquarters of American Express. As the restaurant's name implies, it boasts a porch with a prominent view over Hamilton's harbor, an English-style pub, and a wide outdoor terrace for use in nice weather. (Navigate the stairs carefully as you climb up from Front Street, and be even more careful as you come down after having a drink or two.) Food is available throughout this establishment, even in the pub-style areas you might have thought were reserved only for drinking.

The menu offers routine fare, especially veal and beef dishes, including prime sirloin steak (10 ounces), prime roast rib of beef with Yorkshire pudding, steak with shrimp, and even wild boar in season (a throwback to the days of the early settlers on Bermuda). Lunch features sandwiches, salads, fresh fish, crab cakes, burgers, and oysters. It's all quite competently prepared if you don't have high expectations; otherwise, you might prefer to drop by for a drink and soak up the atmosphere.

Primavera

69 Pitts Bay Rd. ☎ **441/295-2167.** Reservations required. Lunch main courses $16–$22; dinner main courses $19–$25. AE, DC, MC, V. Tues–Fri 11:45am–2:30pm; daily 6:30–10:30pm. Closed Mon in winter. Bus: 7 or 8. ITALIAN.

Primavera, in Hamilton West between Front Street and the Hamilton Princess, is a longtime staple on the dining scene; it is often viewed as an alternative to the more traditional fare served in many of the island's restaurants. The cuisine reflects all regions of Italy, including Sicily, Sardinia, and Rome. We will not pretend that this is the best Italian food in Hamilton. Many diners prefer to eat at Little Venice instead. But what you get here is the type of food that those old rat-packers—the late Dino or the aging Frankie—used to prefer back when they were on the road. You might begin with a choice of either hot or cold antipasti (for example, a cold seafood salad or hot baked clams served in a marinara sauce). You might follow this with soup (perhaps minestrone) or a salad (probably a Caesar). The array of pasta dishes includes tortellini Primavera (the chef's surprise), or a good chicken cacciatore or sautéed veal with fresh vegetables. Top off your meal with an Italian espresso or a frothy cappuccino. The service is impeccable.

Red Carpet Bar and Restaurant
In the Armoury Building, 37 Reid St. ☎ **441/292-6195.** Reservations recommended. Lunch main courses $6.75–$18; dinner main courses $12.95–$26. AE, MC, V. Daily 11:30am–3pm and 6:30–10:30pm. Bar open until 1am. Bus: 1, 2, 10, or 11. ITALIAN/FRENCH.

Located in a 150-year-old building, the Red Carpet serves many Italian dishes even though the atmosphere resembles an English pub. This place does a thriving lunch business, thanks to the many offices nearby. Later, after work, the bar (with its decor of darkly stained wood trim, dark-red carpeting, and dim lights) is a popular place for people to relax with a beer. Lunch offerings include sandwiches, cold platters, and a few hot dishes such as pan-fried fish (including Bermuda tuna and wahoo). Dinners feature a wider choice such as veal scaloppine, veal marsala, chicken cacciatore, filet mignon, and New York strip sirloin. A variety of pasta dishes is also featured. Both Primavera and Little Venice serve better food, but your bill here will probably be more to your liking. What you get is quite good, but undoubtedly rather familiar to those who have been "dining Italian" for years.

Tuscany
Bermuda House, 95 Front St. ☎ **441/292-4507.** Reservations recommended. Lunch pastas $8–$9; lunch main courses $12.75–$14.50; dinner pastas $12.75–$13.25; dinner main courses $18.25–$23.75. AE, DC, MC, V. Mon–Fri 11:45am–2:30pm, Mon–Sat 6:30–10:30pm. Bus: 1, 2, 10, or 11. ITALIAN.

This restaurant has a lot going for it, including its location on the second floor of a balconied building overlooking Hamilton Harbour. With a casual and relaxed atmosphere, it serves good food at reasonable prices. The best recommendation for it, however, is that many of the island's chefs dine here on their night off. Established in 1994, it displays a large mural commemorating the hills of Tuscany, a collection of copper artifacts similar to what you might find in a northern Italian farmhouse, and a narrow balcony with a half-dozen tables suspended above the pedestrian traffic of the harborfront walkway below.

The menu features selections from the entire Italian peninsula, all prepared with a certain Mediterranean flair. The list of pastas alone is worth the trip here, especially the ravioli filled with sautéed zucchini and Ricotta and tossed in a porcini mushroom sauce. Although calling itself "Tuscany," the cuisine here is actually Venetian as exemplified in such dishes as *pesce alla Vicentina* (fillet of baked fish with chopped onions, capers, anchovies, and a touch of cream). A Venetian-style liver dish is prepared with white wine, onions, and sauce—served with or without onions. Pizzas, and quite delectable ones at that, are also served, including one for vegetarians. The Tuscany repertoire emerges again in the famous soup of Florence, *ribollita*, made with chopped spinach and Swiss chard. Service is first-rate.

INEXPENSIVE

Bombay Bicycle Club

In the Rego Furniture Building, 75 Reid St. ☎ **441/292-0048.** Reservations required. Main courses $13.95–$22; fixed-price lunch $11.95. AE, MC, V. Mon–Fri noon–2:30pm; Mon–Sat 6:30–11pm. Bus: 1, 2, 10, or 11. INDIAN/CONTINENTAL.

Indian cuisine is expertly prepared and served in this third-floor upstairs hideaway where you can enjoy lunch or dinner in a relaxed atmosphere. The authentic Indian food served here is flavorful—in fact, it's the best choice for Indian food in Bermuda. However, visitors from such cities as London or New York will find far better choices back home. For lunch, there is "A Taste of India" buffet daily, with a variety of dishes ranging from mulligatawny soup to chicken, beef, lamb, and seafood served with a choice of sauces, in a spicy curry, or roasted in the tandoori oven. The Indian chefs will prepare your dishes with the mild, delicate tastes of coastal India. But true lovers of Indian food often choose instead the "fiery tastes" from the forts of the Moghuls. There are also Indian vegetarian dishes and continental selections. Dress is "smart casual."

Botanic Garden

In Trimingham's, 17 Front St., between Reid and Queen Streets. ☎ **441/295-1183.** Reservations not accepted. Soups and quiches $4.50; seafood salads $7.25–$8.50; sandwiches $3.50–$6; tea 85¢; pastries $1.75–$3. No credit cards. Mon–Sat 9:30am–4:30pm. Bus: 1, 2, 10, or 11. INTERNATIONAL.

Housed on the third floor of the most famous department store in Hamilton, this place attracts shoppers who know good value when they see it. Offering self-service and informality, the Botanic Garden is ideal for morning coffee or afternoon tea. The pastries, pies, and cakes are excellent, especially the banana bread and the gingerbread. An array of sandwiches is served as well.

Chopsticks Restaurant

88 Reid St. ☎ **441/292-0791.** Reservations recommended. Main courses $10.50–$28. Daily noon–2:30pm and 6–11pm. Bus: 1, 2, 10, or 11. CHINESE/THAI.

Although off the beaten track at the east end of Hamilton, Chopsticks offers some of Bermuda's best Chinese and Thai food, including spicy soup, tangy pork ribs, and seafood. The chef specializes in Szechuan, Hunan, Thai, and Cantonese dishes, with an emphasis on fresh vegetables and delicate sauces. The fine food is served by a Bermudian staff.

Chicken dishes, including an excellent jade chicken with spears of broccoli and mushrooms and water chestnuts in a mild Peking wine sauce, are also a specialty. Peking duck is served only for two, and it must be ordered 24 hours in advance. Seafood is also prominent on the menu, exemplified by everyone's all-time favorite— shrimp in lobster sauce. The best Thai dish is green curry chicken—chicken breast strips simmered with onions and bamboo shoots, and served with fresh basil, coconut milk, and a green-curry paste. It can be prepared mild, spicy, or hot. Most of the dishes are the standard ones you'd find in any North American Chinese restaurant, including sweet and sour chicken or beef in oyster sauce. Some dishes, however, have real flair— including duck in red curry. Vegetarians will find a haven here, since there are many vegetable dishes that can be shared.

Fourways Pastry Shop

In the Washington Mall, Reid Street at Queen Street. ☎ **441/295-3263.** Reservations not accepted. Tea or coffee $1.40; sandwiches $3–$5; daily specials $7.50. AE, MC, V (for purchases of $25 or more). Mon–Sat 8am–4:30pm. Bus: 1, 2, 10, or 11. PASTRIES/SANDWICHES.

This is one of Hamilton's most consistently popular lunchtime venues, serving hundreds of the capital's office workers every day. Although the establishment's most popular choices are pastries, sandwiches, and endless cups of tea and coffee, they also offer at least three platters of the day which—when served with something to drink—comprise meals in themselves. Depending on what's available at the market on any particular day, daily specials might include lasagna with a side salad; savory breast of chicken with greens; or a platter of "deep-fried rice" with minced beef or pork.

The Hickory Stick

2 Church St., at Bermudiana Road. ☎ **441/292-1781.** Reservations not accepted. Salads $2.75–$5.50; sandwiches $3.20–$6.75; hot takeaway platters $3–$5.50. No credit cards. Bus: 1, 2, 10 or 11. DELI.

Located near the rose-colored walls of the Princess Hotel in Hamilton, this is the most popular delicatessen and take-out restaurant in the capital, serving 1,000 customers a day, including many of the capital's office workers.

Although one section might remind visitors of a popular coffee shop (scones, doughnuts, and morning coffee provide doses of caffeine for the neighborhood residents), most customers are attracted to the overstuffed sandwiches and takeaway portions of food. Offerings include steaming portions of chicken Parmesan, barbecued spare ribs, and fish cakes; even more popular, however, are the salads, sandwiches, and hot dogs, all of which are often wrapped up and carried away to be eaten as picnic food outdoors. Advance telephone orders are accepted, and this may be a good idea if you don't want to wait for your order to be prepared. Paper napkins and plastic knives, forks, and spoons are provided on request.

Hog Penny

5 Burnaby Hill. ☎ **441/292-2534.** Reservations recommended. Lunch main courses $6.25–$16; dinner main courses $14.95–$45; fixed-price dinner (5:30–7:30pm) $17.50. AE, DC, MC, V. Daily 11:30am–4pm and 5:30–10:30pm. Bus: 1, 2, 10, or 11. ENGLISH/BERMUDIAN.

Bermuda's most famous pub, built and decorated in the British style with dark paneled rooms, offers draft beer and ale. Established in the early 1960s, this pub has fed and assuaged the thirst of hundreds of thousands of visitors ever since. Reservations are strongly advised, because the place is becoming extremely popular. The decor consists of old fishing and farm tools, as well as bentwood chairs and antique mirrors. At lunch you can order pub specials (including shepherd's pie and seafood crêpes) or a tuna salad. The kitchen prepares a number of passable curries, including chicken and lamb. Fish and chips and steak-and-kidney pie are the perennial favorites, and they are comparable to what you'd find in a London pub. Dinner is more elaborate; the menu might include a whole lobster (if available), a fresh fish of the day (perhaps Bermuda yellowfin tuna), and Angus beef (which is excellent). There is nightly entertainment from 9:30pm to 1am; dress is casual.

ⓢ M. R. Onions

Par-la-Ville Road. ☎ **441/292-5012.** Main courses $9.95–$23.50. Early bird 3-course dinner $14.95. AE, DC, MC, V. Mon–Fri noon–2:30pm; daily 5–10pm; bar daily 11:30am–1am. Bus: 1, 2, 10, or 11. AMERICAN/BERMUDIAN.

The name of this popular restaurant and bar—a chicken and ribs kind of place—is a colloquialism. Bermudians are known as onions, and the "M. R." stands for "'em are," or "they are"; hence the name means "they are Bermudians." Resembling an Edwardian-era bar, the decor focuses on brass, potted palms, leaf-green walls, and oak trim. Caricatures of many Bermudians hang on the walls. If you go early, plan to have a drink at the large rectangular bar that fills most of the front room. During happy hour (daily 5 to 7pm), it's a favorite rendezvous for office workers in the neighborhood. Snacks are available in the bar until 10pm. Well-prepared meals are served in a rear dining room; specialties include the house onion soup and fresh fish (including tuna, wahoo, rockfish, and mahimahi). Fish can be charbroiled, pan-fried, or served à la amandine or spicy Cajun blackened-style. Tasty barbecued chicken, ribs, burgers, and steak are also available. Desserts feature mud pie, cheesecake, or a choice from the "sweet trolley." There is a no-smoking dining room.

Pasta Basta

1 Elliott St. ☎ **441/295-9785.** Reservations not accepted. Salads $4.75; pastas $5.75 (half-portion) or $9 (full portion). No credit cards. Mon–Fri 11:45am–11pm; Sat–Sun 5–11pm. Bus: 1, 2, 10, or 11. PASTA.

This is the larger of two restaurants with the same cafeteria-style pasta-and-salad combination. (The other, **Pasta Pasta,** is in St. George's; the slight difference in the spelling of its name has caused a lot of discussion.) In a rather summery setting, customers are offered two kinds of salad (tossed and Caesar) and about a dozen varieties of pasta. Served in full or half-portions, they include two kinds of lasagna (one of which is meatless), plus a frequently changing array of varying shaped pasta topped with a choice of meat, seafood, or vegetarian sauces. When we last visited Pasta Basta, the daily special was shell-shaped pasta with sausage and onions in a pink sauce. This restaurant is a great place to fill up on quite decent food at a reasonable price—don't expect a lot more. *Note:* No wine, beer, or alcohol is served here, and local licensing laws do not permit you to bring your own drinks.

Pink's

55 Front St. ☎ **441/295-3524.** Reservations not accepted. Salads, sandwiches, and hot takeaway platters $3.25–$8. Breakfast croissant with coffee $2.75; salads and sandwiches $3.80–$7.25. Complete picnic boxes $14.50 per person. No credit cards. Mon–Fri 7:30–6pm; Sat 8:30–5pm. Bus: 1, 2, 10, or 11. DELI.

Outfitted in a color scheme of (you guessed it) pink and teal blue, Pink's serves hundreds of Hamilton's office workers every day in the form of nonfried (i.e., health-conscious) breakfasts (fresh-made croissants and scones), and flavorful lunches consisting of well-stuffed sandwiches, the best and largest Caesar salads in Bermuda, and a rather unusual couscous salad. Also available are hot platters such as beef pies or summer chicken (drenched in a sauce of sour cream, yogurt, thyme, and orange juice). One of the greatest things about Pink's is its wide second-floor veranda—the longest porch along Front Street—where canopies protect the outdoor tables from sun and rain.

Portofino

Bermudiana Road. ☎ **441/292-2375.** Reservations recommended. Main courses $9.95–$20.75; pizzas $9.50–$13.75. AE, MC, V. Mon–Fri 11:30–4pm; daily 6pm–midnight. Closed Dec. 25. Bus: 1, 2, 10, or 11. ITALIAN.

The decor of this Italian trattoria evokes the feeling of a warm and inviting place in northern Italy, complete with hanging lamps. It offers well-prepared and reasonably priced specialties, including a classic minestrone; three kinds of spaghetti and all the famous pastas—lasagna, ravioli, and cannelloni; and 17 kinds of pizza (9-inch). There are also such standard and familiar Italian dishes as Venetian-style liver, veal parmigiana, chicken cacciatore, and beefsteak pizzaiola. Your best bet is one of the freshly made specials posted daily. The kitchen is noted for its ice-cream desserts. There is a limited selection of Italian wines.

Rosa's Cantina

121 Front St. ☎ **441/295-1912.** Reservations required only on Fri and Sat. Main courses $7.95–$17.95; lunch from $6.95. AE, MC, V. Daily noon–1am. Bus: 1, 2, 10, or 11. TEX-MEX.

For your Tex-Mex fix, you can fill up here on such bounty as beef and chicken fajitas, zesty chili, nachos, tacos, enchiladas, and burritos (the largest on the island), along with frozen margaritas to put the fire out. To the sound of the music of mariachi bands, you might begin with a hearty and thick black bean soup, and then move on to carne asado (mesquite grilled rib eye steak)—a chef's specialty. The hickory-smoked barbecue ribs are the best in Bermuda. The prices are reasonable and the most desirable seating is on the al fresco balcony.

Ye Olde Cock and Feather

8 Front St. ☎ **441/295-2263.** Lunch sandwiches, salads, and platters $5.75–$14.50; dinner main courses $12.50–$18.75. MC, V. Mon–Sat 11am–10:30pm, Sun noon–10:30pm. Bar open until 1am. Bus: 1, 2, 10, or 11. BRITISH/INTERNATIONAL.

Housed within a centuries-old whiskey warehouse on Front Street (between Burnaby Hill and Queen Street), this is one of the capital's most prominent pubs. According to its staff, the place can be seen in some of Hamilton's oldest photographs. There's a wide veranda overlooking the harbor, and the decor resembles that of a traditional British pub combined with suitably nautical artifacts. Lunch features such dishes as salads, deep-fried cheese sandwiches, seafood combination platters, and beef pies. Dinners are more elaborate, offering such dishes as chicken Dijonnaise and oyster chowder. The food is quite passable, although some people think this is a better place for drinking than for dining. Live evening entertainment is sometimes presented in the bar area, and the crowd can become rowdy whenever the mood strikes.

2 Paget Parish

VERY EXPENSIVE

✪ Fourways Inn

1 Middle Road, Paget. ☎ **441/236-6517.** Reservations in summer 1–2 days in advance. Jacket and tie required for men. Lunch main courses $7.75–$17.50; dinner main courses $26.75–$55; Sunday barbecue $29.50 per person. AE, MC, V. Daily 11:30am–2:30pm and 6:30–9:30pm. Bus: 8. FRENCH/BERMUDIAN.

The Fourways Inn has now become the best restaurant in Bermuda. With a predominantly European staff, it has a certain kind of snobbish appeal. Housed in a former coral stone and cedar 18th-century Georgian home, with interior mahogany beams, the restaurant maintains a traditional Bermudian character. Guests can dine either inside or out, depending on the season. Most evenings, there is a pianist playing and the atmosphere is relaxed. The old kitchen has been turned into the Peg Leg Bar with a whitewashed fireplace.

To complement its ambitious menu, the Fourways has the finest wine cellar on the island. Bermuda's most tempting selection of hors d'oeuvres—hot and cold—is served here, including pan-roasted bay scallops and scampi with ratatouille and a fresh basil purée. A limited but excellent choice of fish is offered nightly, including a lightly char-grilled local tuna with braised scallions, sun-dried tomatoes, and sweet peppers that is perfection itself. The good life filters ever more sweetly into the rest of the exquisite cuisine, which is based on the best seasonal ingredients. The chef's signature dish consists of thin slices of tender veal served with a zesty citrus sauce. A fine selection of fresh vegetables is served nightly. A nonvegetarian acquaintance of ours

---

ⓕ Family-Friendly Restaurants

M. R. Onions *(see p. 109)*   Taking its name from the colloquial name for Bermudians, this is one of the best family restaurants in the city of Hamilton. Kids love the barbecue chicken, ribs, and steak. There's also an array of burgers.

Pink's *(see p. 110)*   Right in Hamilton, this place can serve the needs of the entire family weekdays until 4:30pm. Everything from breakfast to well-stuffed sandwiches, hot platters, and picnic baskets are available.

Rosa's Cantina, in the city of Hamilton *(see p. 111)*   For Tex-Mex fare, this house of chili, burritos, fajitas, nachos, tacos, and enchiladas has no equal on the island. Children are given balloons to help create a festive environment, and they're also offered coloring material and crayons after they have been seated.

Wickets Brasserie & Cricket Club *(see p. 116)*   Children's menus are available at this popular daytime eatery in the Southampton Princess Hotel. If you take your children there before 6:30pm, you can order dinner for them from the low-priced lunch menu, which is still available at that time.

---

came here once and ordered only vegetables; she was extremely pleased with their preparation and taste. At lunch, there are sandwiches and several hot dishes, including a catch of the day.

EXPENSIVE

Norwood Room

In the Stonington Beach Hotel, South Shore Road, Paget. ☎ **441/236-5416.** Reservations required. Jacket and tie required for men in the evening. Lunch main courses $7–$18; fixed-price dinner $46. AE, DC, MC, V. Daily noon–2pm and 7–8:30pm. Bus: 7. CONTINENTAL.

The Norwood Room offers stately dining in a large sun-filled room, decorated in tones of blue and soft yellow. The room is laced with wood beams and a halo of arched windows looking out over the well-maintained lawn and the ocean. The restaurant is part of a state-run hotel training institute (see Chapter 5, "Accommodations"). Although the young staff is inexperienced, they are exceptionally thoughtful and courteous. A pianist or harpist provides music in the evening.

The food served here is splendid and each dish is prepared with care. We always choose the set menu, which is broadly continental; we once had tenderloin of pork stuffed with dried winter fruit in an exotic chili plum dressing, another time it was pan-seared duck breast in a tart orange sauce, flambéed with Gosling's Black Seal rum, and still another time it was grilled fillet of mahimahi with tiger shrimps served over polenta and drizzled with a gingered Malaysian sauce. The chef also prepares a pasta of the day. The last order is taken at 8:15pm.

MODERATE

Ondine's

In the Elbow Beach Hotel, A Wyndham Resort, 60 South Shore Road, Paget. ☎ **441/236-3535.** Reservations recommended. Main courses $19.50–$33. AE, MC, V. Daily 6:30–9:30pm. Bus: 1, 2, or 7. INTERNATIONAL.

If you'd like to dine at a restaurant run by Bermuda's most fabled hotel, you will find Ondine's on the lobby level of the Elbow Beach Hotel. Its large windows overlook the sea, and the service and food are first class, even though the prices are actually moderate. Since the restaurant caters to many traditional palates, it always offers such standbys as grilled New York sirloin or broiled lobster tail. However, there are occasional surprises; recently we were pleased with an appetizer of duck and quail terrine in a raspberry coulis with an essence of Pernod—heavenly. One of the more exotic and popular soups is sweet potato and pumpkin, and another unusual dish is Bermuda "jerk" lamb—heavily seasoned and grilled over an open flame.

INEXPENSIVE

⑤ Paraquet Restaurant

South Shore Road (P.O. Box 173), Paget. ☎ **441/236-9742.** Reservations not required. Breakfast special (until 11am) $7.10; sandwiches $2.90–$9.10; main courses $11.25–$24.25. No credit cards. Bus: 1, 2, or 7. BERMUDIAN.

Located near a major traffic junction on the south shore near the Elbow Beach Hotel, this unpretentious restaurant with a menu straight from the fifties is the center of an apartment cluster of the same name. From your table, you can see a circular formal flower garden, created by the Portuguese owners. Although the lime-colored Formica, tiles, and plants are decidedly coffee shop decor, much of the menu features substantial home-style Bermudian fare. You will find one of the largest sandwich menus on the island (hot and cold), as well as omelets, homemade soups (there is always a fish chowder of the day), and salads. You can order mixed platters, for example, turkey breast and crabmeat, or such grilled dishes as T-bone steak, fried liver and onions, or roast half spring chicken. This is the type of good, wholesome food that Dick and Pat used to enjoy in the White House—not the type of food served when the Kennedys were in residence.

3 Warwick Parish

Pawpaws Restaurant & Bar

87 South Shore Road, Warwick. ☎ **441/236-7459.** Reservations recommended. Lunch main courses $6–$14.75; dinner main courses $14.75–$25.50. MC, V. Daily 11am–10pm. Closed Tues in winter. Bar open until 1am. Bus: 7. CONTINENTAL/BERMUDIAN.

About 3 miles west of Hamilton, this family favorite offers a varied and unusual menu at reasonable prices. On the walls there are murals of pawpaw trees and other scenes, along with trellis work and a few paintings by local artists. With an aura and ambience of a European bistro, Pawpaws attracts everybody from those seeking an upscale diner to the family with kids in tow (there's a children's menu). Lunch features sandwiches and salads as well as the restaurant's signature dish—Pawpaw Montespan—made from green pawpaws, ground beef, and herbs.

In the evening one of the most deservedly popular dishes is the lobster ravioli in a cream-flavored basil sauce with strips of smoked salmon. Equally good is the seafood vol-au-vent. If you're yearning for island cuisine, sample the red snapper in banana sauce. You will also find more classic dishes, including a tender peppersteak in a cognac cream sauce or leg of lamb steak marinated in herbs.

4 Southampton Parish

VERY EXPENSIVE

✪ Newport Room

In the Southampton Princess, 101 South Shore Road. ☎ **441/238-8000.** Reservations recommended. Jacket and tie required for men. Main courses $25–$30. AE, DC, MC, V. Daily 6:30–9:15pm (when the last orders are taken). Closed usually Jan–Feb. Ferryboat from Hamilton. FRENCH.

The Newport Room is unequaled in its sumptuously understated decor, and its French cuisine is among the best in Bermuda. The dining room is entirely paneled in teak and rosewood, with appropriate nautical brass, to evoke the expensive interior of a well-maintained yacht. In the center are exact miniature replicas of two of the winning sailboats from the Newport to Bermuda race.

At the entrance you'll be greeted by a maître d'hôtel stationed beside a ship's compass. Settle into leather armchairs as you peruse the menu, which might list gourmet variations of *cuisine moderne,* such as duck breast with cinnamon and fig sauce. The menu changes often, but all dishes are made from the freshest and best ingredients available. The personal attention and service, the carefully prepared and artfully presented dishes, and the elegant ambience will probably make you feel like J. P. Morgan. A wide array of international wines, served in Irish crystal, complements each dinner.

EXPENSIVE

✪ Henry VIII

South Shore Road, Southampton. ☎ **441/238-1977.** Reservations required for dinner. Jacket required for men. Lunch main courses $6–$12; dinner main courses $20–$30; Sunday brunch $19.50 per person. AE, DC, MC, V. Mon–Sat noon–2:30pm; daily 6:30–10pm; Sun noon–3pm. Bus: 7 or 8. ENGLISH/CONTINENTAL.

This pub/restaurant looks rather gimmicky with its faux Tudor decor, "wenches," and the like, but the food is exceptionally good—far superior to anything that was probably served to Henry VIII in his day. Lying below Gibbs Hill Lighthouse—between the Southampton Princess and the Sonesta Beach Resort—the restaurant is richly decorated with oak furnishings, brass railings, and period-style lighting fixtures—quite suitable for the arrival of good Queen Bess. The food is worth a special trip here. You might want to drop by the split-level Oak Room Bar for some English draft beer and the nightly entertainment.

Hot pub lunches include steak-and-kidney pie, mussel pie, and plain old hamburgers—far superior to the usual pub grub. The Sunday brunch is one of the most well-attended on the island. In the evening the chef turns out whimsically named dishes that are often terrific, including Court Jester, a delectable broiled seafood combination, and steak Anne Boleyn, which is flavored with cognac and simmered in a Madeira sauce. Other notable beef dishes are the peppersteak, with a zesty flavor, and the chateaubriand. Like a first-class London restaurant, the kitchen always prepares a classic mixed English grill.

Lillian's/The Sea Grape

In the Sonesta Beach Resort, South Shore Road. ☎ **441/238-8122.** Reservations recommended. Lillian's, main courses $18–$26; fixed-price menu $38. The Sea Grape, main courses $18–$22. AE, DC, MC, V. Lunch daily in the Sea Grape only, 11:30am–4pm. Dinner daily in both Lillian's and the Sea Grape, 6–10pm. Closed, the Sea Grape only, Oct–Apr. Bus: 7. ITALIAN/ PACIFIC RIM.

Many visitors to Southampton Parish head for one of the Sonesta's restaurants, including Lillian's (an art nouveau eatery specializing in northern Italian cuisine), or the Sea Grape (an outdoor terrace adjacent to the sea). Lillian's is the more glamorous of the two, with a pink and blue decor, an ambitious menu, and a formally correct staff. Menu choices include antipasto such as vegetable lasagna and house-smoked salmon (served with roasted pepper risotto cakes, fennel, and aïoli). You might also begin with Tuscan-style white bean soup made with spinach and Italian sausage. There is good pizza and succulent pastas (either as full or half courses). Main courses might include baked wahoo with grilled polenta or roast Atlantic salmon with a fennel risotto. Roasted rack of lamb with a vegetable lasagna is also noteworthy.

The Sea Grape prides itself on its Pacific-Rim menu. Generally, these include calorie- and cholesterol-conscious "clean" foods where sauces (inspired by Californian, Korean, and Japanese cuisine) are served on the side. Zesty appetizers range from spiced poached pineapple with coconut yogurt and candied ginger to grilled shrimp with a smoked bacon guacamole. Main dishes are often grilled and served with fresh chutneys, salsas, and Yaki Soba noodles. There is usually a daily catch, priced at the market. Our favorite entrée is sesame-crusted pork tenderloin.

✪ Waterlot Inn

In the Southampton Princess, Middle Road. ☎ **441/238-8000.** Reservations required. Jacket and tie required for men at dinner. Main courses $24–$42; Sun brunch $28 adults, $17 children under 12. AE, DC, MC, V. Daily 6:30–9:15pm; Sun brunch 11:30am and 1pm (choice of seatings). Guests are shuttled from the hotel to this waterside inn. MEDITERRANEAN/FRENCH.

One of our all-time favorites, this restaurant ranks among the island's finest dining spots. The service is impeccable, and the culinary repertoire is impressive, inventive, and personalized (even though there are a large number of diners in the evening). Some 300 years ago, merchant sailors unloaded their cargoes directly into the basement of this historic inn and warehouse. Today the best way to approach this inn is still by water, and that's precisely what many Bermudians do, mooring their sailing craft in its sheltered cove. Over the years the inn has attracted such guests as Mark Twain, James Thurber, Eleanor Roosevelt, and Eugene O'Neill. After the landmark building was devastated by a gas explosion in 1976, the Southampton Princess had it renovated and today it's one of their gourmet restaurants.

Diners enjoy a drink in an upstairs bar, where they are entertained by the resident classical pianist. After descending a colonial staircase with white balustrades, they can sit in one of three conservatively nautical dining rooms. Each is filled with captain's or Windsor chairs, oil paintings of old clipper ships, and lots of exposed wood. The bouillabaisse is about as good as it gets this side of the Riviera, although there are many other temptations as well. The grilled veal tenderloin, worthy of inclusion in *Gourmet* magazine, is served with caramelized shallots and onions in a Muscat wine sauce and with young stuffed vegetables. Occasionally we've settled happily for a plate of grilled Mediterranean vegetables, ranging from artichokes to eggplant.

This restaurant is the most popular place on the island for Sunday brunch, attracting both visitors and Bermudians. Thus, you must reserve a place as far in advance as possible. Brunch is buffet-style with all the classic dishes: eggs Benedict, hot and cold meats, turkey platters, lamb dishes, and an array of seafood. There is also a station featuring traditional Bermudian breakfast cuisine. Fashionable clothes are customary, such as a smart blue blazer with tailored Bermuda shorts for men.

MODERATE

Rib Room Steak House

In the Southampton Princess, 101 South Shore Road. ☎ **441/238-8000.** Reservations recommended. Four-course fixed-price menu $35. AE, DC, MC, V. Daily 6:30–9:15pm (when the last orders are taken). Ferryboat from Hamilton. STEAKS/SEAFOOD.

When you look at the menu, you'll think you're in one of London's finest chophouses. Samuel Johnson and James Boswell would have smacked their chops over the roast prime rib of beef with Yorkshire pudding. Many of the juicy and delectably tender beef dishes are broiled over charcoal. The broiled lamb chops are classic, evocative of those served at the Cheshire Cheese in London. For those who prefer fish, the chef will prepare the catch of the day. All dinners come with an extensive salad bar.

The Rib Room sits atop the golf pro shop, near the tee-off point for the 1st hole. As you relax in upholstered armchairs, taking in the panoramic view from the windows, you might want to start your evening with a "Dark and Stormy"—black rum and ginger beer; it's for the adventurous at heart.

Tio Pepe

South Shore Road, Horseshoe Bay, Southampton. ☎ **441/238-0572.** Reservations recommended. Pizzas and pastas $8.50–$17; main courses $21–$23.50. AE, MC, V. Daily 11am–10:30pm. Bus: 7. ITALIAN.

Don't be fooled by the Spanish name. The cuisine is purely Italian and traditional. The establishment serves pizzas, pastas, and the classic cuisines of Italy in generous portions with a bit of Mediterranean pizzazz. You won't find gourmet Italian fare here. However, the friendly atmosphere, the bountiful food, and the prices are right on target. Guests have the choice of sitting on a wide garden-view terrace or in one of three indoor dining rooms. Chianti bottles top off the red and green (colors of Italy) interior. Tio Pepe caters to a Hamilton clientele who appreciate its proximity to the Southampton Princess Hotel and Horseshoe Bay Beach.

Whaler Inn

In the Southampton Princess, 101 South Shore Road. ☎ **441/238-8000.** Reservations recommended. Fixed-price dinner $35. Daily 6:30–9:15pm. Closed Nov–Mar. Ferryboat from Hamilton. SEAFOOD.

Famous for its seafood, this restaurant is perched atop a low cliff overlooking the rocks and pink sands that border the Atlantic near the Southampton Princess. Its landscaped terraces sprout with clusters of sea grape, Norfolk Island pine, and padded iron armchairs. From here you can view the sunsets that redden the lapping waves of one of the island's most secluded beaches. Inside, the Whaler Inn's huge windows provide an airy setting where the panoramic view is the main decor.

Guests choose fixed-price items from a four-course table d'hôte menu. To "bait your appetite," you might begin with baked oysters Rockefeller, Bermuda fish chowder, or something as exotic as roasted pumpkin potato gnocchi served with roasted sunflower seeds. The special main courses will be well-seasoned portions of whatever game fish the local fishers brought in that day, including yellowfin tuna, barracuda, shark, wahoo, or dolphin (the fish). Additional main courses might include a kettle of seafood St. David's style, mussels marinière, and a deep-fried fisher's platter, along with a pan-fried local fish with almonds and bananas. You'll get a full array of excellent Bermuda fish, either broiled or sautéed in butter. Desserts might include banana fritters with black-rum sauce, or Armagnac ice cream with prunes. On Friday nights (usually from June through October), the restaurant features a popular Louisiana Cajun seafood festival, with indoor and outdoor dining, accompanied by a Dixieland band.

INEXPENSIVE

Ⓢ Wickets Brasserie & Cricket Club

In the Southampton Princess Hotel, 101 South Shore Road. ☎ **441/238-8000.** "Healthy start" breakfast buffet $12.50 per person; lunch main courses $7.50–$12.50. AE, DC, MC, V. Daily 7–11am and noon–6:30pm. Ferryboat from Hamilton. INTERNATIONAL.

Outfitted with all the memorabilia of a British-based cricket club, this brasserie and bistro features a health-conscious breakfast buffet with all the requisite low sodium and high fiber, and one of the longest and most comprehensive luncheon menus on the island. The restaurant, situated on the lower lobby level of the Southampton Princess, provides a nice view over the hotel's swimming pool and the more distant ocean. Informal but traditional, the restaurant requests only that guests cover their bathing suits with a shirt. Since it stays open all afternoon until 6:30pm, many Bermudians like to come here for a late lunch or early supper.

Standard menu items include deli-style sandwiches, soups, chowders, pastas, salads, and platters such as grilled steaks, pork chops, and veal. The most popular fish here is grilled grouper with citrus-butter sauce. Children's menus are also available.

5 Sandys Parish

The following restaurants are all located on Somerset Island.

EXPENSIVE

Lantana Restaurant
Somerset Bridge. ☎ **441/234-0141.** Reservations required. Jacket and tie required for men. Fixed-price dinner $45, plus 15% service. No credit cards. Daily 7:30–9pm. Closed Jan 5–Feb 14. Hamilton ferry to Somerset Bridge. CONTINENTAL.

This is an elegant restaurant within an exclusive hotel. Guests sometimes enjoy having a predinner drink near the fireplace in the huge salon before climbing the short flight of steps to the pastel-colored dining room. If you prefer dining in a greenhouse environment, a second room filled with plants has been glassed over with a solarium-style roof. A uniformed staff member will usher you to a table where you will find a hibiscus at each place setting.

The menu changes nightly, and the cuisine is well prepared with only first-rate ingredients, as demanded by guests of this exclusive hotel. Some of the memorable dishes we've sampled include pan-fried sea bass served with toasted pinenuts, basil, and lemon—everything scented lightly with garlic; baked fish fillet with cucumber spaghetti and a delicate beetroot sauce; perfectly cooked and tender sautéed strips of veal served with a carrot mousseline and creamy mushroom sauce topped with a crisp potato cake. Certain nights of the week there is live music for dancing (call for further information). Although most dinners are eaten in the hotel's main dining room, the venue moves to La Plage on Wednesday and Friday nights, where the setting is open-air and less formal (see below). Regardless of the location, the food and prices are the same at dinner.

Tamarisk Dining Room
At Cambridge Beaches, 30 Kings Point Rd. ☎ **441/234-0331.** Reservations recommended for nonresidents. Lunch main courses $9.50–$15.25; set-price five-course dinner $55. No credit cards. Daily 12:30–2:30pm and 7–9pm. Bus: 7. INTERNATIONAL.

Many aspects of this dining room remind one of an upscale country club. Situated within Bermuda's first cottage colony, its newfound focus on cuisine has elevated this establishment to a higher level within the past year. The traditionally styled dining room is outfitted in limed wood, impressive columns, ceiling beams, and shades of pale green. Sliding glass doors extend the dining area during nice weather onto a rambling, eastward-facing terrace that overlooks the bay. Although Princess Margaret has dined here in the past, today you're likely to see groups of lawyers and business leaders, especially after dark.

At lunch there are likely to be platters of chicken-macadamia salad, a signature pita-bread sandwich (stuffed, California-style, with chicken salad, avocado slices, and bean sprouts), and some of the best cheeseburgers in the parish. The dinner menu changes frequently, but nearly always includes a juicy tenderloin of beef with a grain mustard and blanched garlic sauce; "cushions" of lamb served with a Stilton mousse soufflé, red wine sauce, and lentils; and a flavorful thyme-and-garlic roasted monkfish floating on a bed of ratatouille.

MODERATE

Il Palio

64 Main Rd. ☎ **441/234-1049.** Reservations required. Main courses $13.50–$24. AE, DC, MC, V. Tues–Sun 6–10pm. Bus: 8. ITALIAN.

Named after the famous horse race in Siena, Italy, and located in the center of Somerset, this restaurant serves some of the best pizzas on the island—a selection of 9-inch favorites that constitute an entire meal. Of course, the regular and classic Italian cuisine here is also quite good—everything from steak Diane to roast duckling with a zesty green peppercorn sauce. The emphasis is on the tried-and-true, such as fettuccine Alfredo or tender slices of sautéed veal; among the best choices is the pasta primavera and the ground meat and spinach-filled cannelloni. Fresh fish is also recommended, especially the selection that's sautéed with bits of garlic to which pine nuts, capers, and well-seasoned tomato sauce are added. If you arrive early, you can enjoy a drink in the downstairs bar.

La Plage

In the Lantana, Somerset Bridge. ☎ **441/234-0141.** Reservations recommended. Lunch main courses $12–$15; fixed-price dinner $45. No credit cards. Daily 12:30–2:30pm; Wed and Fri 7:30–9pm. Hamilton ferry to Somerset Bridge. INTERNATIONAL.

Walking toward this restaurant will give you a chance to admire the sculpture scattered throughout the gardens of the most exclusive hotel in Sandys Parish. In many ways, it's the perfect luncheon stopover during a tour of Bermuda's West End. The urn-shaped balustrades that separate the terrace from the cove, fresh flowers, and impeccable service resemble what you might find at the edge of a lake in northern Italy. The pier and dock area close to the restaurant create the impression that a yacht might pull up at any moment. You can choose a table near the flowers of the sundeck, or one inside the pink-and-lemon summertime interior. The setting here seems to overpower the food.

Although the food here is fresh and well prepared, it rises to the sublime only on Wednesday and Friday nights, when dinner is served. At lunch you might begin with a Bermuda fish chowder, followed by a choice from an array of offerings—from ordinary sandwiches (peanut butter and bacon) to elaborate fantasies such as salmon mousse, crêpes stuffed with beef and cheese, Bermuda mussel stew, and coquilles St. Jacques. Several salads are also available, including a traditional chef's salad or one made with tropical fruit.

Loyalty Inn

Mangrove Bay, Somerset Village. ☎ **441/234-0125.** Reservations recommended. Lunch main courses $6.25–$15; dinner main courses $25–$46; Sun brunch $23. AE, MC, V. Bar daily 11am–1am. Restaurant, Mon–Sat 11:30am–4pm; Sun noon–3pm; daily 6:30–10pm. Bus: 7 or 8, or ferry from Hamilton to Watford Bridge. INTERNATIONAL.

This 250-year-old converted home, which overlooks Mangrove Bay, looks vaguely like a church. The bar, in the same building, is filled with captain's chairs and a mock fireplace. There's also an outdoor terrace. The restaurant with its decor of cedar paneling and small-paned windows attracts both visitors and locals. The menu of steak, chicken, sandwiches, and seafood is not elaborate or overly special, but the dishes are well prepared and the portions are generous. The classic fish chowder or hearty Portuguese red bean soup might be followed by either the fish plate or tasty scallops and a salad. In the evening, if you have a large appetite, you could order a seafood dinner. The restaurant is about a five-minute walk east of the Watford Bridge ferry landing.

INEXPENSIVE

Frog & Onion

The Cooperage, Old Royal Naval Dockyard. ☎ **441/234-2900.** Lunch sandwiches, salads, and platters $4.50–$9; dinner main courses $9.25–$19.50. MC, V. Restaurant, daily 11am–4pm and 6–9:30pm. Bar, daily (with snacks) Mar–Nov 11am–1am, Dec–Feb noon–midnight. Bus: 8 or ferry from Hamilton. BRITISH.

Located in the former 18th-century cooperage (barrel-making factory) within the Royal Naval Dockyard, this is perhaps the most quintessential British pub in Bermuda. It's facetious name derives from its Franco-Bermudian owners—French-born Jean-Paul Magnin (the Frog) and Bermuda-born Carol West (the Onion). A pint of English lager might be enjoyed within the shadows of the cooperage's enormous fireplace. Many patrons stay on to dine here. At lunch there are sandwiches, salads, lasagna, bangers and mash, and such bar pies as sweet lamb and curry, steak and mussel, and vegetable and cheese. The dinner menu includes all of the lunchtime choices plus a variety of liver, lamb, beef, and chicken dishes; although they don't scale any gastronomic heights, they are well prepared and hearty. The portions are large; no one leaves here hungry.

Pirates Landing

Old Royal Naval Dockyard. ☎ **441/234-5151.** Reservations accepted but usually not needed. Main courses $13–$22; lunch from $7. Daily 11:30am–4pm and 6–10pm. AE, DC, MC, V. Bus: 8 or ferry from Hamilton. INTERNATIONAL.

Overlooking the Great Sound, this relatively new restaurant has a widely diverse menu that pleases most diners. The seating is comfortable, with pine tables and chairs. The costumed serving staff is exceptionally helpful. Most visitors, who come for lunch, sample the standard soups, burgers, pastas, and even grilled specialties. Gyros, all served on pita bread, are spicy delights, especially the 6-inch gyro pizza made with fresh vegetables, pepperoni, and Mozzarella.

At night the kitchen shines brighter, with its chefs searching abroad for inspiration; some of the unusual dishes include: Hanoi beef, lobster-stuffed ravioli with caviar, and Bhuna Gosht Khair-Ed-Din (dry meat marinated and cooked in Indian spices and herbs). Many dishes, including chicken, are grilled. Baked wahoo steak is often featured, and it's beautifully flavored with white wine, garlic, parsley, rosemary, and a butter sauce.

Somerset Country Squire Tavern

10 Mangrove Bay Rd., Somerset Village. ☎ **441/234-0105.** Reservations recommended. Main courses $10–$25. AE, MC, V. June–Sept, daily 11:30am–4pm; off-season, daily 11:30am–3pm; year-round Sun–Thurs, 6:30–9:30pm, Fri–Sat 6:30–10pm. Bar daily 11am–1am. Bus: 7 or 8. BRITISH/SEAFOOD.

You pass through a moon gate arch to reach the raised terrace of this waterside restaurant, located in the center of the village. (This restaurant can be visited on a trip to the Old Royal Naval Dockyard on Ireland Island.) If you don't want to eat within the confines of the limestone blocks and hedges that ring the terrace, go to the interior dining room downstairs. The bill of fare ranges from British "pub grub" to the much better fresh fish caught in local waters, or the traditional roast beef with Yorkshire pudding. Local Bermudian favorites (your best choices here) include curried mussel pie and fresh Bermuda tuna or wahoo. Look for the specialties of the day, but count on charbroiled and barbecued meals. Most of the food here is fairly routine, although the chef is especially proud of his Bermuda fish chowder, a tomato-based soup that some locals believe to be the best in the West End.

There is light entertainment three evenings a week, and barbecues from Sunday through Tuesday.

6 St. George's Parish

EXPENSIVE

Margaret Rose

St. George's Club, Rose Hill, St. George's. ☎ **441/297-1200.** Reservations required. Jacket and tie required for men at night. Main courses $23–$38. AE, DC, MC, V. Sat noon–3pm; Thurs–Tues 7–10pm. Bus: 8, 10, or 11. INTERNATIONAL.

Named after both Princess Margaret and Rose Hill (on which it is located), this fashionably decorated restaurant overlooks the harbor and the old part of town. Candlelight adds to the romantic ambience. Although the menu does change with the seasons, you might begin with the award-winning Bermuda fish chowder or else enjoy an endive-and-rose-petal salad with a pine nut-and-raspberry dressing. The wild-mushroom ravioli served in a thyme butter sauce is also an excellent appetizer. For your main course, you might choose Bermuda fish Picasso (with a mosaic of fresh fruit and ginger), an excellent loin of lamb with an herb-and-garlic stuffing, or an even better breast of Barbary duckling, pink-roasted. Several succulent pasta specialties are always featured.

MODERATE

Carriage House

22 Water St., Somers Wharf. ☎ **441/297-1730.** Reservations recommended. Lunch main courses $7.50–$22.50; dinner main courses $13.50–$45; 4-course early-bird special $19.75 (5:30–6:45pm). Sunday buffet $24.50 per person. AE, DC, MC, V. Daily 11:30am–4:30pm and 5:30–9:30pm; Sun buffet brunch noon–2pm. Bus: 3, 10, or 11. BEEF/SEAFOOD.

Housed in the same old waterfront storehouse as the Carriage Museum, the restored Carriage House specializes in beef and seafood. It retains the 18th-century-warehouse look with two rows of bare brick arches, spruced up with hanging baskets of greenery. Guests can choose to dine outdoors by the harborside. The chef specializes in prime rib, which is always cut to order (and priced according to size) and served with a ramekin of creamed horseradish in the British tradition. Other specialties include English roast spring lamb and tasty versions of Bermuda rockfish, grouper, or snapper. Many dishes are well prepared, especially oven-roasted pork médaillons (served with a leek and port sauce) and panfried médaillons of veal with a creamy mushroom and Pernod sauce. A different soup is offered every day. At lunch, there is a large selection of hamburgers, as well as sandwich platters, Bermuda fish chowder, pastas, soups, and oysters. The dessert choices are always excellent. Casual dress is acceptable.

San Giorgio

Water Street. ☎ **441/297-1307.** Reservations recommended. Lunch main courses $15–$19.50; dinner main courses $15–$19.50; pizzas and pastas $10–$11. MC, V. Mon–Fri noon–2:30pm; Mon–Sat 6:30–9:45pm. Bus: 3, 10, or 11. ITALIAN.

To reach this little Italian restaurant next to the Tucker House Museum, you must climb a short flight of steps from a point opposite Somers Wharf. This is your best bet for Italian dining in the East End (the Italian restaurants in Hamilton are better). The 150-year-old building was originally a private house and later served as the local telephone exchange for St. George's. Today's bistro/trattoria is deliberately informal, with red-and-white-checked tablecloths, a casual dress code, and several

St. George's Dining

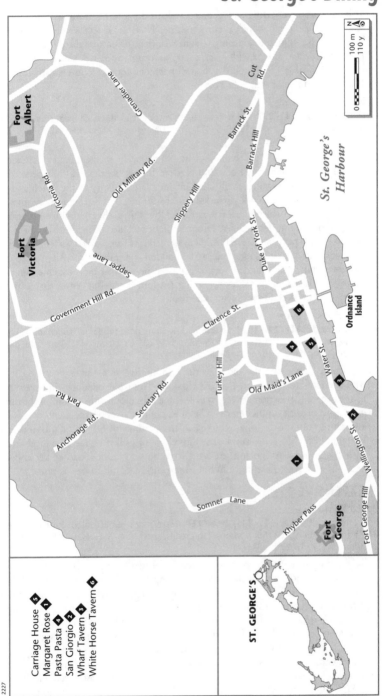

Carriage House 5
Margaret Rose 1
Pasta Pasta 4
San Giorgio 2
Wharf Tavern 3
White Horse Tavern 6

ST. GEORGE'S

artifacts commemorating San Giorgio and his dragon. Most guests begin with a selection of antipasto, which is fairly routine. There are several savory pasta dishes, including tortellini and a creamy lasagna. Among the entrées there is an excellent breast of chicken sautéed with black-cherry-and-rum sauce, a hot shrimp salad, and a hot scallop salad. Fresh broiled wahoo with lemon butter sauce is regularly featured. If it's on the menu, it might be your best bet.

Wharf Tavern

Somers Wharf. ☎ **441/297-1515.** Reservations recommended. Lunch main courses $5.50–$16.50; dinner main courses $8.50–$24. MC, V. Daily 11am–11pm; bar daily 10am–1am. Bus: 3, 10, or 11. SEAFOOD.

Wharf Tavern, situated on Somers Wharf, is a nautically themed, modern restaurant located on the ground floor of a 200-year-old former warehouse. Only pedestrians are allowed nearby, which might account for the popularity of the porch and the window seats, and the darkly paneled bar area inside. The setting is more interesting than the food (which is just standard fare), but this is what Bermudians have been eating and enjoying for decades. Dinners might include curried mussels, Bermuda fish cakes with peas and rice, pan-fried or broiled rockfish, broiled wahoo, oysters on the half shell, steak-and-kidney pie, and a London-style mixed grill. All main courses are served with a salad and a "starch." During the summer months, entertainment is presented seven nights a week beginning at 10pm. There is no cover charge for the entertainment. A children's menu is available.

White Horse Tavern

King's Square. ☎ **441/297-1838.** Reservations recommended for dinner. Lunch main courses $5.75–$23.75; dinner main courses $8.75–$23.75. MC, V. Lunch daily 11:30am–4pm; dinner daily 5:30–10pm. Bus: 3, 10, or 11. BERMUDIAN.

St. George's oldest tavern—and a favorite with tourists—is a restaurant and cedar bar with a terrace jutting into St. George's Harbour. This white building with green shutters may be the most popular tavern in Bermuda. In nice weather (most of the time), guests prefer to sit on the terrace. The most popular item on the menu here is fish and chips (often overdone), cooked in the manner of St. David's Island. The Bermuda fish chowder is good, as is mussel pie or grilled wahoo (the local catch), with mango salsa. At lunch, there are Tavern burgers, fresh salads, and open-faced sandwiches. Finish off with the White Horse chocolate cake. Dress is casual.

INEXPENSIVE

Pasta Pasta

York Street, St. George's. ☎ **441/297-2927.** Reservations not accepted. Salads $5; pastas $5.75 (half-portion), $9 (full portion). No credit cards. Mon–Sat noon–10:30pm; Sun 5–10:30pm. Bus: 8, 10, or 11. PASTA.

This is the smaller and slightly less expensive of two Bermuda restaurants with the same owners and the same pasta-and-salad emphasis. (Because its twin, listed separately under "Dining in Hamilton," has a slight difference in the spelling of its name, there has been a lot of discussion about this in Bermuda.) Decorated in summery colors, this restaurant offers two kinds of salad (tossed and Caesar), and about a dozen types of pasta. Served in full or half-portions, there are two kinds of lasagna (one of which is meatless) and a frequently changing array of varying shaped pasta topped with a choice of meat, seafood, or vegetarian sauces. A lot of the pasta sold here is intended for take-out consumption. Yes, you will find better pasta elsewhere, but not in St. George's. *Note:* No wine, beer, or alcohol is served here, and local licensing laws do not allow you to bring your own drinks.

St. David's Island

Black Horse Tavern

101 St. David's Road. ☎ **441/297-1991.** Reservations recommended. Main courses $13.25–$27. AE, MC, V. Tues–Sat 10am–1am; Sun noon–1am. Bus: 3. INTERNATIONAL.

If you should land here, in a section of the island that Bermudians call "the country," you'll dine with the locals, many of whom maintain (with some justification) that this is the best place for "an authentic taste of Bermuda." It looks like a dusty-rose-colored private home, with green shutters and a rear glassed-in porch that looks over Smith's Sound. Over the years the tavern has hosted many celebrities; a number of the guests arrive in yachts.

You might begin your meal with curried conch stew, shark hash (made with minced puppy shark), fish chowder, or curried mussels. Later choices include sandwiches, burgers, or perhaps a platter of fish and chips or chicken and chips. The chef also prepares a good sirloin steak and a chicken dinner. If your luck holds, the only Bermuda Triangle you'll encounter is a drink made here with pineapple juice, orange juice, black rum, and Bermuda gold liqueur. This place is more of a "regular" restaurant than the equally famous Dennis's Hideaway (see below).

Dennis's Hideaway

Cashew City Road. ☎ **441/297-0044.** Reservations required. Fixed-price dinners $15–$35. No credit cards. Dinner daily 7–10pm. Bus: 3. SEAFOOD.

Dennis Lamb, a burly St. David's islander, is one of the treasures of Bermuda. So is his quaint little eatery, located in the easternmost parish of St. George's. As you approach it, you're likely to see Dennis working in his garden in front (he grows, among other things, the cabbage for his coleslaw and beets for pickling). He'll show you into his fisher's cottage by one of the island's little coves. Once inside, you'll feel you've left Bermuda and are visiting some little pocket-size country with a distinctive personality.

Descended from whalers and pilots—"wooden ships and iron men"—Dennis and his son will offer you dishes that have virtually disappeared from Bermuda's restaurants, dishes that are normally available only in private homes today. For $35, he'll give you "the works," an array of dishes, including conch stew, dolphin (the fish), herb-flavored shark hash, shrimp, conch fritters—you name it (but please don't order the turtle, an endangered species). You may bring your own wine. If you don't want to eat so much, ask for the $15.50 fish dinner. The cottage is accessible by land or sea, and don't dress up.

(*Warning:* This "Pa Kettle" ambience is not for everyone. Some readers give it high marks, claiming they've made at least 20 pilgrimages here during their annual visits to Bermuda. However, some first-time visitors feel that travel writers should never send diners to this grubby place. Thus, we would recommend Dennis's Hideaway only if you're a bit adventurous!)

7 Hamilton Parish

EXPENSIVE

Mikado

In Marriott's Castle Harbour Resort, Paynters Road, Tucker's Town. ☎ **441/293-2040.** Reservations required. Main courses $22–$40; sushi $4.75–$6.25 per order (usually two pieces). AE, DC, MC, V. July–Sept, dinner only daily 6:30–9:30pm; off-season, dinner only Tues–Sun 6:30–9:30pm. Bus: 2 from St. George's. JAPANESE.

Located on the lower level of the Marriott (see Chapter 5, "Accommodations"), this is the only major Japanese restaurant in Bermuda, although sushi is served elsewhere. You pass through lacquered gateways to reach a whimsically art deco version of a Japanese tea garden. For each group of eight diners, an experienced chef prepares *teppan-yaki* style cuisine. Grills placed near each table permit diners to see whatever is cooking. Rare imported fish mixed with very fresh Bermuda fish (such as wahoo) are used for the sushi bar. All the traditional Japanese specialties, including tempura, along with an aromatic saké, are available. Of course, you may be familiar with Japanese food, but you won't find any other place like this on Bermuda; for the island, it's unique. Dress is "smart casual."

✪ Plantation

46 Harrington Sound Rd., Bailey's Bay. ☎ **441/293-1188.** Reservations recommended for dinner. Jackets requested for men at night. Main courses $22–$32; fixed-price dinner $38. AE, DC, MC, V. Lunch daily noon–2:30pm; dinner daily 6:45–9:30pm; bar service from 10am. Closed mid-Dec to mid-Feb. Bus: 1 and 3. BERMUDIAN/SEAFOOD.

The Plantation, a yellow colonial-style building with fireplaces and steep white roofs, is at the site of Leamington Caves. The restaurant's three rooms, with their carpeting, ceiling fans, and rattan furniture, have an inviting ambience. The service and the Bermudian seafood rank among the island's finest. Gastronomic pilgrims from all over the world flock here because it's near the top of everybody's "you-must-dine-here" list when visiting Bermuda. The freshly caught seafood and its careful preparation have placed Plantation on the culinary maps. Our crêpe filled with seafood was served with a light wine-cheese sauce. The main course of charcoal-grilled fish with citrus butter or banana, raisin, and coconut might be too exotic for many diners, but the lamb with apple chutney and Calvados sauce is usually a hit. The desserts are worth saving room for, especially the white chocolate mousse drizzled with a raspberry sauce.

Tom Moore's Tavern

Walsingham Lane, Walsingham Bay. ☎ **441/293-8020.** Reservations required. Jackets required for men at night. Main dishes $21–$35. AE, MC, V. Dinner daily 7–9:30pm. Closed Jan 5–Feb 14. Bus: 1 or 3. FRENCH/CONTINENTAL.

Bermuda's oldest eatery, built in 1652 as a private home, is located on Walsingham Bay, near the Crystal Caves. It was visited in 1804 by the Irish romantic poet Thomas (Tom) Moore, who wrote some of his verses here; he referred to a calabash tree which still stands, some 200 yards from the tavern.

This is also the most famous dining room in Bermuda, having experienced many incarnations. The present tavern was opened in 1985 by two Italians, Bologna-born Bruno Fiocca and his Venetian partner, Franco Bortoli; it quickly became one of the island's most popular upscale restaurants. With its four fireplaces and darkened cedar walls, this landmark establishment serves classical French and Italian cuisine.

Impressions

Had America ever suffered from land hunger . . . she would have seized Bermuda long ago. Wise, she took it not with soldiers, but with tourists, and today she controls it with dollars and an air base. There is nothing to be sorry about. The Bermudans stand on their tradition and their cash tills.

—Cecil Roberts, *And So to America* (1946)

Seafood is a specialty. During the summer months, there is usually a tank of Bermuda lobsters outside. Local fish featured on the menu are likely to include rockfish and yellowtail; these may be your best bet. One reader wrote that he found the place "very expensive, but worth the price, as the service and atmosphere are both top-notch. The cuisine is not light, however. Extremely well-prepared meals contain very rich sauces." He is right; nevertheless, we would like to recommend the chef's specialty—quail filled with goose liver, morels, and truffles, and then baked together in puff pastry. Two other recommendations are sautéed sweetbreads in a creamy basil sauce and Latino-style jambalaya. The setting, the English silver, German crystal, Luxembourg china, and the general ambience can help make a memorable visit.

INEXPENSIVE

Bailey's Ice Cream & Food D'Lites Restaurant

Corner of Wilkinson Avenue and Blue Hole Hill. ☎ **441/293-8605.** Ice cream $1.85 per scoop; sandwiches $3–$4.50 each. No credit cards. Mon–Sat 11am–5:30pm, Sun 11am–6pm. Closed Dec–Feb. Bus: 3 or 11. ICE CREAM/SANDWICHES.

At Bailey's Bay, this ice-cream parlor is located just across from Swizzle Inn (see below). For all-natural ice cream, there is no comparable spot in Bermuda—20 to 25 different flavors are made in the 40-quart ice-cream maker. The parlor is housed in a small Bermuda cottage, with a parking lot. You can enjoy your Bermuda banana, coconut, white chocolate cherries and chips, or other exotic-flavored ice cream at one of the outdoor tables or take it away. A sandwich nook, which uses fresh-baked bread for all sandwiches, is a popular attraction. Also featured are fresh-fruit ices, frozen yogurts, and natural juices.

Swizzle Inn

3 Blue Hole Hill, Bailey's Bay. ☎ **441/293-1845.** Reservations accepted for five or more only. Lunch main courses $5.95–$16.50; dinner main courses $8.50–$20. AE, MC, V. Daily 11am–1am. Closed Mon in Jan and Feb. Bus: 3 or 11. BERMUDIAN/ENGLISH.

Possibly the oldest pub in Bermuda—dating back some 300 years—the home of the Bermuda rum swizzle lies west of the airport, near the Crystal Caves. Thousands of business cards and graffiti cover the walls. All of the food is freshly prepared. The meaty Swizzleburger was voted best in Bermuda; other pub favorites include fish and chips, conch fritters, and shepherd's pie. These dishes are at least a notch above typical Bermudian pub grub. Popular among both Bermudians and visitors at lunch are the Bailey's Bay fish sandwich and onion rings. The larger and more varied dinner menu appeals to a variety of tastes and diets. Dining is available both inside and on the upper and lower patios. Upstairs there is also a nonsmoking room and a gift shop.

8 Smith's Parish

Inlet Restaurant

In the Palmetto Hotel, Harrington Sound Road, at Flatts Village. ☎ **441/293-2323.** Main courses $17–$28; lunch $14. AE, MC, V. Daily noon–2:30pm, 7–9:30pm; light snacks served in pub until 9:30pm. Bus: 10 or 11. INTERNATIONAL.

In creating this restaurant, the owners added a slope-roofed modern extension to a paneled lounge lined with Bermuda cedar. You can sit either near the big windows, which look out over the moon gate, the swimming pool, and the harbor, or in the darker and more intimate recesses of the back.

For lunch there is a selection of sandwiches and burgers; light snacks can be taken outside on the patio in nice weather. The dinner menu is larger and more varied. You might start with a spinach or Caesar salad, or Bermuda fish chowder. Seafood courses include a casserole of shrimp and scallops, or perhaps fresh Bermuda fish, broiled or pan-fried. Each of these dishes is well prepared and is probably your best bet. An attempt has been made to lift the poultry and meat dishes out of the ordinary; for example, the chicken breast is stuffed with pâté and the grilled médaillons of pork are served with an apple brandy sauce.

What to See & Do 7

Bermuda is for fun and leisure. Even the major attractions are designed to be enjoyed without taxing anyone. Because of the island's small size, it's easy to get to know Bermuda parish by parish. After 20 miles or so, you'll run into the sea—so don't rush anywhere.

Even though a lot of people live on a tiny landmass, it doesn't look that way, mainly because the houses have been built quite naturally into the landscape. There are no jarring billboards or neon signs to spoil the countryside, and because there are relatively few cars, you won't experience any traffic jams or polluted air.

In Bermuda something is going on all the time. Sports are always a star attraction, especially golf and tennis. Sailing, horseback riding, and the pink-sand beaches are also appealing. (See Chapter 9, "Beaches, Water Sports, Golf & Other Outdoor Activities.")

As for the sights, from the western tip of Somerset to the eastern end of St. George's, there is much to see in Bermuda, either by bike, ferry, bus, or taxi. You'll need plenty of time, though, since the pace is slow. Cars can travel only 15 mph in Hamilton and St. George's, 20 mph outside the towns. This speed limit is rigidly enforced, and there are severe penalties for any violations.

Bermuda is divided into nine parishes (or counties): Sandys Parish (in the far western end of the island), Southampton Parish, Warwick Parish, Paget Parish (which has the greatest concentration of hotels), Pembroke Parish (seat of the government at Hamilton), Devonshire Parish, Smith's Parish, Hamilton Parish (not to be confused with the city of Hamilton), and St. George's Parish (at the far eastern extremity; also includes the U.S. naval air base and the little island of St. David's).

In the early days these districts, which encompass about 21 square miles, were called "tribes." By the beginning of the 18th century the term "Tribe Road" was used for the boundaries between parishes. Pembroke, because it encloses the city of Hamilton, is the largest parish in population; St. George's has the largest land area.

Many local guidebooks are fond of pointing out that "you can't get lost in Bermuda." Don't believe them! Along narrow, winding roads—originally designed for the horse and carriage—you can get lost, several times, especially if you're looking for an obscure guesthouse along some long-forgotten lane.

You won't stay lost for long, however. Bermuda is so narrow that if you keep going in either an easterly or westerly direction, you'll eventually come to a main road. At its broadest point Bermuda is only about 2 miles wide. The principal arteries are the North Shore Road, the Middle Road, and the South Shore Road, so you'll at least have some indication as to what part of the island you're in.

Sometimes it starts raining almost without warning. Do not continue to drive in drizzly or rainy weather; pull off the road and wait. The skies usually clear rapidly and the road dries quickly. It is easy to have an accident on Bermuda's slippery roads after a rain, especially if you're not accustomed to using a motor scooter.

There are quite a few gasoline stations—called "petrol stations"—here. But once you "tank up," chances are you'll have plenty of energy to get you to your destination; for example, one tank of gas in a motorbike will take you from Somerset in the west to St. George's in the east.

In this chapter we'll go on a do-it-yourself tour, taking in Bermuda parish by parish. You could also take one of the walking tours described in Chapter 8.

SUGGESTED ITINERARIES

After you've landed in Bermuda, you may be eager to explore the island, especially if your time is short. Below is a suggested itinerary for the first five days. A week's visit will let you break up your sightseeing trips with time to relax, enjoy the beach, go boating, or engage in some of the other available sports.

If You Have 1 Day

If you have only one day for sightseeing, we suggest you spend it in the historic former capital of **St. George's.** It has everything from a ducking stool to narrow, alleyway-like streets with quaint names: Featherbed Alley, Duke of York Street, Petticoat Lane, Old Maid's Lane, Duke of Kent Street. You can spend a day exploring British-style pubs, seafood restaurants, shops (several major Hamilton stores have branches here), old forts, museums, and churches. You'll even see stocks and a pillory once used to humiliate wrongdoers.

If You Have 2 Days

Day 1   Spend Day 1 as indicated above.

Day 2   Devote this day to sightseeing and shopping in the city of **Hamilton.** Since it's likely that you'll be staying in one of the hotels in Paget or Warwick, a ferry from either parish will take you right into the city.

In Hamilton, you can always combine sightseeing with shopping, although for many visitors, the shops are more compelling. Try to time your visit to avoid the arrival of cruise ships. On those days, the stores and restaurants in Hamilton can become crowded.

If You Have 3 Days

Day 1–2   Spend Days 1–2 as outlined above.

Day 3   For your third day, take the ferry from Hamilton across Great Sound to **Somerset.** Your cycle can be carried on the boat—you'll need it later. You'll be let off at the western end of Somerset Island in Sandys Parish, where you'll find the smallest drawbridge in the world. It's easy to spend an hour walking around Somerset Village. Then head east until you reach a beach on Long Bay along the northern rim of the island. There are several places for lunch in Sandys Parish (see Chapter 6, "Dining"). The Somerset Country Squire Tavern, a typical village inn, is one of the best. It's near the Watford Bridge ferry stop at the western end of the island.

❓ Did You Know?

- More than 23,000 couples honeymoon here each year.
- Bermudians imported the idea of moon gates, large rings of stone used as garden ornaments, from the Orient centuries ago. Walking through a moon gate is supposed to bring good luck.
- William Shakespeare's 1610 play, *The Tempest*, was inspired by the mysterious island.
- The British ship *Sea Venture*, headed for Virginia, was wrecked on Bermuda's reefs in July 1609.
- Somerset Bridge is the world's smallest drawbridge. Only 22 inches wide, the opening is just large enough for a ship's mast to pass through.
- Bermuda has more golf courses per square mile than any other place in the world; there are eight of them on the island's approximate 21 square miles.
- The first game of tennis in the Western Hemisphere was played in Bermuda by Sir Brownlow Gray, the island's chief justice, in 1873.
- Shallow-water wreck diving is a popular activity. More than 120 shipwrecks have been reported in the waters around Bermuda.
- With the arrival of spring comes the blossoming of Bermuda's Easter lilies, first brought to the island from Japan in the 18th century.
- Bermuda has no pollution and no illiteracy. There is a ban on outdoor advertising and neon signs.
- Bermuda's cruise-ship policy permits only four ships at a time in its harbors.
- There are no automobile rentals in Bermuda; only one person per household is permitted to own an automobile.
- Once believed to be extinct, the cahow bird was rediscovered in Bermuda; today it nests in the late fall and winter months.

After lunch you can go across Watford Bridge to Ireland Island, home of the Maritime Museum. On your way back to Somerset Bridge and the ferry back to Hamilton, you might take the turnoff to Fort Scaur. From Scaur Hill you'll have a commanding view of Ely's Harbour and a vista over Great Sound. If you don't want to go through Somerset again, the ferry at Watford Bridge will take you back to Hamilton.

If You Have 5 Days

Days 1–3   Spend Days 1–3 as outlined above.

Day 4   Make the most of this beach day, heading for Horseshoe Bay Beach in the morning. Spend most of your time there, exploring hidden coves in all directions. You can have lunch right on the beach at a concession stand. In the afternoon visit Gibbs Hill Lighthouse. After a rest at your hotel, sample some Bermudian nightlife.

Day 5   To conclude your stay, head for Flatts Village, which lies in the eastern sector of Smith's Parish. Explore the Bermuda Aquarium, Zoological Garden, and Natural History Museum, and consider an undersea walk offered by the Hartley family (see "Organized Tours," below). Have lunch at the Palmetto Hotel & Cottages, then visit Elbow Beach. Make sure you've purchased your duty-free liquor to take back with you. After having afternoon tea at one of the hotels, arrange to see an island show that evening.

1 The Top Attractions

Although Bermuda is a small island, you really can't see much of it in a day or two. So, if you have more time, you may want to explore it methodically, as many visitors do—parish by parish; that is what we shall do here, visiting the attractions of each parish as we head from east to west. If your time is limited, however, you may want to consider only the following highlights:

- Walking tour of St. George's (covered in this chapter and in Chapter 8, "Bermuda Strolls").
- Walking and shopping tour of the city of Hamilton. The attractions are covered in this chapter and in Chapter 8, "Bermuda Strolls." If you want to combine shopping and sightseeing, read also Chapter 10, "Shopping."
- Maritime Museum at the Royal Naval Dockyard in the West End.
- Bermuda Aquarium, Zoological Garden, and Natural History Museum, along North Shore Road across Flatts Bridge.
- Crystal Caves, on Crystal Caves Road, discovered in 1907.
- Leamington Caves, Harrington Sound Road, with its underground lakes.
- Verdmont, Verdmont Lane, in Smith's Parish. This 18th-century mansion stands on property once owned by the founder of South Carolina.
- Fort Hamilton, Happy Valley Road, a massive Victorian fortification overlooking the city of Hamilton and its harbor.
- Botanical Gardens, South Shore Road, a Shangri-La in the mid-Atlantic.
- Gibbs Hill Lighthouse, the oldest cast-iron lighthouse in the world.
- Horseshoe Bay Beach in Southampton, most photographed of the pink sandy beaches of Bermuda.
- Elbow Beach at Paget, Bermuda's top sun and swim stretch of sand.

2 St. George's Parish

Settled in 1612, the town of St. George's was once the capital of Bermuda, losing that position to Hamilton in 1815. The town was settled three years after Admiral Sir George Somers and his shipwrecked party of English sailors came ashore in 1609. The town was founded by Richard Moore (of the newly created Bermuda Company) and a band of 60 colonists. It was the second English settlement in the New World (Jamestown, Virginia, was the first). Named after England's patron saint, its coat of arms depicts St. George and the dragon. Sir George Somers died in Bermuda in 1610, and his heart was buried in the St. George's area (the rest of his body was taken home to England for burial).

Almost four centuries of history come alive here, and generations upon generations of sailors have set forth from its sheltered harbor. St. George's even played a role in the American Revolutionary War. Bermuda depended on the American colonies for food, and when war came, the food supply became dangerously low. Although Bermuda was a British colony, the loyalties of its people were divided since many Bermudians had relatives living on the American mainland. A delegation headed by Col. Henry Tucker went to Philadelphia to petition the Continental Congress for food and supplies, for which Bermuda was willing to trade salt. George Washington had a different idea, however. He needed gunpowder, and a number of kegs of it were stored at St. George's. Without the approval of the British/Bermudian governor, a deal was consummated that resulted in the gunpowder's being trundled aboard American warships waiting in the harbor of Tobacco

Bay under cover of darkness. In return, the grateful colonies supplied Bermuda with food.

Although St. George's still evokes a feeling of the past, it's actively inhabited. However, when cruise ships are in port, it is likely to be overrun with visitors. Many people prefer to visit St. George's at night when they can walk around and enjoy it in relative peace and quiet. Of course, the major buildings will be closed, but you'll still be able to get a sense of and be able to appreciate the town.

IN TOWN

King's Square, also called Market Square or King's Parade, is the center of life in St. George's. The square is the site of the colorful White Horse Tavern, where you may want to stop for a drink after your tour. Also on the square you'll see a pillory and stock. Honeymooners like to be photographed in them today, but in earlier times they were used in deadly earnest. Victims were sometimes placed in the pillory for a certain number of hours—sometimes with one ear nailed to the post! "Criminals" were burned on the hand or branded, fined in tobacco, nailed to the post, or declared "infamous." Often they had their ears cut off or were forced to "stand in a sheet on the church porch."

The list of offenses for which Bermudians were punished in the early 1600s offers a glimpse into the social life of the time. Along with such "usual" crimes as treason, robbery, arson, murder, and "scandal," punishable offenses included concealing finds of ambergris, exporting cedarwood, railing against the governor's authority, hiding tobacco, being "notorious cursers and swearers," leading an "uncivil life and calling her neighbor an old Bawd and the like," neglecting to receive Holy Communion, acting in any stage play of any kind whatsoever, and playing at unlawful games such as dice, cards, and ninepins.

The street names in St. George's also evoke its history. **Petticoat Lane** (sometimes called Silk Alley) got its name when two recently emancipated slave girls were said to have paraded up and down the lane rustling their new and flamboyantly colored silk petticoats. **Barber's Lane** is also named for a former slave. It honors Joseph Hayne Rainey, a freedman from the Carolinas who fled to Bermuda aboard a blockade runner during the Civil War. He became a barber in Bermuda until the end of the war. At its conclusion he returned to the United States and was elected to Congress, becoming the first black member of the House of Representatives during Reconstruction.

Visitors Service Bureau

King's Square. ☎ **441/297-1642.** Free admission. Summer Mon–Sat 9am–4pm; Nov–Mar Mon–Sat 9:30am–2pm. Bus: 1, 3, 8, 10, or 11 from Hamilton.

Here you can get a map and any information you might need before you set out to explore on your own. The bureau is opposite the Town Hall.

Town Hall

7 King's Square. ☎ **441/297-1532.** Town Hall free; *Bermuda Journey* $3.50 adults, $2 children under 12. Town Hall Mon–Sat 10am–4pm. *Bermuda Journey,* Mon–Thurs 11:15am and 2:15pm, also Sat (May–Nov only) 12:15pm and 2:15pm. Bus: 1, 3, 8, 10, or 11 from Hamilton.

Headed by a mayor, officers of the Corporation of St. George's meet in the Town Hall, which is near the Visitors Service Bureau. There are three aldermen and five common councillors. The Town Hall has a collection of Bermuda cedar furnishings, along with photographs of previous mayors. A half-hour multimedia, audiovisual presentation on the history, culture, and heritage of the colony,

Bermuda Journey (produced by the same group that created *The New York Experience*), is presented on the upper floor of the Town Hall several times a day.

Old State House

Princess Street. ☎ **441/297-1260.** Free admission. Wed 10am–4pm or by appointment; call Ray O'Leary at **441/292-2480.** Bus: 1, 3, 8, 10, or 11 from Hamilton.

Behind the Town Hall is Bermuda's oldest stone building, the Old State House, constructed with turtle oil and lime mortar in 1620. The Old State House, where meetings of the legislative council once took place, was eventually turned over to the Freemasons of St. George's. The government asked the annual rent of one peppercorn and insisted on the right to hold meetings here upon demand. The Masonic Lodge members, in a ceremony filled with pageantry, still turn over one peppercorn in rent to the Bermuda government every April. (Peppercorns were sometimes a form of payment in the old days. In the late 18th century, for example, two small islands off King's Square were sold for a peppercorn apiece. In 1782 Henry Tucker bought Ducking Stool Island, and in 1785 Nathaniel Butterfield bought Gallows Island; several years later Simon Fraser purchased both for 100 peppercorns and made them into one island, today's Ordnance Island.)

For those who have never witnessed the 45-minute spectacle of the annual rent payment, it begins around 11am with the gathering of the Bermuda Regiment on King's Square and the subsequent arrival of the premier, mayor, and other dignitaries, all amid the bellowing introductions of the town crier. As soon as all the principals have taken their places, a 17-gun salute is fired as the governor and his wife make a grand entrance in their open horse-drawn landau. His Excellency inspects a military guard of honor, while the Bermuda Regiment Band plays. The stage is, of course, now set for the presentation of the peppercorn, which sits on a silver plate atop a velvet cushion. Payment is made in a grand and formal manner, after which the Old State House is immediately used for a meeting of Her Majesty's Council.

✪ Frommer's Favorite Bermuda Experiences

Strolling Bermuda's Pink Sands. The pink sand beaches are reason enough to come to the island. Find your favorite cove (perhaps Whale Bay, Astwood Cove, or Jobson's Cove), and stroll aimlessly at dawn, at twilight, or whenever your fancy dictates.

Cycling Across the Land. On a rented bicycle, or maybe a moped built for two, explore Bermuda from end to end. Start in St. George's in the East End and go all the way to the Royal Naval Dockyard in the West End. You don't necessarily have to do this in one day, however.

Following the Deserted Railway Trail. As you follow this intermittent trail from one end of the island to the other, you'll see panoramic seascapes, exotic flora and fauna, and hear the soothing sounds of the island's bird life.

Touring by Horse and Buggy. No one has ever improved on this old-fashioned method of sightseeing and shopping along Hamilton's Front Street. Or, better yet, go on a two-hour shopping tour of Somerset Village in the West End.

Viewing Bermuda from Gibbs Hill Lighthouse. Climb the 185 steps of the oldest cast-iron lighthouse in the world for one of the greatest views of Atlantic Ocean. Springtime visitors may be lucky enough to see migrating whales beyond the shore reefs.

Deliverance

Ordnance Island. ☎ **441/297-1459.** Admission $3 adults, $1 children under 12. Apr–Nov, Mon–Sat 9am–4pm; Dec–Mar, Wed and Sat 10am–4pm. Bus: 1, 3, 8, 10, or 11 from Hamilton.

Across from St. George's town square and over a bridge is Ordnance Island, where visitors can see a full-scale replica of *Deliverance*, a pinnace (small sailing ship) constructed in 1609 by the shipwrecked survivors of the *Sea Venture* to carry them on to Virginia.

A tape recording guides visitors through the ship. Alongside *Deliverance* is the ducking stool, a replica of the horrible contraption used in 17th-century witch trials. Its use is demonstrated on Wednesday and Thursday at noon.

ARGO Adventures owns *Deliverance* and also operates sightseeing and snorkeling adventures aboard its boat, *ARGO,* Bermuda's only high-speed tour boat, taking passengers along the barrier reef, the south shore beaches, the historic forts, and the billionaires' mansions at Tucker's Town. *ARGO* was custom-built to allow access to the most beautiful parts of the island where larger vessels can't gain entrance. Call for details, which change seasonally.

✪ St. Peter's Church

Duke of York Street. ☎ **441/297-8359.** Free admission, but donations appreciated. Daily 10am–4:30pm (guide available Mon–Sat). Bus: 1, 3, 8, 10, or 11 from Hamilton.

From King's Square, head east to the Duke of York Street, where St. Peter's Church, believed to be the oldest Anglican place of worship in the Western Hemisphere, is located. The original church, built by colonists in 1612 almost entirely of cedar with a palmetto-leaf thatch roof, was almost completely destroyed by a hurricane in 1712. Some of the interior, including the original altar from 1615 (still used on a daily basis), was salvaged, and the church was rebuilt in 1713. It has been restored many times since then, providing excellent examples of the architectural styles of the 17th to the 20th centuries. The tower was added in 1814. On display in the vestry is a silver communion service given to the church by King William III in 1697. Before the Old State House was built, the colony held public meetings in the church. The first assize convened here in 1616, and the first meeting of Parliament was held in 1620. The church has Sunday and weekday services.

Graveyard of St. Peter's

Entrance opposite Broad Alley. Bus: 1, 3, 8, 10, or 11 from Hamilton.

Some of the tombstones in this graveyard are more than three centuries old; many tombs mark the graves of slaves. Here you'll also find the grave of Midshipman Richard Dale, an American, who was the last victim of the War of 1812. The churchyard also holds the tombs of Gov. Sir Richard Sharples and his aide, Capt. Hugh Sayers, who were murdered while strolling on the grounds of Government House in 1973.

The Bermuda National Trust Museum

King's Square. ☎ **441/297-1423.** Adults $4, free for children under 12. Apr–Oct, daily 9:30am–4:30pm; off-season, daily 10am–4pm. Closed public holidays. Bus: 1, 3, 8, 10, or 11 from Hamilton.

This was once the Globe Hotel, headquarters of Maj. Norman Walker, the Confederate representative in Bermuda; today it houses relics from the island's involvement in the American Civil War, but from a Bermudian perspective. St. George's was the port from which ships carrying arms and munitions ran the Union blockade. A replica of the Great Seal of the Confederacy is fitted to a Victorian press so that visitors can emboss copies as souvenirs.

Bermuda Attractions

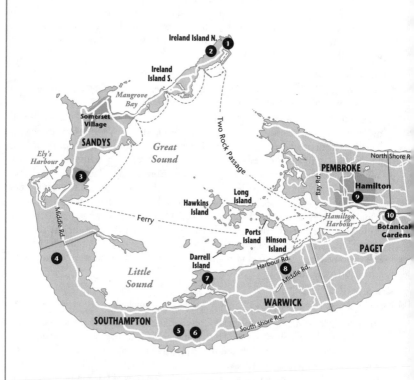

Atlantic Ocean

Ireland Island N.
Ireland Island S.
Mangrove Bay
Somerset Village
SANDYS
Ely's Harbour
Great Sound
Two Rock Passage
North Shore R
PEMBROKE
Bay Rd.
Hamilton
Hawkins Island
Long Island
Hamilton Harbour
Botanical Gardens
Ferry
Middle Rd.
Ports Island
Hinson Island
PAGET
Darrell Island
Harbour Rd.
Little Sound
Middle Rd.
WARWICK
SOUTHAMPTON
South Shore Rd.

DEVONSHIRE PARISH:
Palm Grove ⑬
HAMILTON PARISH:
Bermuda Aquarium, Museum & Zoo ⑮
Bermuda Perfumery ⑲
Crystal Caves ⑱
Leamington Caves ⑰

PAGET PARISH:
Botanical Gardens ⑪

Waterville (House) ⑩
PEMBROKE PARISH (Hamilton City):
Bermuda Historical Society Museum ⑨
Bermuda National Gallery ⑨
Sessions House (Parliament Building) ⑨
ST. GEORGE'S PARISH:
Bermuda National Trust Museum ⑳
Fort St. Catherine ㉒
Ocean View Golf Course ⑫

134

Tucker House Museum

5 Water St. ☎ **441/297-0545.** Admission $4 adults, $3 senior citizens 65 and up, free for children under 12 years. Mon–Sat 10am–4:30pm. Closed public holidays. Bus: 1, 3, 8, 10, or 11 from Hamilton.

This was the home of the well-known Tucker family of England, Bermuda, and Virginia. It displays a notable collection of Bermudian furniture, portraits, and silver. Also in the Tucker House is the Joseph Rainey Memorial Room, where this African American refugee (mentioned above) of the Civil War practiced barbering.

Carriage Museum

22 Water St. ☎ **441/297-1367.** Donation requested. Mon–Fri 9:30am–4:30pm. Closed public holidays. Bus: 1, 3, 8, 10 or 11 from Hamilton.

Much of Bermuda's transportation was by horse-drawn carriage until 1946, when the "automobile age" arrived. Many of these old carriages have been preserved to delight present-day visitors to the island. The museum is in a renovated old Royal Engineers warehouse, on Somers Wharf.

Somers Garden

Duke of York Street. ☎ **441/297-1532.** Free admission. Daily 8am–4pm. Bus: 1, 3, 8, 10, or 11 from Hamilton.

The heart of Sir George Somers was buried here in 1610; a stone column perpetuates the memory of Bermuda's founder. The garden was opened in 1920 by the Prince of Wales (later King Edward VIII and subsequently Duke of Windsor).

Unfinished Cathedral

Blockade Alley. Bus: 1, 3, 8, 10, or 11 from Hamilton.

After leaving Somers Garden, head up the steps to the North Gate, which opens onto Blockade Alley. The structure here is known as the "folly of St. George's." The plan was that this cathedral, begun in 1874, would replace St. Peter's. But the planners ran into money problems, then a schism developed, and—if that weren't enough—a storm swept over the island causing considerable damage to the structure. Result: the Unfinished Cathedral.

St. George's Historical Society Museum

3 Featherbed Alley. ☎ **441/297-0423.** Admission $2 adults, 50¢ children 16 and under. Tues–Thurs 10am–4pm. Bus: 1, 3, 8, 10, or 11 from Hamilton.

In a home built around 1700, this museum contains an original 18th-century Bermuda kitchen complete with utensils from that period. Other exhibits include a 300-year-old Bible, a letter from George Washington, and Native American ax heads. (Some early settlers on St. David's Island were Native Americans, mainly Pequot.)

Old Rectory

At the head of Broad Alley, behind St. Peter's Church. ☎ **441/297-0879.** Free admission, but donations are appreciated. Wed 1–5pm. Bus: 1, 3, 8, 10, or 11 from Hamilton.

Built by a reformed pirate in 1705, this charming old Bermuda cottage was later inhabited by Parson Richardson, who was nicknamed the "Little Bishop." Now a private home, it's administered by the Bermuda National Trust.

Bridge House

1 Bridge St. ☎ **441/297-8211.** Free admission. Mon–Sat 10am–5pm. Mid-Jan to mid-Feb and Sat only, 10am–4pm. Bus: 1, 3, 8, 10, or 11.

This long-established gallery, recently renovated, displays antiques and collectibles, old Bermudian items, original paintings, Bermuda-made crafts, as well as a studio that belongs to Jill Amos Raine, a well-known Bermuda watercolor artist. The house was constructed in the mid-17th century, and was home to several of the colony's governors. Its most colorful owner was Bridger Goodrich, a Loyalist from Virginia, whose privateers once blockaded Chesapeake Bay. So devoted was he to the king that he also sabotaged Bahamian vessels trading with the American colonies. The building is named Bridge House because a bridge used to stand over a muddy creek (filled in now).

ON THE OUTSKIRTS OF TOWN

From its earliest days St. George's has been fortified, and although it never saw much military action, reminders of those former days are interesting to explore. On the outskirts of town, the forts can be reached by Circular Drive.

Nearby, along the coast, is **Building Bay,** where the shipwrecked victims of the *Sea Venture* built their vessel, the *Deliverance,* in 1610.

Gates Fort

Cut Road. No phone. Free admission. Daily 10am–4:30pm. Bus: 1, 3, 8, 10, or 11.

Gates Fort was built in 1609 by Sir Thomas Gates, one of the original band of settlers on the *Sea Venture.* Gates was governor-designate for the colony of Virginia.

Fort St. Catherine

Barry Road. ☎ **441/297-1920.** Admission $2.50 adults, free for children under 12. Daily 10am–4pm. Closed Christmas. Bus: 1, 3, 8, 10, or 11 from Hamilton.

Towering above the beach where the shipwrecked crew of the *Sea Venture* came ashore in 1609 is Fort St. Catherine, completed in 1614 and named for the patron saint of wheelwrights and carpenters. The fortifications have been upgraded over the years. The last major reconstruction took place from 1865 to 1878, so the fort's appearance today is largely the result of work done in the 19th century.

Now a museum, visitors first see a series of dioramas, "Highlights in Bermuda's History." Museum figures are used to depict various activities that took place in the magazine of the fort, restored and refurnished as it was in the 1880s. Large Victorian muzzle–loading cannons can be seen on their original carriages. In the keep, which served as the living quarters of the fort, you can see information on local and overseas regiments that served in Bermuda, a fine small-arms exhibit, a cooking-area display, and an exhibit of replicas of England's crown jewels. There is a short audio-visual show on St. George's defense systems and the forts of St. George's.

3 Hamilton Parish

Around **Harrington Sound,** the sights differ greatly from those of St. George's—more action, less history. Bus no. 1 or 3 from Hamilton will get you here in about an hour. Hamilton Parish is bordered on the east by St. George's and on the southwest by Smith's Parish. The parish encloses Harrington Sound, a landlocked saltwater lake that is 1$\frac{1}{2}$ miles at its widest and 2$\frac{1}{8}$ miles long. It was named for John, first Lord Harrington of Rutland, England.

Some experts believe that back in some prehistoric era, Harrington Sound was a cave that fell in. Its gateway to the ocean is through an inlet at Flatts Village. However, it is believed that there are underwater passages as well, since several deep-sea fish have been caught in the sound.

For the best panoramic view of the north shore, visitors head for **Crawl Hill**—the highest place in Hamilton Parish—just before they come to Bailey's Bay. Crawl is a corruption of the word "kraal," which is where turtles were kept before slaughter. Shelly Bay, named for one of the passengers of the *Sea Venture,* is the longest beach along the north shore.

The **Hamilton Parish Church,** reached by going down Trinity Church Road, stands on Church Bay; built as a one-room structure in 1623, it has been much altered over three and a half centuries.

At Bailey's Bay, Tom Moore's jungle consists of wild woods. The poet Tom Moore is said to have spent many hours writing poetry under a still-standing calabash tree. Since the jungle is now held in private trust, permission must be obtained in order to enter it. It's much easier to pay your respects to the Romantic poet by going to Tom Moore's Tavern (see "Hamilton Parish" in Chapter 6, "Dining").

Bermuda Perfumery

212 North Shore Rd., Bailey's Bay. ☎ **441/293-0627.** Free admission. Apr–Oct, Mon–Sat 9am–5pm, Sun 9am–4:30pm; Nov–Mar, Mon–Sat 9am–4:30pm. Closed Sun in winter. Bus: 1 or 3.

Lili Perfumes are made here. On guided tours, visitors can see the perfume-making process, including the old method of extracting scents from native flowers. Among the fragrances produced are passion flower, Bermuda Easter lily, and oleander jasmine. A small botanic garden with a seating area and walkways provides an attractive resting place. You can also visit the orchid house, which has more than 500 varieties of orchids, and the nature trail, which passes through a large area of the property that is planted with tropical flowers, shrubs, and trees. The perfumery has a gift shop, the Calabash.

✪ Bermuda Aquarium, Museum & Zoo

North Shore Road, Flatts Village. ☎ **441/293-2727.** Admission $6 adults, $3 children ages 5–12, free for children under 5. Daily 9am–4:30pm. Closed Christmas Day. Bus: 10 or 11 from Hamilton or from St. George's. From Hamilton, follow Middle Road or North Shore Road east to Flatts Village; from St. George's, once over the causeway, follow North Shore Road or Harrington Sound Road west to Flatts Village.

Across Flatts Bridge, this complex is home to a wide collection of tropical marine fish, turtles, harbor seals, and other forms of sea life. In the museum you can see exhibits on the geological development of Bermuda, deep-sea exploration, and humpback whales. The complex also has a zoo with Galápagos tortoises, alligators, and monkeys, along with a collection of birds, including parrots and flamingos.

The 140,000-gallon-tank North Rock Exhibit allows visitors to enter an exhibit to experience a coral reef washed by ocean surge. The tank houses a living coral reef, as well as reef and pelagic fish species. The tank holds the first living coral exhibit on this scale in the world, made possible by the Aquarium, Museum, and Zoo's success in the science of coral husbandry.

There is parking for cycles and cars across the street from the aquarium.

✪ Crystal Caves

8 Crystal Caves Rd., off Wilkinson Ave., Bailey's Bay. ☎ **441/293-0640.** Admission $5 adults, $2.50 children ages 5–11, free for children 4 and under. Feb–Mar and Nov–Dec, Sun–Fri 10am–4pm; Apr–Oct daily 9:30am–4:30pm. Closed 2nd and 3rd weeks of Jan. Bus: 1 or 3.

This cave is composed of translucent formations of stalagmites and stalactites, a setting that includes the crystal-clear Cahow Lake. Discovered in 1907, the cave is reached by a sloping path and a few steps. At the bottom, some 120 feet below the surface, is a floating causeway that follows the winding cavern, where hidden lights illuminate the interior. All tours through Crystal Caves are guided.

✪ Leamington Caves

46 Harrington Sound Rd., Bailey's Bay. ☎ **441/293-1188.** Admission $4 adults, $2 children ages 5–11, free for children 4 and under. Mon–Sat 10am–4pm. Closed Dec to mid-Feb. Bus: 1 or 3.

For Spelunkers

Bermuda has one of the highest concentrations of limestone caves in the world. Most of this cave-making activity began during the Pleistocene Ice Age. As early as 1623, the adventurer Captain John Smith complained that he had encountered "vary strange, darke, cumbersome caves."

In Bermuda, nature's patient, relentless underground sculpting is a dream world for even the casual spelunker. Deep in the majestic silence of the earth's interior, you can roam in caverns of great stalactites and stalagmites of gothic grandeur, and of delicacy and beauty.

This awesome underground has been the inspiration for creative achievements as diverse as Shakespeare's *The Tempest* and Henson Associates' "Fraggle Rock" muppets.

You can visit Crystal Caves or Leamington Caves, both reached along Harrington Sound Road *(see p.138 for more information).*

This grotto, which is attached to the Plantation Club, has crystal formations and underground lakes. It was first discovered by a young boy, who noticed a small opening on the rocky hillside that he and his father were clearing for plowing in 1908. He slipped through the hole with a rope and candles and found a wonderland of natural cave splendors some 1.5 million years old. Guided tours take you along lighted walkways with handrails, through the high-vaulted, amber-tinted grotto.

Devil's Hole Aquarium

92 Harrington Sound Rd., ☎ **441/293-2072.** Admission $5 adults, $2 children 12 and under. Daily 10am–5pm. Bus: 1 or 3.

The pool of this former cave is fed by the sea through half a mile of subterranean passages. A natural aquarium, it's stocked with some 400 individual fish, including moray eels, sharks, giant groupers, and massive green turtles. Visitors can tempt the pond's inhabitants with baited but hookless lines. It has been open to the public since 1834.

4 Smith's Parish

Smith's Parish, named for Sir Thomas Smith, a member of the Bermuda Company, faces the open sea on both its northern and southern borders. To the east is Harrington Sound, and to the west, bucolic Devonshire Parish.

The parish encompasses **Flatts Village,** one of the most charming parish towns of Bermuda, reached by bus no. 10 or 11 from Hamilton. This was a smugglers' port for about 200 years. The origin of the name has been lost to history. Once it was the center of power for a coterie of successful "planter politicians" and landowners. Their government ranked in importance second only to that of St. George's, then the capital. People gathered at the rickety Flatts Bridge to "enjoy" such public entertainment as a hanging on the gallows. A so-called blasphemer in 1718 had his tongue bored through with a fire-hot poker. If the offense was serious enough, victims were drawn and quartered here. From Flatts Village you'll have nice views of both the inlet and Harrington Sound.

At the top of McGall's Hill, which you can visit after seeing the Verdmont mansion (see below), is **St. Mark's Church.** Another church, built in 1746, once stood near the site of St. Mark's. When it became unsafe, a local family, the Trotts, donated land for the construction of St. Mark's. Work began on the new church in 1846, and the first services were held on Easter Sunday in 1848. Subsequent additions—such as the chancel—continued to be made up until the end of the 19th century. St. Mark's Church was based on the same designs used for the Old Devonshire Parish Church.

✪ Verdmont

6 Verdmont Lane, Collectors Hill, Smith's Parish. ☎ **441/236-7369.** Admission $4 adults, children under 12 free. Apr–Oct, Tues, Fri, Sat 10am–4pm; Nov–Mar, Mon–Fri 10am–4pm. Closed one week in either Jan or Feb (dates vary). Bus: 1 from Hamilton or St. George's.

This is an 18th-century mansion of special significance to Americans who are interested in colonial and Revolutionary War history. It stands on property that was owned in the 17th century by William Sayle, who left Bermuda to found South Carolina on the American mainland and then became its first governor. The house was built before 1710 by John Dickinson, a prosperous ship owner who was also Speaker of the House of Assembly in Bermuda from 1707 to 1710. Verdmont passed to Mr. Dickinson's granddaughter, Elizabeth, who married the Hon. Thomas Smith, collector of Customs. Their oldest daughter, Mary, married Judge John Green, a Loyalist who came to Bermuda in 1765 from Philadelphia. During and after the American Revolution, Green was judge of the Vice-Admiralty Court and had the final say on prizes brought in by privateers. Many American shipowners lost their vessels because of his decisions. The house, which is now administered by the National Trust, contains many antiques, china, and portraits, along with the finest cedar stair balustrade in Bermuda.

Spittal Pond Nature Reserve

South Shore Road. ☎ **441/236-6483.** Free admission. Daily sunrise to sunset. Bus: 1 or 3.

Follow the rather steep Knapton Hill Road west to South Shore Road, turning at the sign for Spittal Pond, Bermuda's largest wildlife sanctuary. The most important of

---

Nature Reserves

The National Trust in Bermuda has wisely protected the island's nature reserves. If you play by the rules—that is, don't disturb animal life or take plant life for a souvenir—you can explore many of these natural wonderlands, which are one of the most rewarding reasons to visit Bermuda, if you enjoy hiking along nature trails.

The best and largest of these is Spittal Pond Nature Reserve in Smith's Parish *(see p.140)*, along South Shore Road. Birders, especially from November through May, are drawn to the reserve to see herons, ducks, flamingos, terns, and many migratory fowl (the latter can't be seen after March).

This 60-acre untamed seaside park is always open to the public with no admission charge. The Department of Agriculture (call **441/236-4201** for information) offers guided tours of the refuge.

The island abounds with other places of natural wonder. Craggy formations shaped over the centuries out of limestone and coral dot the beaches along the southern coast, with towering cliffs forming a backdrop. The best of these is Natural Arches, one of the most photographed sights in Bermuda. Two limestone arches which took nature centuries to carve rise 35 feet above the beach. This natural attraction is signposted almost at the end of South Shore Road, directing you to Castle Harbour Beach.

the National Trust's open spaces, it occupies 60 acres and has about 25 species of waterfowl, which can be seen annually from November to May. Visitors are asked to stay on the scenic trails and footpaths provided. Bird-watchers in particular like to visit in January, when as many as 500 species of birds can be observed wintering on the pond.

5 Devonshire Parish

As you wander its narrow lanes, you can, with some imagination, picture yourself in the original Devon in England. The parish takes its name from the first Earl of Devonshire. It is a lush, hilly parish, rarely spoiled by commercial intrusions.

Along North Shore Road is **Devonshire Dock,** long a seafarer's haven, near the border of Pembroke Parish. Fishers still bring in such catches as grouper and rockfish, so you can shop for dinner if you're staying at a nearby cottage with a kitchen. During the War of 1812 British soldiers came to Devonshire Dock to be entertained by local women.

At the **Arboretum** on Montpelier Road, you'll discover one of the most tranquil oases in Bermuda, an open space with a wide range of Bermudian plant and tree life, especially conifers, palms, and other subtropical trees. It was created by the Department of Agriculture, Fisheries, and Parks.

Along South Shore Road, you can visit the **Edmund Gibbons Nature Reserve,** west of the junction with Collector's Hill. This portion of marshland, owned by the National Trust, provides living space for a number of birds and rare species of Bermuda flora. It's open daily at no charge. Visitors must stay out of the marshy area.

Old Devonshire Church

Middle Road. ☎ **441/236-3671.** Free admission. Daily 9am–5:30pm. Bus: 2.

A major attraction of the parish is the Old Devonshire Parish Church, which is believed to have been built on this Middle Road site in 1624, although the present foundation dates from 1716. An explosion virtually destroyed the church on Easter in 1970, but it was reconstructed. Today the church is very tiny, almost resembling a vicarage rather than a church. Some of the church's contents survived the blast, including its silver from 1590, which may be the oldest on the island. The church, designed by Sir George Grove and built of limestone, has an early English–style high pitched roof. The Old Devonshire Parish Church stands northwest of the "new" Devonshire Parish Church, which dates from 1846.

Palm Grove

38 South Shore Rd. No phone. Free admission. Mon–Thurs (inclusive) 8:30am–5pm. Bus: 1.

One of the delights of Devonshire Parish, this private estate lies 2^1/$_2$ miles east of Hamilton. It is famous for its pond with a relief map of Bermuda in the middle of it. Each parish is an immaculately manicured grassy division. The site, which has well-landscaped flower gardens, opens onto a view of the sea.

6 Pembroke Parish (City of Hamilton)

The city of Hamilton is in Pembroke Parish—a peninsula that opens at its northern rim onto the vast Atlantic Ocean and on its southern side onto Hamilton Harbour. Its western border is on Great Sound. The parish is named after the third Earl of Pembroke, a power in the Bermuda Company of 1616. Nearly one-fourth of Bermuda's population lives in Pembroke Parish, most of them in the capital of Hamilton.

The ideal way to see Hamilton, or the parish itself for the first time is to sail in through Hamilton Harbour, past the offshore cays. You'll join fishers and the yachting set and cruise ships.

The Irish poet Tom Moore and the American humorist Mark Twain publicized the glories of Bermuda, but, for the British at least, the woman who put Bermuda on the tourist map was Princess Louise. The daughter of Queen Victoria, she spent several months in Bermuda in 1883. Her husband was the governor-general of Canada, so she traveled to Bermuda to escape the fierce northern cold. Although in the 20th century Bermuda hosted many royal visitors, including Queen Elizabeth II, Princess Louise was the first royal personage to set foot in the colony. And once she arrived, she turned up all over the island, meeting and visiting with its friendly people and winning their respect and admiration. When she returned to Canada, she told reporters that she'd found the Shangri-La of tourist destinations.

In 1852 the cornerstone was laid for the Hamilton Hotel, Bermuda's first hotel, which was completed in 1863. It survived until 1955, when it was destroyed by fire. When the Hamilton Princess Hotel opened in 1887, it overshadowed the Hamilton Hotel and became the hotel of choice for the island. Over the years it has had a colorful history, especially when it was taken over by Allied agents during World War II.

If Princess Louise were to visit Bermuda today, she would probably stay at **Government House,** which stands on North Shore Road and Langton Hill. Not open to the public, it is the residence of the governor of the island. The spacious grounds may be viewed by applying to the governor's aide-de-camp. A Victorian residence, it has housed many notable guests, including Queen Elizabeth II and her husband, Prince Philip, as well as Prince Charles, Sir Winston Churchill, and President John F. Kennedy. The saddest moment for Government House was in 1973, when Gov. Sir Richard Sharples and his aide, Capt. Hugh Sayers, along with the governor's dog, Horsa, were assassinated while they were walking on the grounds. This tragedy led to a state of emergency in Bermuda.

While touring Pembroke Parish, visitors are fond of looking at **Black Watch Well,** located at the junction of North Shore Road and Black Watch Pass. Excavated by a detachment of the Black Watch Regiment, the well was ordered to be dug in 1894, when Bermudians were suffering through a long drought.

CITY OF HAMILTON

Hamilton has been the capital of Bermuda since 1815. Once known as the "Show Window of the British Empire," both Mark Twain and Eugene O'Neill, who lived in places that opened onto Hamilton Harbour, cited its beauty.

A stroll along Front Street will take you by some of Hamilton's most elegant stores, but you'll want to branch off into the little alleyways to check their shops and boutiques. If you get tired of walking or shopping (or both), you can go down to the docks and take one of the boats or catamarans waiting to show you the treasures of Little Sound and Great Sound.

On certain days you may be able to see locals buying their fresh fish—that is, fish that had not already been earmarked for restaurants—right from the fisherpeople who sell the "catch of the day" at Front Street docks. Although rockfish seems to be the most abundant, you'll also see snapper, grouper, and many other species. In the 1930s, seaplanes used to land passengers right in Hamilton Harbour.

Most Bermudians consider the winter months too cold for Bermuda shorts, but come May, all the businesspeople along Front Street seem to don a pair. The British military introduced these shorts to Bermuda in the early part of this century. By the 1920s and 1930s the shorts had become quite fashionable, although they were not acceptable at dinner parties or at church services. Originally the shorts were worn with a white shirt, tie, jacket, and knee stockings; it was considered "daring" to wear the shorts 5 inches above the knee. But to go beyond that and wear Bermuda short-shorts could have led to ticketing by the police in the years after World War II.

Most people come to Hamilton to shop, but there are also many sightseeing attractions. Named for a former governor, Henry Hamilton, it was incorporated as a town in 1793. Because of Hamilton's central location and its large, protected harbor, it was chosen as the island's new capital in 1815, replacing St. George's. Since Hamilton encompasses a total of only 182 acres of land, most visitors explore it on foot.

Today Hamilton is the hub of the island's economy; however, long before it became known as the "showcase of the Atlantic," it was a modest outlet for the export of Bermuda cedar and fresh vegetables.

Hamilton boasts the largest number of eating and drinking establishments in Bermuda, especially on or near Front Street. These restaurants charge a wide range of prices, and there are many English-style pubs if you'd like to go on a pub crawl. Although there is a huge conglomeration of bars, religion isn't neglected—there are 12 churches within the city limits, one or two of which merit a sightseeing visit.

Hamilton should be seen not only on land but also from the water, and you can do so with one of frequent boating tours of the harbor and its coral reefs. If you're visiting from other parishes, the ferry will let you off at the western end of Front Street, which is ideal if you'd like to drop by the **Visitors Service Bureau** and pick up a map. It is located near the Ferry Terminal. The staff here also provides information and helpful brochures. Hours are 9am to 4:45pm Monday through Saturday.

To return to the parishes of Paget, Warwick, and Sandys, ferries leave daily between 6:50am and 11:20pm. On Saturday and Sunday, there are fewer departures.

Opposite the Visitors Service Bureau stands the much-photographed **"Bird Cage,"** where one used to be able to see a police officer directing traffic. Such a sight is rare now. For many years visitors wondered if the traffic director was for real or placed there for tourist photographs.

Nearby is **Albouy's Point,** site of the Royal Bermuda Yacht Club, founded in 1844. The point, named after a 17th-century professor of "physick," is a public park overlooking Hamilton Harbour.

Bermuda Historical Society Museum

13 Queen St., Par-la-Ville Park. ☎ **441/295-2487.** Free admission. Mon–Sat 9:30am–12:30pm and 2–4:30pm. Bus: 1, 2, 10, or 11.

After leaving the harbor, proceed up Queen Street to the public library and the Bermuda Historical Society Museum, which has a collection of old cedar furniture, antique silver, early Bermuda coins (hog money), and ceramics that were imported to Bermuda by early sea captains, plus the sea chest and navigating lodestone of Sir George Somers, whose flagship, *Sea Venture,* became stranded on Bermuda's reefs in 1609. You will also find portraits of Sir George and Lady Somers, as well as models of the ill-fated *Sea Venture,* along with models of *Patience* and *Deliverance.*

The museum is located in **Par-la-Ville Park** on Queen Street. It was designed by William Bennett Perot, Hamilton's first postmaster—from 1818 to 1862—who was somewhat eccentric. As he delivered mail around town, he is said to have placed letters in the crown of his top hat in order to preserve his dignity.

Perot Post Office

Queen Street, at the entrance to Par-la-Ville Park. ☎ **441/295-5151.** Free admission. Mon–Fri 9am–5pm. Bus: 1, 2, 10, or 11.

Bermuda's first stamp was printed in this landmark building. Beloved by collectors from all over the world, the stamps, signed by Perot, are considered priceless. It is said that Perot and his friend, Heyl, who ran an apothecary shop, conceived the first postage stamp in order to protect the post office from cheaters. People used to stop off at the post office and leave letters, but not enough pennies to send them. The postage stamps were printed in either black or carmine.

Philatelists can purchase contemporary Bermuda stamps in this same post office. For its 375th anniversary, Bermuda issued a series of stamps honoring its discovery in 1609. One stamp portrays the admiral of the fleet, Sir George Somers, along with Sir Thomas Gates, the captain of the *Sea Venture*. Another depicts the settlement of Jamestown, Virginia, which was on the verge of extinction when Sir George and the survivors of the Bermuda shipwreck finally arrived with supplies late in 1610. A third shows the *Sea Venture* stranded on the coral reefs of Bermuda. Yet another shows the entire fleet, originally bound for Jamestown, leaving Plymouth, England, on June 2, 1609.

Hamilton City Hall & Arts Centre

17 Church St. ☎ **441/292-1234.** Free admission. City Hall, Mon–Fri 9am–5pm; Bermuda Society of Arts, Mon–Sat 10am–4pm. Bus: 1, 2, 10, or 11.

The City Hall, also home of the Bermuda Society of Arts, is an imposing white structure with a giant weather vane and wind clock to tell maritime-minded Bermudians which way the wind is blowing. Completed in 1960, the building is the seat of Hamilton's municipal government. The theater on the first floor is the venue for stage, music, and dance productions throughout the year, and is also the main site of the Bermuda Festival. The **Bermuda National Gallery** (see below) is also situated here.

Since 1956 the Bermuda Society of Arts has encouraged and provided a forum for contemporary Bermuda artists, sculptors, and photographers. Its gallery, with ever-changing exhibitions, displays the work of local artists as well as visiting artists. Although their goals are often shared, this society is a separate entity from the newer Bermuda National Gallery.

Bermuda National Gallery

City Hall, 17 Church St. ☎ **441/295-9428.** Admission $3 adults; children under 16 admitted free. Mon–Sat 10am–4pm, Sun 12:30–4pm. Bus: 1, 2, 10, or 11.

Located in the east wing of City Hall, the Bermuda National Gallery is home of the Masterworks Foundation Bermudiana Collection, with work by such artists as Georgia O'Keeffe, Winslow Homer, Charles Demuth, Albert Gleizes, Ogden Pleissner, and Jack Bush. The Masterworks Foundation was established in 1987 to return to the island works of art that depict Bermuda and to exhibit them.

The Bermuda National Gallery is also home to the Hereward T. Watlington collection, which includes 15th- to 19th-century paintings by such masters as Reynolds, Gainsborough, and de Hooch. The gallery also displays smaller paintings and watercolors collected by the Bermuda Archives and National Trust.

While a National Gallery for Bermuda has been long overdue, Bermuda's humid climate and damaging sunlight made it necessary to build a gallery with proper climate control and lighting. As a result, the **Bermuda Fine Art Trust** was developed and incorporated by an Act of Parliament in 1982. In 1988, the Hon. Hereward T. Watlington bequeathed his collection of European paintings to the people of Bermuda on condition that they be housed in a European-standard climate-controlled environment. The Corporation of Hamilton offered the use of the East Exhibition Room of City Hall and made a financial contribution toward the construction of a proper facility.

Cathedral of the Most Holy Trinity

Church Street. ☎ **441/292-4033.** Free admission. Daily 7:15am–5pm. Bus: 1, 2, 10, or 11.

The Bermuda Cathedral on Church Street is the so-called mother church of the Anglican diocese. It became a cathedral in 1894 and was formally consecrated in 1911. A comprehensive restoration and enhancement program has just been completed. The building features a reredos, stained-glass windows, and the carvings of the choir stalls.

Sessions House

21 Parliament St. ☎ **441/292-7408.** Free admission. Mon–Fri 9am–12:30pm and 2–5pm. Bus: 1, 2, 10, or 11.

This Italian Renaissance–style structure was originally built in 1819. Its clock tower was added in 1887 to commemorate the Golden Jubilee of Queen Victoria. The House of Assembly meets on the second floor, and visitors are permitted in the gallery (call **441/292-7408** to learn when meetings are scheduled). On the lower level, the chief justice presides over the Supreme Court.

7 Paget Parish

Visitors flock to Paget for its south shore beaches, the best on the chain of islands. Named after the fourth Lord Paget, the parish has a lot of historic homes and gardens, but most of them are not open to public view, except on special occasions. During the springtime College Weeks, the Elbow Beach Hotel is the center of most activities.

Visitors who stay in one of Paget's many hotels often use the ferry service—there are docks at Salt Kettle, Hodson's, and Lower Ferry. One can also "commute" by ferry to Warwick Parish or Sandys Parish to the west.

Paget Parish is the site of **Chelston,** on Grape Bay Drive, the official residence of the U.S. consul-general; it is open only during the Garden Club of Bermuda's open-houses-and-gardens program in the spring. Chelston is situated on $14^{1}/_{2}$ acres of landscaped grounds overlooking South Shore Road.

✪ Botanical Gardens

Point Finger Road, South Shore Road. ☎ **441/236-4201.** Free admission. Daily, sunrise to sunset. Bus: 1, 2, or 7. If you're on a bike or moped, turn left off Middle Road onto Tee Street. At Berry Hill Road, go right. About half a mile farther on the left is the signposted turnoff to the gardens. Take a right fork to the parking lot on the left.

This 36-acre landscaped park is one of Bermuda's major attractions, with hundreds of flowers, shrubs, and trees all clearly identified; it is also riddled with pathways. Attractions include collections of hibiscus and subtropical fruit, an aviary, banyan trees, and even a garden for the blind. The property is maintained by the Department of Natural Resources. It's best to take one of the 90-minute walking tours that depart at 10:30am on Tuesday, Wednesday, and Friday, in season, from the Visitor Centre; the cafe there sells sandwiches and salads (soup and chili in winter). From mid-November through March, tours are scheduled only on Tuesday and Friday. You can always visit on your own, however.

Waterville

5 The Lane (Harbour Road), corner of Pomander Road. ☎ **441/236-6483.** Free admission. Mon–Fri 9am–5pm. Shop: Mon–Sat 10am–4pm. Bus: 8 from Hamilton.

Built before 1735, this is one of the oldest houses in Bermuda, home of seven generations of the prominent Trimingham family. From the cellar storage rooms of this house in 1842, James Harvey Trimingham started the business that was to become Trimingham Brothers, Ltd.—one of Bermuda's finest Front Street shops. Waterville is now the headquarters of the Bermuda National Trust, housing its offices, reception rooms, and shop—Trustworthy. Major renovations were undertaken in 1811, and the house has been restored in this period's style. The two main rooms have also been furnished in this period, mainly with Trimingham family heirlooms specifically bequeathed for use in the house. Waterville is just west of the Trimingham roundabout, quite close to the city of Hamilton.

Paget Marsh
Middle Road. ☎ **441/236-6483.** Free admission. Mon–Fri 9am–5pm by special arrangement. Bus: 8 from Hamilton.

Paget Marsh comprises 25 acres of unspoiled native woods and marshland, with vegetation and birdlife of ecological interest. Since it is a fully protected area with few trails, prospective visitors should call the number given above to make special arrangements and obtain a map from the Bermuda National Trust.

Birdsey Studio
5 Stowe Hill, Paget. ☎ **441/236-6658.** Mon–Fri 10am–1am, Sat 9am–noon. Bus: 8 from Hamilton.

One of Bermuda's best-known painters, Alfred Birdsey, arrived from his native England when he was 7 years old. Around 1990, he radically changed his style from the calendar-style art he now disdains to bold, powerful canvases with bright colors and forceful themes. Watercolors begin at $40 each; oils range from $100 to around $500.

8 Warwick Parish

Famed for its two golf courses, this western parish was named after the second Earl of Warwick, a shareholder in the Bermuda Company of 1610.

Warwick Long Bay, on South Shore Road, with public conveniences, is one of the finest beaches on Bermuda and constitutes the major attraction of the parish. Nearby, you can go inside **Christ Church,** across from the Belmont Hotel on Middle Road, daily from 9am to 4pm. Built in 1719, it is one of the oldest Scottish Presbyterian churches in the New World.

9 Southampton Parish

This parish is a narrow strip of land opening at its northern edge onto Little Sound and on its southern shore onto the Atlantic Ocean. It is bordered by Warwick Parish to the east and Sandys Parish to the west. The U.S. Naval Air Station Annex is also located here. If you see red flags hoisted in the area, take care; they're there to warn of aerial firing.

Known for its beaches, the parish was named after the third Earl of Southampton. **Horseshoe Bay** is one of Bermuda's most attractive public beaches, with changing rooms, a snackbar, and space for parking.

✪ Gibbs Hill Lighthouse
Gibbs Hill, Lighthouse Road, between South Shore Road and Middle Road. ☎ **441/238-0524.** Admission $2, free for children under 5. Daily 9am–4:30pm. Bus: 7 or 8 from Hamilton.

The main attraction of this parish is the Gibbs Hill Lighthouse, built in 1846. It is the oldest cast-iron lighthouse in the world. Although there is a 185-step climb to the top, the panoramic view of Bermuda and its shoreline from the outlook balcony make the climb worthwhile. The lighthouse keeper will explain the workings of the machinery. In spring, visitors may spot migrating whales beyond the south shore reefs.

10 Sandys Parish

Some visitors to Bermuda head directly for Sandys Parish and spend their entire time there; they feel that the far western tip is special, with its rolling hills, lush countryside, and tranquil bays. Comprising a group of islands, the parish was named in honor of Sir Edwin Sandys, one of the shareholders of the original Somers Island (Bermuda) Company, as well as a director of the Virginia Company and the East India Company.

Somerset Island, site of Somerset village, pays tribute to Sir George Somers of *Sea Venture* fame; Sandys Parish is often called Somerset. This area has always stood apart from the rest of Bermuda. For example, during the U.S. Civil War, when most Bermudians sympathized with the Confederates, Sandys Parish supported the Union side.

To explore this tip of the fishhook of Bermuda, it is best to take a ferry (the fare is $3); the trip from Hamilton to Watford Bridge is 45 minutes. Bikes can be taken aboard the ferry (there is a charge of $3 for motor-assisted cycles). Ferries also stop at Cavello Bay, Somerset, and the Royal Naval Dockyard. The **Visitors Service Bureau** is on Somerset Road near St. James Church (☎ **441/234-1388**). From May through November it's open Monday through Saturday from 10am to 4pm. After leaving Fort Scaur (see below), you can continue over the much-photographed 17th-century **Somerset Bridge,** the world's smallest drawbridge. When it's open for marine traffic, the space between the spans is a mere 22 inches at road level—just large enough to allow the mast of a sailboat to pass through.

On Somerset Road is the **Scaur Lodge Property,** an open area that includes the site of Scaur Lodge, a Bermuda cottage that was severely damaged by a waterspout that moved up on land, turning into a tornado and driving across this neck of Somerset Island. This typical Bermuda steep-shoreline hillside is open daily at no charge.

Sandys Parish has areas of great natural beauty, including **Somerset Long Bay,** a public beach, which the Bermuda Audubon Society is developing into a nature preserve; and **Mangrove Bay,** a protected beach right in the heart of **Somerset Village.** You can take pictures from the public wharf. Try to walk around the old village; it's filled with typically Bermudian houses and some shops.

✪ Fort Scaur

Ely's Harbour, Somerset Rd. ☎ **441/234-0908.** Free admission. Daily 9am–4:30pm. Closed Christmas. Bus: 7 or 8 from Hamilton.

On the highest hill in Somerset, this fort was part of a ring of fortifications constructed in the 19th century, during a period of troubled relations between Britain and the United States. Intended as a last-ditch defense line for the Old Royal Naval Dockyard, the fort was skillfully constructed, taking advantage of the land contours to camouflage its presence from detection at sea. The fort has subterranean passages and a dry moat that stretches across the land from Ely's Harbour to Great Sound. Opened to visitors in 1957, Fort Scaur has become one of Somerset's most popular tourist attractions. From the fort one can view Ely's Harbour and Great Sound; using the free telescope, one can see such far-away points as St. David's Lighthouse and Fort St. Catherine. There are picnic tables, benches, and restrooms available. The fort is encompassed by 22 acres of parkland filled with interesting trails, picnic areas, a rocky shoreline for fishing, and a public dock.

Gilbert Nature Reserve

Main Road. ☎ **441/236-6483.** Free admission. Nature reserve daily sunrise to sunset. Bus: 7 or 8 from Hamilton.

In the center of the island lies the Gilbert Nature Reserve—5 acres of unspoiled woodland. It bears the name of the family that owned the property from the beginning of the 18th century until 1973, when it was acquired by the Bermuda National Trust (in conjunction with the Bermuda Audubon Society).

St. James' Anglican Church

90 Somerset Road. ☎ **441/234-0834.** Free admission. Daily 8am–6pm. Bus: 7 or 8 from Hamilton.

This is one of the most beautiful churches in Bermuda. It was constructed on the site of a structure that was destroyed by a hurricane in 1780. The present church was built nine years later; a unique feature is that the altar faces west instead of the customary east. This happened because a road to the west of the church was inadequate, and so a new road was cut through to the east side of the church. The north and south aisles of the church were added in 1836, the entrance gate in 1872, and the spire and chancel in 1880. The church was struck by lightning in 1939, but was restored shortly thereafter.

11 Ireland Island

A multimillion-dollar cruise-ship dock has been built and a tourist village has emerged in this historic area, used by the British navy until 1951. The area also houses the Bermuda Maritime Museum, the Neptune Theatre, the Crafts Market, and the Bermuda Arts Centre. Ferries from Hamilton stop at Ireland Island, at the extreme west end of Bermuda, once each hour from 7am to 6pm. The fare is $3 each way. A bus leaves Hamilton for the Royal Naval Dockyard Monday through Saturday every 15 minutes from 8am to 8pm. The trip takes one hour and costs $2.50 for adults, half price for children.

The **Royal Naval Dockyard** has been transformed into a park, with Victorian street lighting and a Terrace Pavilion and bandstand for concerts. Vendors can be found pushing carts filled with food, dry goods, and local crafts. There is a full-service marina with floating docks, along with a marina clubhouse and showers.

When this dockyard, which had been on British Admiralty land, was sold to the Bermudian government in 1953, it marked the end of British naval might in the western Atlantic.

Bermuda Maritime Museum

Old Royal Naval Dockyard, Ireland Island. ☎ **441/234-1333.** Admission $7.50 adults, $3 children under 18. Daily 10am–4:30pm. Closed Christmas. Transportation: Ferry from Hamilton. Bus: 7 or 8.

In a large 19th-century fortress, built by convict labor, the museum exhibits artifacts, models, and maps pertaining to Bermuda's nautical heritage. Its most famous exhibit is in the 1837 Shifting House, which was opened in 1979. Here you can see such artifacts as gold bars, pottery, jewelry, silver coins, and other items recovered from 16th- and 17th-century shipwrecks, including the *Sea Venture*. Most visitors come here to gaze at the Tucker Treasure.

A well-known local diver, Teddy Tucker, made a significant find in 1955 when he discovered the wreck of the *San Antonio*, a Spanish vessel that had gone down off the coast of Bermuda in a violent storm in 1621. One of the great treasures of this find, the Pectoral Cross, was stolen in 1975 just before Queen Elizabeth II officially opened the museum. The priceless original cross was replaced by a fake. To this day, the original cross has never been recovered, and its mysterious disappearance is still the subject of much discussion.

The fortress's massive buildings of fitted stone, with their vaulted ceilings of English brick, are alone worth a visit. So are the 30-foot defensive ramparts; the underground tunnels, gunports, and magazines; and the water gate and pond for entering by boat from the sea. Exhibits in six large halls illustrate the island's long, intimate connection with the sea—from Spanish exploration to 20th-century ocean liners, from racing dinghies to practical fishing boats, from shipbuilding and privateering to naval exploits. The Shifting House has shipwreck exhibits, including some earthenware and pewter that belonged to the English settlers on their way to Jamestown aboard the *Sea Venture* (wrecked in 1609).

As you enter the Parade Ground at the entrance to the museum, you'll notice a 10-foot-high figure of King Neptune. This comes from the HMS *Irresistible,* recovered when the ship was broken up in 1891; it has now been duplicated in Indiana limestone. The **Queen's Exhibition Hall** houses general maritime exhibits, including those on navigation, whaling, and cable and wireless. A "Bermuda in Five Hours" exhibit focuses on Pan American's early "flying boats." The building itself was constructed in 1850 for the purpose of storing 4,860 barrels of gunpowder.

The **Forster Cooper Building** (from 1852) of the museum illustrates the history of the Royal Navy in Bermuda, including the Bromby Bottle Collection. This exhibit was opened in 1984 by Princess Margaret. The Boatloft houses part of the museum's boat collections, including the century-old fitted dinghy *Victory,* the 17-foot *Spirit of Bermuda,* and the *Rambler,* the only surviving Bermuda pilot gig. On the upper floor, the original dockyard clock, which is still working, chimes the hours and the quarter-hours.

One of the most enjoyable ways to see the dockyard is on a guided walking tour, many of which are Free admission. The tours change frequently, so it is best to check with the Visitor Service Centre at the dockyard to see what may be available at the time of your visit.

Bermuda Craft Market

In the Cooperage Building, 4 Freeport Rd. ☎ **441/234-3208.** Free admission. Daily 10am–5pm. Transportation: Ferry from Hamilton. Bus: 7 or 8.

This market is the place to watch local artists at work and to buy their wares. Established in 1987, it offers items made from Bermuda cedar, candles, clothing, dolls, fabrics, hand-painted goods, jewelry, metal and gem sculpture, needlework, quilts, shell art, glass panels, and woven-cane goods, among other things.

Bermuda Arts Centre

4 Freeport Rd. ☎ **441/234-2809.** Free admission. Daily 10am–5pm. Ferry from Hamilton. Bus: 7 or 8.

Works by local artists are featured in this gallery, with exhibits changing about every six weeks. An eclectic range of original art and prints are for sale. Local artists in residence now include a cedar sculptor, a watercolorist, and a silversmith/jewelry maker.

12 Especially for Kids

Families with children can enjoy a wide variety of activities April through October, for example, sailing, water skiing, snorkeling, or glass-bottom boat trips; tennis; visits to museums and caves; and a wide array of walking tours.

Most resorts offer specific children's activities, and there are special family packages. Most of the larger properties will also provide babysitting services for minimal fees.

Here are some of the favorite activities for kids:

Bermuda Aquarium, Museum & Zoo *(see p.138)* This provides a learning experience about the undersea world. Hand-held cassette tapes enable one to listen to a history of marine life while visiting live exhibits of Bermuda's native fish.

Bermuda Maritime Museum *(see p.148)* Entire families take equal delight in viewing the exhibits of Bermuda's nautical history in this authentic Victorian fortress museum.

Bermuda Railway Trail *(see p.162)* A nature walk for the whole family, this 21-mile trail can be followed in sections, according to your stamina and interests. There are strolls overlooking the seashore and along quiet tree-lined alleyways.

Devil's Hole Aquarium *(see p.139)* The first established attraction in Bermuda—founded in 1834—this aquarium is located near Harrington Sound. Kids toss baited but hookless lines to feed fish and turtles in this natural marine environment.

Crystal Caves *(see p.138)* Two boys chasing a runaway ball in 1907 discovered an enormous cavern surrounded by an underground lake. Easy walkways take parents and children down into the caverns of the crystal cave in Hamilton Parish.

Undersea Walk (see "Organized Tours," below) Explore the ocean floor with "helmet diving." Following a predive educational lecture aboard the ship, children can walk along the ocean floor for face-to-face encounters with friendly sea creatures.

Horseback Riding (see Chapter 9, "Beaches, Water Sports, Golf & Other Outdoor Activities") Spicelands Riding Center accepts riders over 21 years of age, but the Lee Bow Riding center is well equipped for younger riders.

13 Special-Interest Sightseeing

FOR THE ARCHITECTURE LOVER

All of Bermuda should interest the architecture lover. Mark Twain wrote of the whiteness of Bermuda houses and roofs: "It is exactly the white of the icing of a cake, and has the same emphasized and scarcely perceptible polish. The white of marble is modest and retiring compared with it . . . clean-cut fanciful chimneys—too pure and white for this world—that will charm one's gaze by the hour."

For more details and lore, see "Bermuda Style" in Chapter 2, "Introducing Bermuda." The **town of St. George's**—the oldest and most historic settlement—is likely to hold the greatest fascination for architecture buffs (see Chapter 8, "Bermuda Strolls").

The **Old State House** is the oldest stone house in Bermuda (constructed in 1620). The governor at the time, Nathaniel Butler, believed he was erecting the house in an Italianate style. He ordered the workmen to use a combination of turtle oil and lime as mortar. This established a style for subsequent buildings in Bermuda.

Many architects have wanted to finish the **Unfinished Cathedral** in St. George's, reached by going up Blockade Alley. Construction was launched in 1874, but then a schism developed in the church and then there was no money to continue the project.

The **Old Rectory** in St. George's, now a private residence, was built by a former pirate in 1705. Located on Broad Alley, it is distinguished by its Dutch doors, chimneys, shutters, and what is called a "welcoming arms" staircase.

From an architectural point of view, one of the most intriguing structures in St. George's is **St. Peter's Church,** on Duke of York Street. This is the oldest Anglican Church in the Western Hemisphere, dating from 1620. It was constructed to replace an even older structure (from 1612) that had been poorly built from posts and palmetto leaves. A storm destroyed that church in 1712. The present St. Peter's was rebuilt and enlarged in 1713. In 1833, the galleries on each side of the church were added. The section around the triple-tier pulpit is believed to be the oldest part of the structure, dating from the 1600s. The first governor of the island, Richard Moore, ordered construction of the dark red Bermuda cedar altar in 1615. It is the oldest surviving piece of woodwork from the colonial period.

Also in St. George's, **Tucker House,** on Water Street, was built of native lime-stone. The house is furnished in an interesting manner, mostly with pieces from the mid-1700s and early 1800s.

Another notable architectural monument in Bermuda is **Verdmont,** situated on Verdmont Lane in Smith's Parish. Dating from around 1710, it was once owned by a wealthy shipowner. There have been many other owners during its long history, including an American Loyalist, John Green, who fled from Philadelphia to Bermuda at the end of the War of American Independence. Built to resemble an English manor house, Verdmont has a striking double roof and a quartet of large chimneys. Each room has its own fireplace. The style of the sash windows was once fashionable in certain English manor houses.

FOR THE LITERARY ENTHUSIAST

Bermuda has long been a haven for writers. It has figured in many works of literature, beginning with Shakespeare's play *The Tempest.* Shakespeare never visited the island himself but was inspired by accounts he had read or heard of it.

The Irish poet Thomas Moore (1779–1852), who visited Bermuda for several months in 1804, was moved by its beauty to write:

> *Oh! could you view the scenery dear*
> *That now beneath my window lies.*

Moore left more memories—literary and romantic—than any other writer who came to Bermuda. He once stayed at Hill Crest Guest House in St. George's (see Chapter 5, "Accommodations"). He soon became enamored of Nea Tucker, the adolescent bride of one of the most prominent men in town. "Sweet Nea! Let us roam no more," he once wrote of his beloved.

It is said that the lovesick poet would gaze for hours upon Nea's veranda, hoping that she'd appear. A jealous Mr. Tucker one day could tolerate this no more and banished the poet from his property. Moore was chased down a street that now bears the name Nea's Alley—to commemorate this unrequited romance.

One of the most popular restaurants in Bermuda is Tom Moore's Tavern (see Chapter 6, "Dining"). The building was once the home of Samuel Trott, who built it in the 17th century. Unlike the jealous Tucker, the descendants of Samuel Trott befriended Moore, who often visited the house. In his writing, Moore immortalized the calabash tree on the Trott estate; he liked to sit under this tree and write his verse.

Following in Moore's footsteps, many famous writers visited Bermuda in later years. There are no literary shrines, however, to any of them.

For Americans it was Mark Twain who helped make Bermuda a popular tourist destination. He published his impressions in the *Atlantic Monthly* in 1877–78 and in his first book, *The Innocents Abroad.* So enamored did he become of the island that, as he wrote many years later to a correspondent, he would fain choose it over heaven.

[Many Britons in Bermuda, to their dislike,] find that while the colony is supposedly and unquestionably British—nationally, legally, officially—it is in very many senses dominated by the United States, is utterly dependent on the United States and can well be regarded, and not by cynics alone, as the only British colony which is more like an American colony, run by Bermudians, on Britain's behalf, for America's ultimate benefit.

—Simon Winchester, *The Sun Never Sets: Travels to the Remaining Outposts of the British Empire* (1985)

After Twain, Eugene O'Neill came to Bermuda in 1924, and returned several more times, at least through 1927. While here, he worked on *The Great God Brown, Lazarus Laughed,* and *Strange Interlude.* O'Neill was convinced that cold weather adversely affected his ability to write. He also thought that Bermuda would "cure" him of alcoholism. His daughter, Oona, was born here (she later married Charlie Chaplin). At first, O'Neill and his family rented cottages on what is now Coral Beach Club property. Later, O'Neill bought the house "Spithead," in Warwick. In 1927, however, his marriage ended, and O'Neill left his family—and Bermuda.

During the 1930s, several eminent writers made their way to Bermuda, in hopes of finding idyllic surroundings and perhaps a little inspiration: Sinclair Lewis, who spent all his time cycling around "this gorgeous island"; Hervey Allen, who proved more prolific, writing *Anthony Adverse,* his prodigious best-selling novel, at Felicity Hall in Somerset; and James Ramsey Ullman, who wrote *The White Tower* on the island. James Thurber also made several trips during this time; on one trip he stayed long enough to finish *13 Clocks* at Lantana in Somerset.

In 1956 Noël Coward came with his longtime companion, Graham Payn, to escape "the monstrously unjust tax situation in England." He was not, he said, "really mad about the place," yet he purchased "Spithead" in Warwick (O'Neill's former home), and stayed some two years, working on *London Mornings,* his only ballet, and the musical *Sail Away.* The house is now privately owned.

Other well-known authors who visited Bermuda over the years include Rudyard Kipling, C. S. Forester, Hugh Walpole, Edna Ferber, Anita Loos, John O'Hara, E. B. White, and Philip Wylie.

Although perhaps not as internationally prominent, Bermuda's own writers include William S. Zuill, a former director of the Bermuda National Trust who wrote *The Story of Bermuda and Her People,* an excellent historical account, and Nellie Musson, Frank Manning, Eva Hodgson, and Dale Butler (the latter four have written of the lives of African-Bermudians).

14 Organized Tours

A major sightseeing attraction in Bermuda is to take one of the glass-bottom-boat **Reef Roamer Cruises.** The best of these is *Reefs and Wreck,* where passengers can observe the wreck of the HMS *Vixen,* reef fish, and coral formations. Two-hour tours leave daily at 10am and 1:30pm, and cost $30 for adults.

The **Bermuda Island Cruise** offers a chance to see Bermuda in a day. One of the cruise highlights is a stop at the historic Royal Naval Dockyard with time for shopping, sightseeing, and a visit to the Maritime Museum. A hot and cold buffet is served in St. George's, where participants can do more shopping and sightseeing. Cruises leave daily at 10am and return at 4pm.

In the evening, the **Pirate Party Night at Hawkins Island** includes a buffet dinner, music from the Island Fever Band, and a Hot Spice Limbo show, with gombey dancers and a complimentary bar. The cost is $65 per adult, half price for children 7–12, free for children 6 and under. Children under 18 must be accompanied by a parent. Departures are at 7pm on Tuesday, Wednesday, Friday, and Saturday, returning at 10:30pm.

The cruises are operated by **Bermuda Island Cruises, Ltd.,** P.O. Box 2249 in Hamilton (☎ **441/292-8652**); they can be booked over the phone or at various hotel tour desks.

BDA Water Tours Ltd., P.O. Box 1572, Hamilton (☎ **441/236-1500**), offers two- and three-hour trips, most of which include the sea gardens; passengers board glass-bottom boats to view the wonders of coral reefs and fish. Also available are a variety of water trips, ranging from two-hour sea-garden tours to snorkeling and dinner cruises. You can call 24 hours a day for information.

In order to study climate change and the "greenhouse effect," a U.S. nonprofit organization, the **Bermuda Biological Station for Research, Inc.,** has been given an annual grant of some $500,000 by the U.S. National Science Foundation to study the carbon cycle. The Bermuda Biological Station has collected the world's most comprehensive data on the oceanographic absorption of human-released carbon dioxide, since it has tracked carbon dioxide levels for more than 40 years over a 13-mile area southeast of Bermuda. The station has also has compiled an extensive record on acid rain in the North American atmosphere.

Vacationers to Bermuda can learn firsthand what these scientists are studying at the station by taking a free hour-long guided tour of the grounds and laboratory in St. George's. Guides explain what scientific studies are being conducted in Bermuda and how they relate to the overall world environment. They also discuss the island's natural areas, including the coral reefs, protected by strict conservation laws, and how humans have produced changes in the fragile ecological environment.

The special educational tours at 10am on Wednesday are conducted by trained volunteers and by scientists who are actually carrying out the study projects. Before 10am visitors should assemble in the Biological Station's main building. Coffee and snacks are served, for which a donation is requested.

For information on the tours, contact the Bermuda Biological Station for Research, Inc., 17 Biological Lane, Ferry Reach, St. George's (☎ **441/297-1880**).

8

Bermuda Strolls

You can cover much of Bermuda on foot, especially the harbor city of Hamilton and the historic town of St. George's. Indeed, if you had the time you could walk—or, if you prefer, cycle—through all of the parishes to see the major attractions of each. But most visitors would rather devote their vacation time to less taxing pursuits, such as lying insouciantly on the beach or playing a leisurely game of golf.

If, however, you are among the hardy few and do not mind a little physical exertion if the reward promises to exceed the effort, then you should certainly consider taking one or perhaps all three of the walking tours suggested below. For the best way to familiarize yourself with any new place—city, town, or village—is by strolling through it and experiencing its sights and sounds at close range.

WALKING TOUR 1
City of Hamilton

Start: The Visitors Service Bureau/Ferry Terminal.
Finish: Fort Hamilton.
Time: 2¹/₂ hours.
Best Time: Any sunny day.
Worst Time: When cruise ships are anchored in Hamilton Harbour.

Begin your tour along the harborfront at the:

1. **Visitors Service Bureau/Ferry Terminal.** (You might want to take an orientational ferry ride around the inner harbor; that way, you'll get an overview of Hamilton before concentrating on specific landmarks or monuments. Or you could take the ferry ride at the end of the tour.) Pick up some free maps and brochures of the island here.

   From the bureau, you will emerge onto Front Street, Hamilton's main street and principal shopping area. Before 1946, there were no automobiles here, but today its busy traffic includes small automobiles (driven only by Bermuda residents), buses, mopeds, and bicycles. You'll also see horse-drawn carriages, which are the most romantic (and the most expensive) way to see Hamilton.

   Observe the docks in back of the Ferry Terminal. Here is where you board ferries to the parishes of Warwick and Paget (for a description of their attractions, see Chapter 7, "What to See & Do"). You can also take a ferry across Great Sound, going to the West End (Somerset).

Walk directly south of the Ferry Terminal toward the water, taking a short side street between the Visitors Service Bureau and the large Bank of Bermuda. You'll come to:

2. **Albouy's Point,** a small grassy park with benches and trees that open onto a panoramic vista of the boat- or ship-filled harbor. Nearby is the Royal Bermuda Yacht Club, an elite rendezvous for both the Bermudian and American yachting set—including lots of the rich and famous—since the 1930s. To use the word *royal* in its name, special permission had to be given by Prince Albert, Queen Victoria's consort, in London. The club sponsors the widely televised Newport-Bermuda Yacht Race.

After taking in the view, walk directly north, crossing Point Pleasant Road, to the:

3. **Bank of Bermuda,** which can be visited Monday through Friday from 9:30am to 3pm. On its mezzanine you can see Bermuda's most extensive coin collection—at least one sample of every coin minted in the United Kingdom since the time of King James I (the early 17th century). Many Spanish coins used in colonial days are also displayed. You can also see the most famous Bermudian money—the first coins ever minted on the island—called "hog money." In use since the early 1600s, the hog coin is stamped on one side with the ill-fated *Sea Venture* and on the other side with a wild hog, the main source of food (excepting fish) for the early settlers. Look for an 1887 £5 piece depicting Queen Victoria; its issuance led to a protest throughout the British Empire, for critics claimed that the queen's small crown made her look foolish.

Upon leaving the bank, head east along Front Street to the point where it intersects with Queen Street. This is the site of the:

4. **"Birdcage,"** the most photographed sight in Bermuda. Here you'll sometimes find a policeman (or perhaps a policewoman) directing traffic. If the "bobbie" is a man, he's likely to be wearing regulation Bermuda shorts. The traffic box, which was named after its designer, Michael "Dickey" Bird, stands at Heyl's Corner, named for an American southerner, J. B. Heyl, who operated an apothecary shop nearby in the 1800s.

Continue north along Queen Street until you reach:

5. **Par-la-Ville Park,** which was once a private garden attached to the town house of William B. Perot, the first postmaster of Bermuda, who designed the gardens in the 19th century. He collected rare and exotic plants from all over the globe, including an Indian rubber tree which was seeded in 1847. Mark Twain wrote that he found the tree "disappointing" in that it didn't bear rubber overshoes and hot-water bottles.

Also opening onto Queen Street at the entrance to the park is the:

6. **Bermuda Historical Society Museum,** 13 Queen Street, which is also the Bermuda Library. It's filled with curiosities, including cedar furniture, collections of antique silver and china, hog money, Confederate money, a 1775 letter from George Washington, and other artifacts. The library has many rare books, including a 1624 edition of John Smith's *General Histoire of Virginia, New England and the Somers Isles.* If you'd like to rest and catch up on your reading, you'll also find a selection of current local as well as British newspapers and periodicals here.

Next door is the:

7. **Perot Post Office,** which was run by William Perot from 1818 to 1862. It is said that he'd go down to collect the mail from the clipper ships, but would put it under his top hat in order to maintain his dignity. As he proceeded through town, he'd greet his friends and acquaintances by tipping his hat, thereby delivering their mail at the same time. He started printing stamps in 1848. A Perot stamp is extremely valuable today since only 11 are still known to exist; several are owned by Queen Elizabeth II. The last time a Perot stamp came on the market, in 1986, it fetched $135,000.

   Continue to the top of Queen Street, then turn right onto Church Street to reach:

8. **Hamilton City Hall,** 17 Church Street, which dates from 1960 and is crowned by a white tower. The bronze weather vane on top is a replica of the *Sea Venture*. Portraits of the queen and paintings of former island leaders adorn the main lobby. The Bermuda Society of Arts holds frequent exhibitions at this hall. The Benbow collection of stamps is also on display here.

   ☕ TAKE A BREAK   The **Fourways Pastry Shop** at Washington Mall and Reid Street was recommended in Chapter 6, "Dining." Located on the ground floor of a shopping and office complex, it serves the most irresistible pastries in town. You can also order ice cream, tartlets, quiches, and croissant sandwiches, along with espresso and cappuccino.

   In back of Hamilton City Hall, opening onto Victoria Street, lies:

9. **Victoria Park,** a cool, refreshing oasis frequented by office workers on their lunch break. It features a sunken garden, ornamental shrubbery, and a Victorian bandstand. The 4-acre park was laid out in honor of Queen Victoria's Golden Jubilee in 1887. Outdoor concerts are held here in summer.

   Cedar Avenue is the eastern boundary of Victoria Park. If you follow it north for two blocks, you reach:

10. **St. Theresa's,** a Roman Catholic cathedral that is open daily from 8am to 7pm. Dating from 1927, its architecture was inspired by the Spanish Mission style. It is one of half a dozen Roman Catholic churches in Bermuda; its treasure is a gold and silver chalice—a gift from Pope Paul VI when he visited the island in 1986.

    After seeing the cathedral, retrace your steps south along Cedar Avenue until you reach Victoria Street. (Cedar Avenue now becomes Burnaby Street.) Continue south on this street until you come to Church Street and then turn left. A short walk along this street (on your left) will bring you to the:

11. **Bermuda Cathedral,** or the Cathedral of the Most Holy Trinity as it is sometimes called. This is the seat of the Anglican Church of Bermuda, and it towers over the city skyline. Its style is neo-gothic, characterized by stained-glass windows and soaring arches. The lectern and pulpit duplicate those of St. Giles in Edinburgh, Scotland.

    Leave the cathedral and continue east along Church Street to the:

12. **Sessions House (Parliament Building),** on Parliament Street, between Reid and Church Streets, which is open to the public Monday through Friday from 9am to 5pm. The Parliament of Bermuda is considered the third oldest in the world, after Iceland's and England's. You can see political action, Bermuda-style, from the Visitors' Gallery. The speaker is attired in full wig and flowing black robes.

    Continue to walk south along Parliament Street until you approach Front Street, where you should turn left toward the:

Walking Tour—City of Hamilton

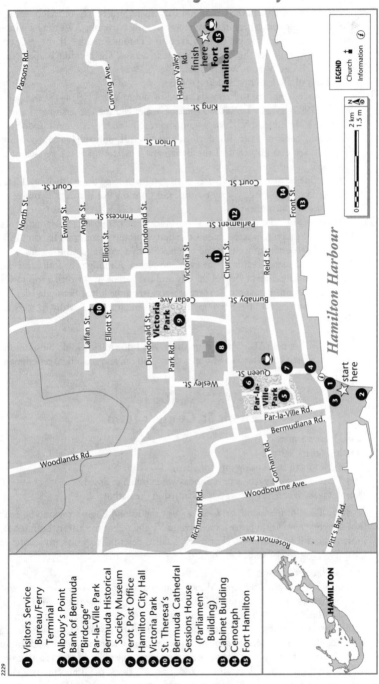

LEGEND
✝ Church
ⓘ Information

N

0   2 km
     1.5 m

Hamilton Harbour

1. Visitors Service Bureau/Ferry Terminal
2. Albouy's Point
3. Bank of Bermuda
4. "Birdcage"
5. Par-la-Ville Park
6. Bermuda Historical Society Museum
7. Perot Post Office
8. Hamilton City Hall
9. Victoria Park
10. St. Theresa's
11. Bermuda Cathedral
12. Sessions House (Parliament Building)
13. Cabinet Building
14. Cenotaph
15. Fort Hamilton

HAMILTON

2229

13. **Cabinet Building,** between Court and Parliament Streets. The official opening of Parliament takes place here in late October or early November. Wearing a plumed hat and full regalia, the governor makes his "Throne Speech." If you visit on a Wednesday, you'll see the Bermuda Senate in action. The building is open Monday through Friday from 9am to 5pm.

In front of the Cabinet Building is the:

14. **Cenotaph,** a memorial to Bermuda's dead in World War I (1914–18) and World War II (1939–45). In 1920 the Prince of Wales laid the cornerstone. (Later, in 1936, as King Edward VIII, he would abdicate to marry an American divorcée, Wallis Simpson, and later still, during World War II, now the Duke of Windsor, he would serve as governor of the Bahamas.) The landmark is a replica of the Cenotaph in London.

Continue east along Front Street until you reach King Street, then head north until you come to Happy Valley Road. Go right on this road until you see the entrance (on your right) to:

15. **Fort Hamilton,** an imposing old fortress on the eastern outskirts of Hamilton. The Duke of Wellington ordered its construction to protect Hamilton Harbour. Filled with underground passageways and complete with a moat and 18-ton guns, it was considered outdated before it was even completed. Although the fort never fired a shot, it permits a great view of the city and the harbor (it is worth a trip just for the view). In summer, try to be there at noon when the kilted Bermuda Isles Pipe Band performs a skirling ceremony on the green, accompanied by dancers and drummers.

TAKE A BREAK After your stroll, wind down with some old-fashioned tea at the **Fort Hamilton Tea Shoppe,** where you can also order light refreshments.

WALKING TOUR 2
Historic St. George's Town

Start: King's Square.
Finish: Somers Wharf.
Time: 2 hours (not counting interior visits).
Best Time: Any sunny day except Sunday when much is closed.
Worst Time: When a cruise ship is anchored in the harbor.

At the east end of the island, St. George's was the second English town to be established in the New World (after Jamestown in Virginia). For the history buff, it holds more interest than Hamilton. (For more detailed descriptions of its attractions, see Chapter 7, "What to See & Do.")

We'll begin the tour at:

1. **King's Square,** also known as Market Square and King's Parade, the very center of St. George's. Only about 200 years old, it's not as historic as St. George's itself. This was formerly a marshy part of the harbor—at least when the shipwrecked passengers and crew of *Sea Venture* first saw it. At the water's edge stands the Visitors Service Bureau, where you may want to pick up additional information. Displayed on the square is a replica of the pillory and stocks that were formerly used to punish criminals, and, in many cases, the innocent. You could be severely punished here for such alleged "crimes" as casting a spell over your neighbor's turkeys. Head south across the small bridge to:

Walking Tour—Historic St. George's Town

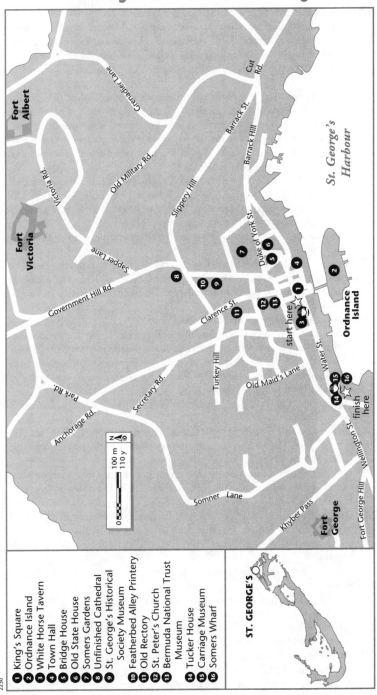

1. King's Square
2. Ordnance Island
3. White Horse Tavern
4. Town Hall
5. Bridge House
6. Old State House
7. Somers Gardens
8. Unfinished Cathedral
9. St. George's Historical Society Museum
10. Featherbed Alley Printery
11. Old Rectory
12. St. Peter's Church
13. Bermuda National Trust Museum
14. Tucker House
15. Carriage Museum
16. Somers Wharf

ST. GEORGE'S

2. **Ordnance Island,** jutting into St. George's Harbour. The British army once stored gunpowder and cannons here, but today the island houses *Deliverance,* a replica of the vessel that carried the shipwrecked *Sea Venture* passengers on to Virginia. Alongside the vessel is a ducking stool, a contraption used in 17th-century witch trials. Retrace your steps across the bridge to King's Square. On the waterside stands the:

3. **White Horse Tavern,** a restaurant jutting out into St. George's Harbour. (For more details, see Chapter 6, "Dining.") Consider the tavern as a possible spot for lunch later. It was once the home of John Davenport, who came to Bermuda in 1815 to open a dry goods store. Davenport was considered a bit of a miser, and upon his death some £75,000 in gold and silver was discovered stashed away in his cellar. Across the square stands the:

4. **Town Hall,** near the Visitors Service Bureau. This is the meeting place of the Corporation governing St. George's. It has antique cedar furnishings and a collection of photographs of previous Lord Mayors. *Bermuda Journey,* a multimedia audiovisual presentation, is shown here several times a day.

   From King's Square, head east along King Street, cutting north on Bridge Street. There you'll come to the:

5. **Bridge House,** 1 Bridge Street. Constructed shortly after 1700, this was once the home of several governors of Bermuda. Furnished with 18th- and 19th-century antiques, it is now home to an art gallery and souvenir shop. Return to King Street and continue east to:

6. **Old State House,** which actually opens onto Princess Street, at the top of King Street. This is the oldest stone building in Bermuda, dating from 1620, and was once the home of the Bermuda Parliament. It is the site of the ancient Peppercorn Ceremony, in which the Old State House pays the government "rent" of one peppercorn annually. (See Chapter 7, "What to See & Do," for details on this grand ceremony filled with pageantry.)

   Continue your stroll down Princess Street until you come to the Duke of York Street, the entrance to:

7. **Somers Gardens.** The heart of Sir George Somers, the admiral of the *Sea Venture,* is buried here. The gardens, featuring palms and other tropical plants, were opened in 1920 by the Prince of Wales.

   Walk through Somers Gardens and up the steps to the North Gate onto Blockade Alley. If you look up the hill, you'll see what is known as "the folly of St. George's"—the:

8. **Unfinished Cathedral,** which was intended to replace St. Peter's (see below). Work began on the church in 1874, but eventually came to an end; the church was beset by financial difficulties and a schism in the Anglican congregation.

   After viewing the ruins, turn left onto the Duke of Kent Street, leading down to the:

9. **St. George's Historical Society Museum,** at the corner of Featherbed Alley and the Duke of Kent Street. An example of 18th-century architecture, the house has a collection of Bermudian historical artifacts and cedar furniture. Around the corner on Featherbed Alley is the:

10. **Featherbed Alley Printery,** which has a working replica of the type of printing press invented by Johannes Gutenberg in Germany in the 1450s. Go up Featherbed Alley and straight onto Church Street. At the junction with Broad Lane, look to your right to see the:

11. **Old Rectory,** at the head of Broad Alley, behind St. Peter's Church. Now a private home, but administered by the National Trust, it was built in 1705 by a reformed pirate. If you'd like to go inside, it is open only on Wednesday and Friday from 10am to 4pm.

   After seeing the Old Rectory, you can go through the back of the churchyard entrance, opposite Broad Alley, to reach:

12. **St. Peter's Church.** The church's main entrance is on Duke of York Street. This is believed to be the oldest Anglican place of worship in the Western Hemisphere. In the churchyard you'll see many headstones, some dating back three centuries. The assassinated governor, Sir Richard Sharples, was buried here. The present church was built in 1713, with a tower added in 1814. Across the street is the:

13. **Bermuda National Trust Museum.** When it was the Globe Hotel, this was the headquarters of Major Norman Walker, the Confederate representative in Bermuda. It was once a hotbed of blockade-running.

   As you continue west along Duke of York Street, you will reach Barber's Lane, which honors Joseph Hayne Rainey. A former slave from South Carolina, Rainey and his French wife fled to Bermuda at the outbreak of the Civil War. He became a barber in St. George's but eventually returned to South Carolina, where in 1870 he was elected to the U.S. House of Representatives—the first African American to serve in Congress.

   Nearby is Petticoat Lane, also known as Silk Alley. The name dates from the 1834 emancipation, when two former slave women who'd always wanted silk petticoats like their former mistresses, finally got some and then paraded up and down the lane to show off their new finery.

   Continue west until you reach:

14. **Tucker House,** which opens onto Water Street. This was the former home of a prominent Bermudian family, whose members have included an island governor, a treasurer of the United States, and a captain in the Confederate Navy. The building houses an excellent collection of antiques, including silver, portraits, and cedar furniture. One room is devoted to memorabilia of Joseph Hayne Rainey. Diagonally across from the Tucker House is the:

15. **Carriage Museum,** 22 Water Street. Housed here are some of the more interesting carriages used in Bermuda until 1946, when the automobile arrived. In the same building as the Carriage Museum, is:

   ☕ **TAKE A BREAK**   **Carriage House**, 22 Water St., Somers Wharf (☎ 441/297-1730), a former waterfront storehouse. It is an excellent place for lunch in St. George's. You can sample sandwich platters along with the famous Bermuda fish chowder. Soups and salads are also available, as are juicy burgers.

16. **Somers Wharf,** a multimillion-dollar waterfront restoration project, that now includes shops, restaurants, and taverns.

WALKING TOUR 3
Sandys Parish

Start: Somerset Bridge.
Finish: Somerset Long Bay Park.
Time: 7 hours.
Best Time: Any sunny day.
Worst Time: When the weather's bad.

The Bermuda Railway Trail

One of the most unusual sightseeing adventures in Bermuda is following the Bermuda Railway Trail (or parts thereof), which stretches for 21 miles along the old railroad right-of-way across three of the interconnected islands that make up Bermuda. Opened in 1931, the Bermuda Railway ceased operations in 1948. Once the island's main source of transportation, the train gave way to the automobile.

Before setting out on this trek, arm yourself with a copy of *the Bermuda Railway Trail Guide*, obtainable at the Bermuda Department of Tourism in Hamilton or at the Visitors Service Bureau in Hamilton or St. George's. You're now ready to hit the trail of the old train system that was affectionately called "Rattle and Shake." Constructing this rail line may have been one of the most costly ever on a per-mile basis. There are many ways to explore the trail: horseback, bicycle, moped, or the ever-trusty feet.

Although the line covered 21 miles stretching between St. George's in the east and Somerset in the west, a 3-mile stretch has been lost to roads in and around the capital city of Hamilton. For the most part, however, the trail winds along an automobile-free route, permitting some views of Bermuda not seen by the general public since the end of World War II.

In the West End of Bermuda, the trail begins near the Watford Bridge, but there are many convenient points of access. In the East End, it is most convenient to pick up the trail on North Shore Road.

Along the way, you'll see something of the 5-acre Gilbert Nature Reserve (described on p.148). You'll also see some of the rare Bermuda cedar, which nearly vanished as a result of the blight that struck the island in the early 1940s. Along the trail, too, is much greenery and semitropical vegetation, such as the poinsettia, oleander, and hibiscus. You can also see and visit Fort Scaur, the 1870s fortress in Sandys Parish.

Sandys (pronounced as if there were no "y"), the far western parish of Bermuda, consists of Somerset Island (the largest and southernmost), Watford, Boaz, and Ireland Islands. When Bermudians cross into Somerset via Somerset Bridge, they say they are "up the country."

The area is characterized by craggy coastlines, beaches, nature reserves, fisher's coves, old fortifications, winding lanes, and sleepy villages. All the major attractions lie along the main road from Somerset Bridge to the Royal Naval Dockyard, which is at the end of Ireland Island.

Although we are classifying this as a walking tour, you may want to rent a bicycle or moped to help you cover the longer stretches.

From the center of Hamilton, you can take a ferry to Somerset. Check the schedule: Some boats take 30 minutes to get there, whereas others take up to an hour. The longer trip will give you a more leisurely opportunity to enjoy the waters of Bermuda's Great Sound. You can bring your cycle or moped aboard the ferry. You can also see the West End by public bus (for details, see Chapter 7, "What to See & Do").

To begin the tour, take the ferry from Hamilton to:

1. **Somerset Bridge,** which links Somerset Island with the rest of Bermuda. It was among the first three bridges to be constructed in Bermuda in the 1600s, and is said to be the smallest drawbridge in the world—its opening is just wide enough

Walking Tour—Sandys Parish

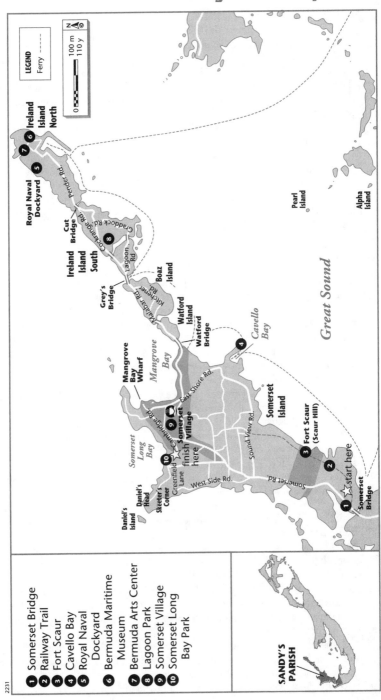

LEGEND
Ferry - - - - -

100 m
110 y
0

Ireland Island North

Royal Naval Dockyard

Ireland Island South

Cut Bridge

Grey's Bridge

Pender Rd.

Craddock Rd.

Cockburn Rd.

Lagoon Rd.

Malabar Rd.

Kitchener Rd.

Boaz Island

Watford Island

Watford Bridge

Cavello Bay

Great Sound

Pearl Island

Alpha Island

Mangrove Bay Wharf

Mangrove Bay

Somerset Long Bay

Daniel's Island

Daniel's Head

Skeeter's Corner

East Shore Rd.

Cambridge Rd.

Somerset Village

Greenfield Lane

West Side Rd.

Somerset Island

Sound View Rd.

Fort Scaur (Scaur Hill)

Somerset Rd.

Somerset Bridge

start here

finish here

1. Somerset Bridge
2. Railway Trail
3. Fort Scaur
4. Cavello Bay
5. Royal Naval Dockyard
6. Bermuda Maritime Museum
7. Bermuda Arts Center
8. Lagoon Park
9. Somerset Village
10. Somerset Long Bay Park

SANDY'S PARISH

163

2231

to accommodate a sailboat mast. Near the bridge you can take a look at the old Somerset Post Office and see an 18th-century cottage known as Crossways.

After viewing this, walk up Somerset Road about 75 yards to the entrance to the:

2. **Railway Trail,** which is restricted to pedestrians, cyclists, and bikers. This trail follows the path of old "Rattle and Shake," the Bermuda Railway line that once ran the entire length of the island. Since you may not walk the whole railway trail (although some hearty visitors do just that), it might interest you to know that this particular section of the trail—between Somerset Bridge and Sound View Road—is considered one of the most attractive on the island. Parts of the trail open onto the coast, affording panoramic vistas of the Great Sound.

The trail goes across the parkland of Fort Scaur, with its large moat. If you're there around noontime, you might want to consider this as a picnic spot. If you can spend all day in Somerset (highly recommended), you might also want to take time out for a swim before returning to your walking or cycling. Others prefer to have lunch at Lantana, one of the most exclusive cottage colonies on Bermuda (see Chapter 5, "Accommodations").

Follow the signposts to:

3. **Fort Scaur,** which covers 22 acres and opens onto Somerset Road. In the 1870s, the British feared an attack from the United States, and so they built this fort on the highest hill in Somerset to protect Her Majesty's Royal Naval Dockyard. A huge dry moat was cut right across Somerset Island. Visitors can wander at leisure around this fort, which proved unnecessary, since the feared U.S. invasion never materialized. If you stand on the ramparts, you'll be rewarded with a marvelous view of Great Sound. Through a free telescope, you can see such distant sights as St. David's Lighthouse and Fort St. Catherine in the East End of Bermuda. If you take the eastern moat all the way down to the Great Sound shore, you'll find ideal places for either swimming or fishing.

After exploring the fort grounds, resume your walk along the railway track and continue north for more than a mile until you come to Sound View Road. Turn right and stroll along this sleepy residential street, which has some of the finest cottages in Bermuda. Continue around a wide arc, passing Tranquility Hill and Gwelly and Saltsea Lanes. When you come to Scott's Hill Road, take a right and go about 85 yards to East Shore Road.

At the first junction, take a little road—Cavello Lane—that branches off to the right; it will take you to:

4. **Cavello Bay,** a sheltered cove and a stopping point for the ferry from Hamilton. Wait for the next ferry and take it (with your cycle or moped) either to Watford Bridge or directly to:

5. **Royal Naval Dockyard.** You could spend an entire afternoon here since there is so much to see. On Ireland Island, the dockyard is a sprawling complex that covers 6 acres. The major attraction here is the:

6. **Bermuda Maritime Museum,** which was opened by Queen Elizabeth II in 1975. Visitors can cross a moat in order to explore the keep and the 30-foot-high defensive ramparts. There is an exhibit of Bermuda's old boats, documenting the island's rich maritime history.

Across the street from the Maritime Museum is the Old Cooperage Building, site of the Neptune Cinema. Adjacent to the cinema is the Craft Market, where interesting items are on sale. Next door, call at the:

7. **Bermuda Arts Center,** which was opened in 1984 by Princess Margaret. Showcasing the visual arts and crafts of the island, this nonprofit organization is staffed by volunteers.

From the dockyard, it's a long walk to Somerset Village, yet many people who have walked or cycled the distance feel that this was one of the highlights of their Bermuda trip. Some of the best beaches are found here, so if you get tired along the way, take time out for a refreshing dip in the ocean.

Leave by the dockyard's south entrance, walking down Pender Road about half a mile. Cross Cockburn's Cut Bridge, heading for Ireland Island South. Go straight along Cockrange Road, which will take you to:

8. Lagoon Park. Enter the park as you cross over the Cut Bridge onto Ireland Island South. The park, which is crisscrossed by walking trails, has a lagoon populated with ducks and other wildfowl. There are places for picnicking in this park, which is free and open to the public.

To continue, cross Grey's Bridge to Boaz Island, and walk or cycle along Malabar Road. On your right you'll see the calm waters of Mangrove Bay. You'll eventually arrive at:

9. Somerset Village, one of the most charming in Bermuda. One road goes through the village. Although you could do some shopping here, most of the stores are just branches of larger stores in Hamilton.

TAKE A BREAK Somerset Country Squire Tavern (for details, see Chapter 6, "Dining"). At this English-style pub, you can order sandwiches or burgers, as well as such pub grub as steak-and-kidney pie or "bangers and mash" (sausages and mashed potatoes). The kitchen is also noted for its desserts.

Follow Cambridge Road west to:

10. Somerset Long Bay Park, which is always open. Families like this park because of its nice beach and shallow waters opening onto Long Bay. You can also picnic in the parkland. The nature reserve here is operated by the Bermuda Audubon Society, and the pond attracts migrating birds in both spring and autumn, including the Louisiana heron, the snowy egret, and the purple gallinule.

9

Beaches, Water Sports, Golf & Other Outdoor Activities

Although people visit Bermuda mainly for its beaches (see below), it also offers a large variety of outdoor sports: In fact, its sports facilities are better than those found on most of the Caribbean or Bahamian islands. The most popular sports in Bermuda are tennis and golf, but sailing ranks high as well. You'll find a fair number of tennis courts and professionally designed golf courses around the island where you may practice your swing, often with players of better than average ability. But if you hesitate to pick up a racket or golf club because your game has been somewhat neglected of late, fear not: Your Bermudian partner, on the court or on the links, would deem it quite improper to remark that your game was anything but superb; and if a word of friendly criticism is ever offered, be assured that it will be as gentle as the ocean breezes that sweep over the island.

1 Beaches

Bermuda is one of the world's leading beach resorts, its miles of pink-sand shoreline broken now and then by cliffs to form sheltered coves. Many stretches have shallow water for some distance out and sandy bottoms, making them safe for children and nonswimmers. Hotels and private clubs often have their own private beaches, but there is no shortage of public facilities in Bermuda, which are supervised by the Parks Division of the Department for Agriculture and Fisheries.

At most of the public beaches you'll find public restrooms and usually a place nearby for drinks or snacks. Although you will find dozens of appropriate spots for sunbathing, swimming, and beach-combing, here is a listing of the island's most famous, arranged clockwise beginning with the south shore beaches closest to the city of Hamilton.

Elbow Beach One of the consistently popular beaches in Bermuda, Paget Parish's Elbow Beach incorporates almost a mile of (occasionally interrupted) pale pink sand and the swimming facilities of at least three hotels into its perimeter. A $3.50 fee is charged for visitors who are not staying at one of these hotels. Because of the protective coral reefs that surround it, Elbow Beach is one of the safest on the island; it is the beach of choice among foreign college students who vacation on Bermuda during Easter break. The Elbow Beach Hotel/A Wyndham Resort (☎ **441/236-3535**) offers umbrellas and beach chairs for rent; toilet facilities are available. Adjacent to the paid facilities is the free public beach. Take bus no. 7 or 8 from Hamilton.

Astwood Cove   Situated within Warwick Parish, at the bottom of a steep and winding road that intersects with South Shore Road, this beach has no problem with overcrowding during most of the year because of its remote location. Astwood Park provides a lovely green backdrop to the beach itself. Take bus no. 7 or 8 from Southampton.

Warwick Long Bay   Very different from the sheltered coves of nearby Chaplin and Horseshoe Bays (see below), this popular beach features a half-mile stretch of sand, one of the longest on the island. Against a backdrop of scrubland and low grasses, the beach lies on the southern side of South Shore Park, in Warwick Parish. Despite the frequent winds, the waves are surprisingly small because of an offshore reef. Jutting above the water less than 200 feet offshore is a jagged coral island which, because of its contoured shape, appears to be floating above the water's foam. There are restrooms at the beach's western end.

Chaplin Bay   Straddling the boundary between Warwick and Southampton Parishes, this small but secluded beach disappears almost completely during storms or exceptionally high tides. Geologists tend to admire the open-air coral barrier that partially separates one half of the beach from the other. Chaplin Bay, like its more westerly (and more famous) neighbor, Horseshoe Bay (see below), lies at the southern extremity of South Shore Park. Take bus no. 7 or 8 from Hamilton.

Horseshoe Bay Beach   Bermuda's most famous beach is at Horseshoe Bay, South Shore Road, Southampton Parish, where the Beach House (☎ **441/238-2651**) provides lockers, changing rooms, toilets, and showers, as well as food, drinks, and rental equipment for the beach or surf. You can also buy suntan lotion and other sundries you may need. Take bus no. 7 or 8 from Hamilton.

Church Bay   Although this beach lies along Bermuda's southwestern edge, at the point in Southampton Parish where the island hooks off to the northeast (and where the waves pound the shore mercilessly), it is sheltered by rows of offshore reefs. Marine life abounds within the relatively calm waters, much to the delight of snorkelers and swimmers. And if you're just planning to lounge in the sun, the beach offers unusually deep pink sands. Take bus no. 7 or 8 from Hamilton.

Somerset Long Bay   Whenever offshore storms trouble the waters northwest of Bermuda, the water here is considered unsafe for swimming. Because its bottom isn't always sandy or of a consistent depth, many people feel this beach is better suited to beachwalking than actual swimming. Nevertheless, it appeals to those who are looking for seclusion. The undeveloped parkland of Sandys Parish shelters it from the rest of the island, and the beach's crescent shape and length—about a quarter of a mile— make it unusual by Bermudian standards. You'll find restrooms, changing facilities, and panoramic sunsets. You can either take bus no. 7 or 8 from Hamilton or approach it via Cambridge Road in Sandys Parish.

Shelly Bay Beach   Situated on the north shore of Hamilton Parish within a cove whose encircling peninsula partially shelters it from mid-Atlantic waves, this public beach offers abundant pink sand, changing rooms, a shop where you can buy

The Best Public Beaches

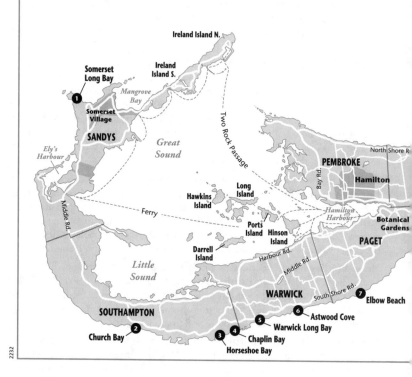

Atlantic Ocean

Ireland Island N.

Somerset Long Bay

Ireland Island S.

Mangrove Bay

Somerset Village

SANDYS

Ely's Harbour

Great Sound

Two Rock Passage

North Shore R.

PEMBROKE

Bay Rd.

Hamilton

Long Island

Hawkins Island

Ferry

Ports Island

Hinson Island

Hamilton Harbour

Botanical Gardens

PAGET

Darrell Island

Harbour Rd.

Middle Rd.

Little Sound

Middle Rd.

WARWICK

South Shore Rd.

Elbow Beach

SOUTHAMPTON

Astwood Cove

Warwick Long Bay

Church Bay

Chaplin Bay

Horseshoe Bay

2232

souvenirs and film, a snack bar, and facilities where you can rent lounge chairs, beach towels, and snorkeling equipment.

Tobacco Bay Beach   This is the most popular beach on St. George's Island, especially among those who come for the day to visit the historic town of St. George's. With its broad open sands, this beach looks more like those on the southern shore than those on the north side. Its pale pink sand is sheltered within a coral-sided cove just a short walk west of Fort St. Catherine and St. Catherine Beach (see below). Look for the area's Beach House, Naval Tanks Hill, St. George's (☎ **441/293-9711**), which offers equipment rentals, toilets, changing rooms, showers, and a snack bar. Take bus no. 10 or 11 from Hamilton.

John Smith's Bay   This is the only public beach in Smith's Parish, and as such, tends to be popular with residents of Bermuda's eastern end. Long, flat, and richly scattered with pale pink sand, this beach usually has a lifeguard during warm weather. There are toilet and changing facilities on site. Take bus no. 1 from Hamilton.

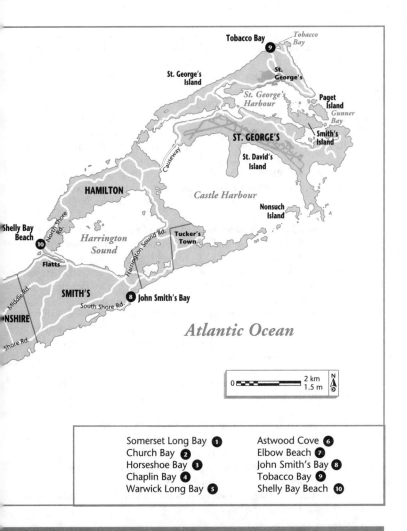

Somerset Long Bay ❶	Astwood Cove ❻
Church Bay ❷	Elbow Beach ❼
Horseshoe Bay ❸	John Smith's Bay ❽
Chaplin Bay ❹	Tobacco Bay ❾
Warwick Long Bay ❺	Shelly Bay Beach ❿

2 Snorkeling & Diving

SNORKELING

Marine biologists have always claimed that far more lies below the surface of the sea than what usually appears above it. If you're a snorkeling enthusiast, a handful of Bermuda-based companies are ready, willing, and able to help you, or else you can be adventurous and do it on your own.

The best places to go snorkeling are at any of the public beaches (see "Beaches," above). Many hotels that are right on the beach will either lend or rent you fins, masks, and snorkels, as well as advise you of the best sites in your area, so you don't have to travel far.

Die-hard snorkelers—some of whom visit Bermuda every year—as well as many snorkeling Bermudians, prefer Church Bay to all other spots for snorkeling. Church Bay lies on the south shore, west of the Southampton Princess Golf Course and Gibbs Hill Lighthouse. This little cove, which seems to be waiting for a movie camera, is carved out of coral cliffs. Well protected and filled with snug little nooks in the coral, another advantage is that the reefs are fairly close to land. However, the seas can be rough (as is true anywhere in Bermuda), so caution is always advised.

At the eastern end of the south shore, John Smith's Bay, situated to the east of Spittal Pond Nature Reserve and Watch Hill Park, is another preferred spot, especially if your hotel is in the east. Even more convenient, especially for snorkelers staying at St. George's or at a hotel near the airport, is Tobacco Bay, directly north of St. George's Golf Course. Another good spot for snorkelers is West Whale Bay, although it is small. This bay lies along the south shore at the west end of Southampton. It is west of the Port Royal Golf Course. Yet another area preferred by many snorkelers is along the north shore of Devonshire, north of the Ocean View Golf Course.

Bermuda is known for the gin-clear purity of some of its waters, as well as for its vast array of coral reefs. Both inshore and offshore wrecks can be discovered, and this adds to the thrill of snorkeling.

If you don't like cold water, the best snorkeling is from May through October, although snorkeling is a year-round pursuit. Wet suits are often worn in winter when the water temperature is in the 60s.

The waters of the Atlantic can be rough at any time of the year, especially in winter. Therefore, winter snorkelers should head for the more sheltered waters of Castle Harbour and Harrington Sound, both large bodies of water in the East End. The rewards for the snorkeler here are the bizarre coral formations, the underwater caves, the grottoes, and especially the schools of brilliantly-hued fish.

If you don't go on a snorkeling cruise, it's better to rent a small boat (see "Sailing," below), some of which have glass bottoms. Rentals are for variable periods of time.

Some of the best snorkeling sites are only accessible from a boat; others can be reached by swimming, but it would be a long swim. Of course, if you rent a boat, the rental company will give you advice. Because of the many reefs around Bermuda, there are countless wrecked boats. If you're not familiar with Bermuda's waters, you should stay in the sounds, harbors, and bays, especially in Castle Harbour and Harrington Sound. If you want to make a trip to the reefs, it's better to take one of the recommended snorkeling cruises.

Bermuda Water Sports

At the Grotto Bay Beach Hotel, Hamilton Parish. ☎ **441/293-2640.** May–Nov booking hours daily 9am–1pm and 6–9pm. Bus: 1, 3, 10, or 11.

This group offers a glass-bottom snorkel cruise aboard a 60-foot motorized catamaran. Priced at around $37 for a $3^1/_2$-hour cruise, the cost includes free use of snorkeling equipment and the expertise of a crew well-versed in the marine life of Bermuda's offshore reefs. The special design of this boat allows it to anchor in very shallow waters, which is ideal for the novice or nonswimmer. There's a cash bar and a freshwater shower on board, as well as recorded music, which makes the experience something like a private party.

Bermuda Water Tours

P.O. Box HM 1572, Hamilton Parish HMGX. ☎ **441/236-1500.** Booking hours 24 hour a day. Bus: 1, 2, 10, or 11.

This group offers snorkeling tours twice daily between April 1 and mid-November (weather permitting) from the docks near Hamilton Harbour's Ferryboat Terminal.

The large glass-bottom boats are well equipped with a cash bar, showers, and an ample assortment of free snorkeling equipment. On the return trip, complimentary rum swizzles and soft drinks are served. A $3^1/_2$-hour tour costs $39. A dinner cruise with open bar is $59 daily from 6:30 to 9:30pm.

Salt Kettle Yacht Charters

Salt Kettle, Paget Parish. ☎ **441/236-4863.** May 15–Oct 15 Mon–Fri 9:30am and 1:30pm and Sat 9:30am only. Call 9am–5pm Mon–Sat. Ferryboat from Hamilton every 30 minutes.

Salt Kettle offers snorkeling cruises on a 35-foot cruiser (without a glass bottom) daily Monday through Saturday. The $40, four-hour trip includes free use of snorkeling equipment. The boat stops above offshore reefs teeming with marine life, as well as at the sites of two underwater shipwrecks whose rusted hulks remind one of the many maritime disasters that influenced the early history of Bermuda. Rum swizzles and soft drinks are included in the price.

DIVING

Bermuda's waters are considered to be the clearest in the western Atlantic; this plus the reefs, wrecked ships, variety of marine life and coral formations, and underwater grottoes make Bermuda ideal for scuba diving. Diving here is not as dramatic as in the Cayman Islands, but it may be more suitable for novices who can learn the fundamentals and go diving in about 20 to 25 feet of water on the same day as their first lesson.

Although scuba fanatics dive all year, the best diving months are May through October. The sea is the most tranquil at that time and the water temperature is moderate (it averages 62° Fahrenheit in the spring and fall and 83° Fahrenheit in summer).

Weather permitting, scuba schools function daily, and all dives are overseen by fully licensed scuba instructors. Most dives are conducted from a 40-foot dive boat, and a wide range of dive sites are covered. Night dives and certifications are offered as well.

Helmet Diving

Helmet diving enjoys great popularity in Bermuda. Underwater walkers, clad in helmets that are fed air through hoses connected to the surface, stroll along the sandy bottom in water to depths of 10 to 12 feet. It's even possible to walk underwater with contact lenses. These walks are considered safe for anyone from 5 to 85 years of age, even nonswimmers. These undersea walks are conducted among the coral reefs. Participants can feed dozens of rainbow-hued fish, which take food right from your hands. You will also be able to see sponges breathing and coral feeding.

The original undersea walk offered by Bronson Hartley can be arranged by writing or calling Mr. Hartley at 5 North Shore Rd., P.O. Box FL 281, Flatts FL BX, Bermuda (☎ **441/292-4434**). Anybody can take part in this adventure, which was featured twice in *Life* magazine. It's as simple as walking through a garden, and you won't even get your hair wet. A helmet is placed on your shoulders as you climb down the ladder of the boat to begin your guided walk. The skipper and host, Mr. Hartley, personally conducts the tours. His ability to train fish in their natural habitat has been acclaimed in many publications. His 50-foot boat, *Carioca*, leaves Flatts Village daily at 10am and 2pm. The underwater wonderland walk costs $45 per adult or $30 for children under 12. Bus no. 10 or 11.

In general, Bermuda reefs are still healthy despite the talk about dwindling fish and dying coral formations. Sometimes, in addition to the rainbow-hued schools of fish, you'll find yourself swimming with a barracuda.

All dive shops display a map of wreck sites that can be seen, nearly 40 in all, the oldest of which dates back to the 17th century. Although it is believed there may be a total of some 300 wreck sites, those that are mapped are the best known and in the best condition. Dive depths to these sites vary between 25 and 85 feet. Inexperienced scuba divers may want to stick to the wreck sites off the western part of Bermuda, since these tend to be in shallower water—perhaps no more than about 32 feet. Snorkelers sometimes frequent these shallow wreck sites as well.

As mentioned, many of the hotels have their own water sports equipment. If not, there are several independent establishments that rent equipment.

Note: Spearfishing is not allowed within 1 mile of any shore, and spearguns are not permitted in Bermuda.

Blue Water Divers Co. Ltd.

Robinson's Marina, Southampton. ☎ **441/234-1034.** Daily 8am–6pm. Bus: 6 or 7.

Bermuda's oldest and largest full-service scuba-diving operation offers introductory lessons and dives at $85 for a half-day. Daily one- and two-tank dive trips cost $65 and $80, respectively, with a $15 reduction if you have equipment. Snorkeling trips are $34 per half day. Full certification courses are available through PADI, NAUI, and SSI. All equipment is provided. Reservations are necessary.

Fantasea Diving

Darrell's Wharf, Harbour Road, in Paget Parish (☎ **441/236-6339**), is a year-round operation, except for two weeks in February or March when the weather's rough. It arranges daily dives at 8am and again at 1pm. Its Discover Scuba course costs $85 for 3¹/₂ hours, and cameras are available to rent. Its popular reef and wreck dive at various depths costs $45 for three hours. A two-tank dive may appeal to experienced divers who want to see wrecks and reefs; it lasts 4¹/₂ hours and costs $65. Finally, a night dive for experienced divers only is a special feature at $55. Snorkeling trips can also be arranged.

Nautilus Diving Ltd.

At both the Southampton and Hamilton Princess Hotels (☎ **441/238-2332** or **441/295-9485**), is one of the leading dive operators on the island. It functions year-round from 8am to 5:30pm, offering a "Discover Scuba" resort course that's quite popular. It costs $95 for three hours, and all dives are from a 40-foot boat. Its one-tank dive for $50 goes to reef or wreck dives, and a two-tank dive, including a view of a shipwreck and the exploration of a reef in 25 to 30 feet of water, costs $70. This is a PADI, five-star center.

South Side Scuba Water Sports

At Sonesta Beach Resort, South Shore Road, Southampton, and Grotto Beach Hotel, 11 Blue Hill Rd., Hamilton Parish (☎ **441/293-2915** for information about both locations). Call the day before, 7:30am–5:30pm. Bus: 7 to Sonesta; 1, 3, 10, or 11 to Grotto Bay.

South Side Scuba is known for its daily two-tank wreck and reef dives, costing $75. A Resort Course lesson plus dive is $95. A single-tank dive goes for $45, and you can snorkel off the boat for $20. Deduct $10 if you have your own diving gear, except for Resort Courses; otherwise, the rates include all equipment. The company has two fully equipped, custom-built fiberglass dive boats with the latest approved safety gear.

3 Other Water Sports

PARASAILING

Marriott's Castle Harbour Resort

Paynters Road, Hamilton Parish. ☎ **441/293-2543.** Daily 8am–5pm (July–Sept until 7pm).
Bus: 2 from St. George's.

Parasailing here is from a Nordic Ascender, and up to six persons are taken out in a boat at a time. Single parachute rides cost $50 per person. If space is available, you can go along for just the boat ride for $15.

SAILING

Bermuda is one of the world's sailing capitals. Sail-yourself boats are available on a 2-hour, half-day (4-hour), or full-day (8-hour) basis.

Mangrove Marina Ltd.

End of Cambridge Road, Mangrove Bay, Somerset. ☎ **441/234-0914.** Daily 9am–5pm.

Mangrove Marina is the best outlet for renting Boston whalers for island-hopping on your own. A 13-foot Boston whaler (25 and 30 hp) carries four and costs $60 for 2 hours, or $135 if you want to keep it 8 hours. The smaller $11^{1}/_{2}$-foot Boston whaler with 15 hp carries three and costs $45 for 2 hours or $95 for 8 hours. It's also possible for 4 persons to rent a 15-foot Open Bowrider at 30 hp, costing $65 for 2 hours, or $150 for 8 hours. This outfitter provides a lot of extras, such as Bimini tops, special maps, a ladder, a viewing box, and a fish and coral ID card.

Pompano Beach Club Watersports Centre

36 Pompano Beach Rd., Southampton ☎ **441/234-0222.** Daily 7:30am–midnight.

This one of the island's best outfitters, mainly because of its varied and modern self-drive boats. These include the O'Brien Windsurfer, holding one passenger—either novice or experienced—costing $12 for 1 hour or $36 for four hours. One or two persons can also rent an Aqua Finn sailboat for the same price, which is also the charge for a Dolphin paddleboat. A Buddy Board (a kayak-type with a viewing window) is rented to a single person for $10 per hour or $30 for 4 hours. Aqua-eye Viewing boards are also popular at $10 per hour or $30 per 4 hours. Finally, kayaks are rented to one person for $10 per hour or $30 per 4 hours. A $25 deposit is required on all rentals.

Southside Scuba Water Sports

Grotto Bay Beach Hotel, 11 Blue Hole Hill, Hamilton Parish. ☎ **441/293-2915.** Daily 9am–5pm. Bus: 1, 3, 10, or 11.

Southside Scuba rents Sunfish for $60 (4 hours) or $100 (8 hours). A Broadsailer costs $20 per hour or $50 for 4 hours, and a kayak goes for $12 per hour. A wide range of other equipment is also available for rent, including Paddle Cats and Puffers.

Bermuda Caribbean Yacht Charter

2A Light House Rd., Southampton Parish. ☎ **441/238-8578** after 6pm. Daily 9am–5pm. Bus: 7 or 8.

Yachts for charter with a licensed skipper can be rented at a number of places, including Bermuda Caribbean Yacht Charter. Offering a keen insight on the islands, Captain Hal White, the owner of the 52-foot ketch *Night Wind,* operates from April to November and charges $320 for a half day (10am–pm and 1:30pm–4pm), or else $500 for a full day for six passengers. Any additional person pays an extra $20.

WATERSKIING

You can waterski in the protected waters of Hamilton Harbour, Great Sound, Castle Harbour, Mangrove Bay, Spanish Point, Ferry Reach, Ely's Harbour, Riddells Bay, and Harrington Sound. May through September is the best time for this sport. Bermuda law requires that water-skiers be taken out by a licensed skipper. There are only a few boat operators for this sport, and charges fluctuate with fuel costs. Rates include the boat, skis, safety belts, and usually an instructor. Hotels and guesthouses can assist with arrangements.

Island Water Skiing

Grotto Bay Beach Hotel, Hamilton Parish. ☎ **441/293-2915.** Apr–Nov daily 8am–7:30pm, weather permitting. Closed Dec–Mar. Bus: 1, 3, 10, or 11.

Up to three persons are taken out for skiing on board a Barefoot Nautique. It costs $40 for 15 minutes, $60 per half hour, or $95 for 1 hour.

Bermuda Waterski Centre

Robinson's Marina, Somerset Bridge. ☎ **441/234-3354.** May–Oct daily 8am–7:30pm; variable hours the rest of the year. Bus: 6 or 7.

Up to five people can go waterskiing with a specially designed Ski Nautique. Lessons are available. The per-person charge is $50 for a half-hour of skiing, $90 for 1 hour.

4 Golf

Since the first course was laid out in 1922, golf has been one of Bermuda's most popular sports. It can be played year-round, but early spring, winter, and fall offer the best seaside golf conditions. You must arrange your starting time at any of the eight courses in advance through the management of your guesthouse or hotel. Women's and men's clubs, either right- or left-handed, are available at each course, and most leading stores in Bermuda sell golf balls.

Tournaments are held throughout the year, with top players participating. For information, contact the **Bermuda Golf Association,** P.O. Box HM 433, Hamilton HM BX, Bermuda (☎ **441/238-1367**).

The Castle Harbour Hotel golf course is considered one of the most scenic courses on the island, whereas the Port Royal, designed by Robert Trent Jones, is a challenge to your golfing expertise. Two famous courses—the Mid Ocean Club at Tucker's Town and the Riddells Bay Golf and Country Club—are private, and introduction by a member is required before you can play there. Certain deluxe hotels can sometimes secure playing privileges at the Riddells Bay Golf and Country Club. One of the most photographed golf courses in Bermuda is at the Southampton Princess Hotel, where rolling hills and flowering shrubs add to the players' enjoyment.

The golf courses listed below that are part of a hotel complex also permit nonguests to use their facilities. All of these golf courses have pros, and you can take lessons if you wish.

Belmont Hotel, Golf & Country Club

Between Harbour and Middle Roads, Warwick Parish. ☎ **441/236-1301.** Daily 7am–5pm. Ferry from Hamilton.

A Scotsman, Emmett Devereux, designed this 18-hole, par 70, 5,777-yard course in 1923, and its layout has long been a challenge to golfers. All golfing magazines write of its par-five 11th hole, with a severe dogleg left with a blind tee shot. It's sometimes difficult to finish uphill at number 18. Crystal caves under the turf sometimes cause the ball to roll unpredictably. In spite of these disadvantages, golf pros recommend the Belmont for beginning golfers. The first hole is said to be "confidence building." It is estimated that with a 9 or 10 handicap, golfers will shoot in the 70s at Belmont, but there are no guarantees. Most of the course is inland and, unlike many golf courses in Bermuda, this one provides few views of the Atlantic. *Warning:* On weekends it is typical to have rounds of five hours or more. Although greens fees are free for hotel guests, carts (available for $36) are mandatory; fees for nonguests are $80, including cart. A full set of golf clubs rents for $25. This course can also be played as a 9-hole course.

Castle Harbour Golf Club

Tucker's Town, Hamilton Parish. ☎ **441/293-2040.** Daily 7:30am–6pm. Bus: 22. Exit off Harrington Sound Road, follow Paynter's Road to Castle Harbour resort entrance.

This 18-hole, par 71, 6,440-yard course was designed by golf architect Charles Banks. This resort championship course features challenging tee shots. The first tee by the clubhouse has often been compared to a "crow's nest" by golfing magazines. It gives you an immediate sense of what to expect with this course, a panorama of Castle Harbour's blue-green waters with the darker Atlantic in the distance. As you look down over the fairway, you'll think you're seeing the course from a helicopter. Winds sweeping in from the Atlantic make this course a constant challenge. Sometimes the greens are elevated, especially the 190-yard, par-three 13th hole, lying atop an embankment that rises about 100 feet. Golfers consider the 235-yard, par-three 18th hole as the hardest finishing hole on the island, especially if the Atlantic decides to send a wind out of the north just at that time. There are not as many sand traps here as on other Bermuda courses. This is one of the more expensive courses to play, but at least part of the money is used to maintain the best-kept greens on the island. Greens fees are $100 for 18 holes. There are no caddies. A full set of clubs rents for $25; gas golf carts rent for $21 per person (golf carts are mandatory).

Ocean View Golf Course

2 Barkers Hill Rd., Devonshire. ☎ **441/295-9092.** Daily 7:30am–6:30pm. Bus: 2.

This course has 9 holes, par 35, 2,940 yards. Back in the 1950s, this was a club for African Bermudians. Later, as other clubs started to admit black players, the course fell into disrepair. The government spent some $2 million to restore the course; although it has been vastly improved, its old reputation lives on. In the center of Bermuda (Devonshire Parish), this course offers panoramic views of the ocean from many of its elevated tees. Many golfers consider the terrain "unpredictable"; that, combined with rambling hills, make the course more challenging than it first appears. A few holes have as many as six tees. Winds from the Great Sound might have a greater effect on your score than you might think. The green on the 177-yard, par-three 5th hole has been cut into the coral hillside. Since it is draped with semitropical vines, golfers sometimes have the eerie feeling that they are hitting the ball into a Bermudian cave. Weekdays this course has tended to be the least crowded of any in Bermuda. However, as improvements are made to the course, this might change. Greens fees are $28 (for 9 holes or the course played for 18 holes). There are no caddies. A full set of clubs rents for $16; gas golf carts rent for $17 for 9 holes, $30 for 18 holes.

Port Royal Golf Course

Middle Road, Southampton Parish. ☎ **441/234-0974.** Daily 7am–5pm. Bus: 7 or 8.

This is an 18-hole, par 71, 6,565-yard public course. Jack Nicklaus might be found at the much-publicized 16th hole, a favorite for photo layouts in golf magazines.

The Best Golf Courses

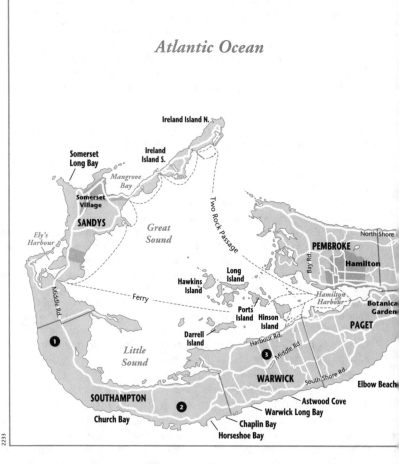

Both the 16th and the 15th hole ring the craggy cliffs around Whale Bay. Sometimes winds from the Atlantic taunt golf balls hit from these holes. The 7th and 8th holes are, respectively, a dogleg par five and a windy par three. Port Royal is so popular that some avid golfers have reserved starting times a year in advance. Golf architect Robert Trent Jones designed the course along the oceanside terrain, and the course is owned and operated by the Bermuda government. Greens fees are $60 Monday through Friday, $65 weekends. There are no caddies. A full set of clubs rents for $16, golf carts for $30, and handcarts for $7. The clubhouse, which overlooks the ocean and the 9th and 18th greens, boasts a bar and a restaurant serving breakfast, lunch, and dinner.

Southampton Princess Golf Club

101 South Shore Rd., Hamilton. ☎ **441/238-0446.** Daily 7am–5pm. Bus: 7 or 8.

On the grounds of one of the most luxurious hotels in Bermuda, this 18-hole, par 54, 2,684-yard course occupies not only the loftiest but one of the most scenic settings on the island. Elevated tees, strategically placed bunkers, and plenty of

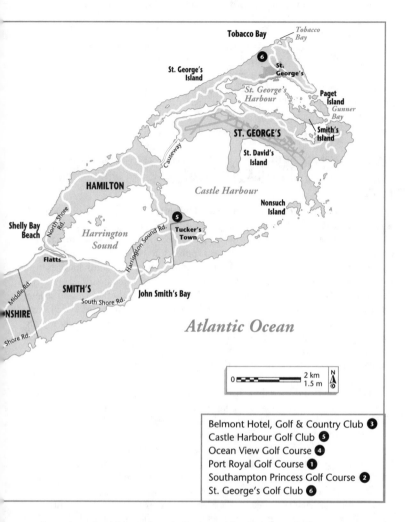

Belmont Hotel, Golf & Country Club ③
Castle Harbour Golf Club ⑤
Ocean View Golf Course ④
Port Royal Golf Course ①
Southampton Princess Golf Course ②
St. George's Golf Club ⑥

water hazards make this course a challenge; golfers have been known to use every club in their bag when the wind blows in from the Atlantic. Against the backdrop of the Gibbs Hill Lighthouse, the 16th hole was designed in a cup ringed by flowering bushes. The vertical drop on the 1st and 2nd holes is almost 200 feet. Even experienced golfers like to "break in" on this course before taking on some of Bermuda's more challenging courses. Because of the hotel's irrigation system, we have often found this course to be green while some of the others experienced a "summer brown-out." Greens fees (including mandatory cart) are $51 for hotel guests and $55 for visitors. There are no caddies. The charge for renting clubs is $15 per 18 holes.

St. George's Golf Club

1 Park Rd., St. George's Parish. ☎ **441/297-8067.** Apr–Sept, Mon–Fri 8am–5:30pm; Sat-Sun, 7:30am–5:30pm. Off-season, Mon–Fri 8am–4:45pm, Sat–Sun 7:30am–4:45pm. Bus: 6, 8, 10, or 11.

Redesigned by Robert Trent Jones Jr., this 18-hole, par 62, 4,043-yard course is the newest of the Bermuda government's golf courses. Lying on a headland at the northeastern tip of the island, it is within walking distance of St. George's. Links run along the hillsides, providing players with panoramic vistas of the ocean; winds coming in off the ocean will also have a significant effect on your game. On some of the par threes, players need everything from a nine-iron to a driver to reach the green. The greens are the smallest on the island; some appear to be no more than two dozen feet across. The abundant salt air makes the greens slick. Usually, the course is not crowded at midweek. Greens fees for 9 or 18 holes are $35. There are no caddies. A full set of clubs rents for $16; gas golf carts go for $28 to $30, and handcarts for $5.

5 Other Outdoor Activities

BICYCLING

With a year-round average temperature of 70° Fahrenheit, the weather in Bermuda is often ideal for bicycling unless you encounter a rainy day, when you may get splashed by passing vehicles. However, if conditions are balmy, you can have fun cycling, stay in shape, and take a hands-on approach to your sightseeing.

Push-bikes (or pedal bikes), the term Bermudians use to distinguish bicycles from mopeds, are a popular form of transport. Bicycles can be rented hourly, daily, or for the entire period of your Bermuda holiday. For information about cycle and scooter rentals, see "Getting Around" in Chapter 4. All of the recommended cycle liveries also rent bicycles, and many hotels have them available for guest use, with or without a fee. Rental costs are generally $10 to $15 for the first day, and then $5 per day for each additional day. Both 3-speed and 10-speed pedal bikes are usually available. It's always a good idea to call one of these cycle liveries as far in advance as possible, since demand is great, especially from April through October.

Much of the island's terrain consists of flat stretches, although the hills provide what the government refers to as "challenges." Some of these climbs are steep, especially the roads that run north and south along the island. The South Shore Road in Southampton and Warwick Parishes often leaves bikers huffing and puffing.

Most roadways are well paved and maintained. Although the island's speed limit is 20 mph for all vehicles, one should exercise caution when riding a bike or scooter on Bermuda's roads: The roads are narrow and winding, and the traffic, especially during the day, tends to be heavy with Bermudians riding in their cars. The operators of most vehicles are considerate of cyclists, but a car can approach suddenly without honking. The government discourages unnecessary blowing of horns. You might even be overtaken by fellow cyclists, since bicycle racing is one of the most popular sports in Bermuda.

In spite of all the tourist material extolling the glories of bicycle riding in Bermuda, the truth is that the roads are not suitable for beginning riders. You need to give careful thought about where it might be safe for youngsters to ride. Some of the most interesting trails for cyclists are in Devonshire and Smith's parishes, and the hills there will guarantee that you get your exercise for the day. But the beautiful landscapes will make all of your efforts seem worthwhile. Spittal Pond, a wildlife sanctuary, is great for cycling; there are biking paths running along scenic shoreline cliffs. It is one of the most rewarding destinations for the cyclist. Another good choice for beginning riders is the Bermuda Railway Trail (see Chapter 8).

If you're a real demon on a bike, you can go farther west and experience the challenge of pumping up to Gibbs Hill Lighthouse, the oldest cast-iron lighthouse in the Western Hemisphere. The panoramic view from the foot of the lighthouse will make your trip worth the effort.

Bird-Watching

There is a nucleus of bird-watching enthusiasts in Bermuda, but there are not many organized tours. Visiting bird-watchers are advised to make arrangements for tours with local enthusiasts.

Bird-watchers might contact David Wingate, conservation officer for the Bermuda government at ☎ **441/236-4201** or Eric Amos at ☎ **441/236-9056.** They occasionally—but not always—advise by phone of the island's best retreats, walkways, and hideaways. Before calling, pick up a copy of David Wingate's *Check List and Guide to the Birds of Bermuda* or Eric Amos's *A Guide to the Birds of Bermuda*, both of which are available at local bookstores.

You can also contact the Bermuda Audubon Society, P.O. Box 1328, Hamilton HM, Bermuda (☎ **441/293-7394**), for information about any organized field trips for birding in Bermuda.

If you'd like to enjoy a picnic while on a bicycle outing, head for Sandys Parish. First cross Somerset Bridge, the smallest drawbridge in the world, then pedal along Somerset Road to Fort Scaur Park. Once there, you can enjoy a panoramic view of Ely's Harbour while eating outdoors.

Only the hardiest cyclist can probably traverse the 21-mile length of Bermuda in one day. For most people, it's far better to focus on a small section of the island at one time. Decide what interests you parish by parish and proceed from there. To save cycling time, you can take your bike aboard various ferries, then begin cycling once you reach your desired destination. Bicycles are carried free on the ferries.

Another interesting bicycle option is the Bermuda Railway Trail (see p. 162), which is restricted to bicyclists and pedestrians. The Railway Trail can be divided into seven sections, each of which has its own character. It is up to you to decide how much of the trail you would want to cover in one day, and what sections you would want to focus on.

The trail begins in Sandys Parish, where the Gilbert Nature Reserve and the Heydon Trust Estate provide contrasting views of rural Bermuda. The first part of the trail ends at Somerset Bridge.

The second section of the trail begins as you cross into Southampton Parish. A sense of 19th-century Bermudian life is felt here; Southampton includes much of Bermuda's 500 acres of arable land, as well as examples of traditional manor houses.

Entering Warwick Parish, the trail skirts Little Sound and then passes through an allspice forest. Approaching the island's central area, the West End's woodlands and fields become dotted with Bermuda's traditional old houses, some still featuring domed water tanks and old stone butteries. The trail then rises above Paget Marsh—a National Trust Nature Reserve—which includes Bermuda's oldest palmetto forest and a wide variety of bird life. The tour of Paget Parish ends with a ride through a 450-foot-long railway tunnel, partially covered with the thick roots of a rubber tree.

Picking up beyond Hamilton, Bermuda's capital city, the trail leads to Palmetto House, built in the shape of a cross and virtually unchanged since the 1700s.

After crossing a cricket pitch, or field, while moving from Devonshire into Hamilton Parish, the trail then edges the wild coastline along Bailey's Bay.

The final section of the trail is in the Parish of St. George's, where the windswept coast is rocky and rugged. The mariner's landmark of Sugarloaf Hill offers a panoramic seascape and view of St. George's.

FISHING

Bermuda is considered one of the world's finest fishing centers, especially in light tackle fishing. Blue marlin catches have increased dramatically, and Bermuda can also add bill-fishing to its already enviable reputation. Fishing is a year-round sport in Bermuda, but is best from May through November. No license is required.

Visitors may obtain fishing information from the International Game Fish Association representative for Bermuda: Tom Smith (☎ 441/238-0112).

Bermuda Game Fishing Association, P.O. Box HM 1306, Hamilton HM FX, Bermuda, is an advisory body that represents all the IGFA-affiliated clubs in Bermuda and serves as caretaker for all local records and world records held locally.

DEEP-SEA FISHING

Wahoo, amberjack, blue marlin, white marlin, dolphin, tuna, and other varieties can be found in these waters. In addition, Bermuda offers the necessary equipment to help you fish for them.

Bermuda Sportsfishing

Creek View House, 8 Tulo Lane, Pembroke HM 02, Bermuda. ☎ **441/295-2370.** Daily 7am–10pm. Bus: 1, 2, 10, or 11.

Bermuda Sportsfishing is run by the De Silva family, who have been in business for many years. They charge $600 for a half day of fishing and $850 for a full day. If you give them enough notice, the family can assemble a group of six, in which case the charge per person is only $100 for a half day with all equipment included in the price. Boats range in size from 34 to 38 feet.

REEF FISHING

Reef fishing is likely to turn up such catches as greater amberjack, almaco jack, great barracuda, little tunny, Bermuda chub, gray snapper, yellowtail snapper, and assorted bottom fish. Three major reef bands lie off Bermuda's shore. The closest one begins about $1/2$ mile offshore, and stretches for nearly 5 miles. The Challenger Bank is about 14 miles offshore, and Argus Bank is the most distant—at about 30 miles. Of course, the farther out you go, the more likely you are to turn up larger fish.

Several charter companies offer either half- or full-day charters. Arrangements can be made through Bermuda Sportsfishing (see "Deep-Sea Fishing," above).

SHORE FISHING

This type of fishing turns up such catches as bonefish, palometa (pompano), gray snapper, and great barracuda. Locals and most visitors prefer shore fishing at Spring Benny's Bay or West Whale Bay. Great Sound and St. George's Harbour are other promising grounds.

Activities directors at hotels can usually help make fishing arrangements for you; if they can't, go to **Mangrove Marina, Ltd.,** end of Cambridge Road, Mangrove Bay, in Somerset (☎ 441/234-0914). A rod, reel, and tackle can be rented there at $6 for four hours or $10 a day. A $20 deposit is required.

HORSEBACK RIDING

Spicelands Riding Centre

Middle Road, Warwick Parish. ☎ **441/238-8212.** Call the day before, 9am to 5pm, to make arrangements. Bus: 8.

Here you'll find trail rides for $35 per person for 1 hour. The popular early morning ride, a 1½-hour jaunt followed by a continental breakfast, costs $45 per person. From May to October, evening rides costing $35 are offered, Monday through Friday.

Lee Bow Riding Stables

1 Tribe Rd., Devonshire Parish. ☎ **441/236-4181.** Make reservations one day in advance; call daily 9am to 5pm. Bus: 3.

Lee Bow is especially geared for children ages 6 to 18, although riders of all ages are accommodated, often in small groups of no more than four. Instruction is available. Lessons and trail rides are given for $25 per hour.

TENNIS

Nearly all the big hotels, and many of the smaller ones, have courts, most of which can be lit for night play. It's best to bring your own tennis clothing and sneakers with you to Bermuda, since a tennis outfit may be required. Colored tennis togs, so popular in America, arrived in Bermuda some time ago—tennis outfits no longer have to be white.

Each of the facilities listed below has a tennis pro on duty, and lessons can be arranged. In case you didn't come prepared, you can rent rackets and buy balls at each place.

Government Tennis Stadium

Cedar Avenue, Pembroke Parish. ☎ **441/292-0105** to reserve a court and to arrange lessons. Mon–Fri 8am–10pm, Sat–Sun 8am–7pm. Bus: 1, 2, 10, or 11.

There are three clay and five Plexicushion courts. To play here costs $5 per adult and $3 per junior. An extra $6 is charged for playing at night. Tennis attire is mandatory. Rackets rent for $4 per hour; balls cost $6 per can.

Elbow Beach Hotel/A Wyndham Resort

60 South Shore Rd., Paget Parish. ☎ **441/236-3535.** Call for bookings daily 9am–5pm. Bus: 1, 2, or 7.

At the Elbow Beach Hotel, there are five LayKold courts (one for lessons only). Hotel guests are charged $8 (others pay $12) to play here. Two of the courts are lit for night play, when hotel guests pay $12 and visitors are charged $15.

Port Royal Golf Course

Off Middle Road, Southampton Parish. ☎ **441/234-0974.** Daily 8am–10pm. Bus: 7 or 8.

The Port Royal Golf Course also has tennis facilities. The four Plexipave courts cost $8 to play during the daytime; night play is $12 to cover the lights and court costs.

Southampton Princess

101 South Shore Rd., Southampton Parish. ☎ **441/238-1005.** Call daily 9am–5pm to make arrangements. Bus: 7 or 8.

This has Bermuda's largest tennis court layout, with 11 Plexipave courts, three of them lit for night play. Hotel guests pay $10 per hour and outsiders are charged $12 per hour; there is a $2 surcharge for lights at night. Rackets rent for $6 per hour, and balls cost $6 per can.

6 Spectator Sports

In this tradition-bound British colony, the most popular spectator sports are cricket, soccer, field hockey, and the not terribly genteel game of rugby. Boating, yachting, and sailing are also popular, since there are many opportunities to participate in these water sports.

An overview of these sports is given below; the Bermuda Department of Tourism can provide dates and venues for upcoming events.

CRICKET   Its arcane rules have been memorized and are understood by far more Bermudians than you might have imagined. If you arrive in midsummer (the game's seasonal high point), you'll probably see several regional teams practicing on cricket fields throughout the island. Each match includes enough pageantry to remind participants of the game's imperial antecedents, and enough conviviality (picnics, socializing, and chitchat among the spectators) to provide sociological insights into Bermuda. The year's most important cricket event—the Cup Match Cricket Festival—takes place in late July or early August. Then, playoffs between Bermuda-based and visiting teams are scheduled at the St. George's Cricket Club, Willington Slip Road (☎ **441/297-0374**), and at the Somerset Cricket Club, Broome Street off Somerset Road (☎ **441/234-0327**). Over the rest of the year, these organizations keep in close touch with the various cricket-related activities throughout the island.

FIELD HOCKEY   One of the great women's competitive sports is field hockey, played with curved wooden mallets. Each team—usually clad in knee socks and either shorts or kilts—tries to drive a small white ball into the opposing team's net. Bermuda has several teams that compete against one another on Sunday afternoons between October and April. In September, Bermuda welcomes huge numbers of field hockey enthusiasts from throughout the Atlantic basin. They come for the Hockey Festival, which is held at the National Sports Club, Middle Road, Devonshire Parish (☎ **441/236-6994**). Admission is usually free.

GOLF   Enthusiasts claim that Bermuda offers some of the finest all-around golfing terrain in the world. Part of this is due to the climate, which supports lush driving ranges and putting greens. In addition, the ever-present golfers play at surprisingly high levels. Golf tournaments are held throughout the year, culminating in the annual, much publicized Bermuda Open in early October. Both amateurs and professionals are welcome to vie for one of the most sought after golfing prizes in the world.

HORSERACING   If you are one of the horse-loving set, check to see what events may be taking place at the National Equestrian Centre, Vesey Street in Devonshire (☎ **441/234-0485**). Beginning in September and lasting through Easter, harness races are staged about twice a month. One of the major equestrian events is held in October, the FEI/Samsung Dressage Competition and Show-Jumping. More details are available from the Bermuda Equestrian Federation, P.O. Box DV-583, Devonshire DV BX (☎/fax **441/234-0485**). If you can't reach this organization on the phone (which is quite likely), ask at the tourist office or check the local newspaper for news of events.

RUGBY   A blend of American-style football and European soccer, this rough 'n' tumble game attracts many aficionados within Bermuda. Rugby players (devoid of protective padding) from several hotly competitive local teams seem to revel in this violent sport. The Easter Rugby Classic, attracting teams from throughout the

British Commonwealth, is the final event in the island's rugby season, which runs from September to April. The venue for virtually every rugby game in Bermuda is at the National Sports Club, Middle Road, Devonshire Parish (☎ **441/236-6994**).

SOCCER This fast-paced game is attracting increasing numbers of fans on both sides of the Atlantic. Bermudians view soccer as an important part of elementary education, and therefore actively encourage this sport for children and teenagers. In early April, teams from countries around the Atlantic and Caribbean compete for the Diadora Youth Soccer Cup, with players in three different age divisions. Games are held on various fields and playing grounds throughout the island. More accessible to visitors at other times, however, are the many games among high school athletic teams, held regularly throughout the year.

YACHTING Bermuda has never hesitated to capitalize upon its geographical position in the mid-Atlantic to lure the yachting crowd. The yacht-racing season runs every year from March to November, with most races scheduled for weekends. Most races take place within the relatively calm waters of Bermuda's Great Sound. Although it can be confusing to watch these races from land because of the shifting sightlines, the best land vantage points include Spanish Point, the islands northeast of Somerset, and Hamilton Harbour. Even better views are available from the decks of privately-owned boats that anchor near the edge of the race course. Despite the confusion of newcomers who watch these carefully choreographed regattas, the sight of a fleet of racing craft with spinnakers and pennants aloft is always exciting.

In late June, Bermuda is the final destination in two of the most important annual yacht races: the Annapolis-Bermuda Race and the even more prestigious Newport-Bermuda Race. Both provide enough visual distraction and maritime pageantry to keep even the most demanding maritime devotees enthralled. Participating yachts range from 30 to 100 feet in length, and their skippers are said to be among the most dedicated in the world.

Around Halloween, the autumn winds propel dozens of less exotic racing craft through the waters of the Great Sound. These compete in a series of one-on-one playoffs for the King Edward VII Gold Cup International Match Racing Tournament.

The island's yachting events are by no means limited to the above-mentioned international competitions. Bermuda's sheltered bays and windswept open seas provide year-round enticement for anyone who has ever wanted to experience the thrill of a snapping jib and taut mainsail.

10 Shopping

Retailers on less prosperous islands have claimed that Bermuda's continuing popularity is due to its superb climate and its many years of skilled marketing. Indeed, no one has ever accused the Bermudians of not knowing how to market themselves or their rich inventories of retail goods. Bermuda, perhaps better than any other island in the world, draws upon its British antecedents to produce a large array of charming and desirable shops and stores, both large and small. Even if your goal is only to window-shop (a highly engrossing activity in its own right), you'll find ample quantities of some of the most realistically priced, elegant merchandise anywhere. Much of it literally seems to beckon through the display windows for the attention of vacationing visitors.

What produces this alluring jumble of salable goods? Some of it may have to do with the inherent sense of conservative style that permeates much of Bermuda. Most stores take full advantage of their location within charming cottages or historically important buildings. Shopkeepers are generally both polite and discreet, and the merchandise is often unusual and well made. Despite the fact that much of it seems to have an upscale quality and innate tastefulness, it tends to be significantly less expensive than you might have expected.

Some frequent visitors to Bermuda take careful stock of their needs for porcelain, crystal, silverware, jewelry, timepieces, and perfume, perhaps anticipating several months in advance a needed wedding gift. The island is filled with merchandisers of fine tableware that is priced 25% to 50% less than you might have found at home. Famous makers whose goods fill the shops of Bermuda include Royal Copenhagen, Wedgwood, and Royal Crown Derby. Crystal is also an excellent bargain in Bermuda, with many of the finest manufacturers in Europe and North America providing wide selections of glittering merchandise. For a fee, all of these items can be shipped, usually in well-wrapped packages that minimize breakage.

Liquor is also a good buy. U.S. citizens are allowed to bring back 1 liter duty-free. But even with U.S. tax and duty, you can save between 35% and 50% on liquor purchases, depending on the brand. Liqueurs offer the largest savings.

Antique lovers appreciate the mixture of the British aesthetic and mid-Atlantic charm. And, naturally, anyone interested in carrying home a piece of the island's nautical heritage will find oversized ship's propellers, captain's bells, brass nameplates, scale models of the sailing ships of long ago, or perhaps an old-fashioned ship's steering wheel from a salvaged shipwreck. Then there is the island's wealth of antique engravings, 19th-century furniture, modern artwork, and handmade pottery and crafts, all of which could become elegant heirlooms. In fact, the island's material (and salable) allures are almost endless.

Other good buys are "Bermudiana"—products make in Bermuda or manufactured elsewhere exclusively for local stores. They include cedarwood gifts, carriage bells, coins commemorating the 375th anniversary of the island's settlement, flower plates by Spode, pewter tankards, handcrafted gold jewelry, traditional-line handbags with cedar or mahogany handles, miniature cottages in ceramic or limestone, shark's teeth polished and mounted in 14-karat gold, decorative kitchen items, Bermuda shorts (of course), silk scarves, and watches with Bermuda-map or longtail faces.

How does Bermuda maintain prices that many visitors consider low and/or at least extremely fair? Many of the merchandisers buy their inventories directly from manufacturers in Europe or North America, thereby avoiding high distribution costs. Duties imposed on goods imported into Bermuda are low, and there is no sales tax. In fact, some prices are low enough, and the merchandise tempting enough, to equalize whatever import duties might be imposed upon them by your government's customs.

Most of Bermuda's best shops are along Front Street in Hamilton. Here, where shopping is relaxed and casual, you'll come across many good buys. Among the choicest items are imports from Great Britain and Ireland, such as Shetland and cashmere sweaters, Harris tweed jackets, Scottish woolen goods and tartan kilts, and even fine china and crystal—many costing appreciably less than in their country of origin.

Although many items might be priced considerably less than Stateside, be aware that this isn't always the case—in fact, some items seem to be overpriced; you should be familiar with prices back home before committing yourself to serious purchases.

1 The Shopping Scene

The best and widest choice of shopping is in Hamilton (see "Hamilton Shopping A to Z," below). Although most shops are on **Front Street,** you may want to explore the back streets as well, especially if you're an adventurous shopper.

The Emporium on Front Street, a restored building constructed around an atrium, houses a number of shops, including jewelry stores. **Windsor Place** on Queen Street is another Bermudia-style shopping mall.

The "second city" of **St. George's** also has many shops, stores, and boutiques, including branches of famous Front Street stores. King's Square, the center of St. George's, is filled with shops; the other major centers are **Somers Wharf** and **Water Street.**

Don't overlook the shopping possibilities of the West End either. **Somerset Village** in Sandys Parish has many shops. But of even greater interest may be the **Royal Naval Dockyard** area on Ireland Island. Here you can visit the Craft Market, Island Pottery, and the Bermuda Arts Centre, and you'll see local artisans at work.

STORE HOURS   Stores in Hamilton, St. George's, and Somerset are generally open Monday through Saturday from 9am to 5:30pm. When large liners are in port, stores may stay open in the evening or even open on Sunday.

FINDING AN ADDRESS   Some Front Street stores post numbers on their build-ings; others do not. Sometimes the number posted or used is the "historic" number of the building, which has nothing to do with the modern number. But somehow it all works out: You can always ask for directions, since most Bermudians are will-ing to help. Outside Hamilton, don't expect to find numbers on buildings at all, or even street names in some cases.

SALES TAX & DUTY   There is no sales tax in Bermuda. Bermuda is not a "duty-free" island. Depending on which country you're returning to, you may have to pay duty (see "Visitor Information, Entry Requirements, Customs & Money," in Chap-ter 3, "Planning a Trip to Bermuda").

"IN-BOND" (DUTY-FREE) SHOPPING   Goods such as liquor and cigarettes can be purchased at in-bond, or duty-free, prices—often at a saving of around 35%—and should be ordered several days in advance of your departure. You cannot con-sume these items in Bermuda; you must pick them up at the airport when you depart. They must be listed on your country's Customs Declaration Form. Liquor purchases should be made at one of the island stores, since the airport doesn't have an in-bond liquor store.

Note: As with various countries and territories, including several in the Caribbean, Bermuda is covered by the U.S. law regarding "Generalized System of Preferences" status. That means that if at least 35% of an item has been crafted in Bermuda, you can bring it back duty-free, regardless of how much you spent. If you've gone beyond your $400 allotment, make a separate list for goods made in Bermuda. That will make it easier for Customs and ultimately, for yourself.

2 Hamilton Shopping A to Z
ANTIQUES
Heritage House
2 Front St. West. ☎ **441/295-2615.**

The Heritage House sells nautical prints, English antiques, old maps, modern porcelain, and the largest collection of fine art on the island. The store was completely overhauled in 1995, with many new gift items added, including one of the best collections of costume jewelry in town. Look for their large collection of "Halcyon Days" pillboxes. Open Monday through Saturday from 9am to 5pm.

Pegasus
63 Pitts Bay Rd. (Front St. West). ☎ **441/295-2900.**

Pegasus has a wide range of antique prints, engravings, and magazine illustrations. This is the best you'll find anywhere in Bermuda. The inventory is varied, with old maps of many different regions of the world, and more than 1,000 literary, sporting, medical, and legal caricatures from Vanity Fair. These cost $40 to $200, depending on the subject. The hand-colored engravings of birds, fruits, and flowers are worth framing and sometimes cost as little as $40 each. Owner Robert Lee and his wife, Barbara, scour the print shops of the British Isles to stock this unusual store. Most prints range from the late 1700s to the late 1800s and are carefully grouped accord-ing to subject. The authenticity of whatever you buy is guaranteed in writing. They also offer ceramic house signs, costing $95 and up each, made at a small pottery in England. Each is unique, since the buyer chooses the design, after which the "house" and the house name or a number and street are hand-painted to specifications. The shop also carries a wide range of English greeting cards, many with botanical designs. All maps, lithographs, and engravings are duty-free and will not affect your take-home quota. The shop is across the street from the Princess Hotel in Hamilton. Open Monday through Saturday from 10am to 5pm.

ART

Windjammer Gallery
Corner of Reid and King Streets. ☎ **441/292-7861.**

Housed in a yellow cottage, this gallery exhibits paintings and bronze sculptures by local and international artists. It also carries an extensive selection of cards, prints, and limited editions, including photographs and signed silk-screen prints. Adjacent to the gallery is the last private garden in Hamilton, used for the display of life-size sculpture. There is a second gallery at 95 Front St. (☎ **441/292-5878**). Open Monday through Saturday from 10am to 5pm.

ARTS & CRAFTS

Masterworks Foundation Gallery
Bermuda House Lane, 97 Front St. ☎ **441/295-5580.**

Established in 1987 by a group of international philanthropists, this foundation showcases paintings by renowned European, Bermudian, and North American artists. Serving to some extent as the island's most visible arts center, it sponsors frequent art exhibitions which have included works by Georgia O'Keeffe (painted during the early 1930s in Bermuda), as well as seascapes by Winslow Homer and watercolors by local artist Ogden Pleissner. The foundation also arranges guided art and architectural tours around the island and coordinates other artistic endeavors and exhibitions throughout the year. Open Monday through Saturday from 10am to 4pm.

Ronnie Chameau Boutique
Trimingham's, 37 Front St. ☎ **441/292-1387.**

Noted local artist Ronnie Chameau, known throughout the island for her charming handmade dolls, crafts doll-shaped ornaments from such natural ingredients as banana leaves, hazelnuts, and grapefruit leaves, gathered from her own and her friends' gardens. Suitable as Christmas gifts, each ornament has a unique personality, is priced under $20, and is individually boxed and gift-wrapped. Ms. Chameau also makes dolls with historically authentic costumes of the late 19th century and wooden Bermuda doorstops, each designed to look like a Bermuda cottage, and priced at $65. Open Monday through Saturday from 9am to 5pm.

BEACHWEAR

Calypso
45 Front St. ☎ **441/295-2112.**

Calypso sells casual, fun fashions (including unusual garments from around the world), and carries the most comprehensive selection of swimwear in Bermuda. There are also Italian leather goods, espadrilles, hats, bags, pareos, Italian ceramics, and whimsical gift items. Calypso is also the exclusive island retailer of Louis Vuitton luggage and accessories. There are branches at both the Southampton and Hamilton Princess Hotels, the Sonesta Beach Hotel, the Coral Beach Club, and the dockyard. Open Monday through Saturday from 9am to 5:30pm.

BOUTIQUES

Aston & Gunn
2 Reid St. ☎ **441/295-4866.**

This shop sells the kind of career-oriented clothing preferred by professionals throughout the island. Although most of the clothing is for men (imported from Germany and Holland), there is a small women's department as well. In addition to the usual collection of shirts, ties, jackets, and suits, Aston & Gunn is the exclusive island distributor of Calvin Klein undergarments. Open Monday through Saturday from 9am to 5:30pm.

Bananas
Front Street West (opposite the Bank of Bermuda). ☎ **441/295-8241.**

Bananas offers colorful, good-quality "Bermuda signature" items. You'll find T-shirts, jackets, beach bags, and beach umbrellas that will let your friends know where you've been. The store has several branches. Open Monday through Saturday from 10am to 5pm.

Davison's
27 and 73 Front St. ☎ **441/292-2083.**

Sportswear with a Bermudian flair is the specialty of this emporium of clothing, clothing accessories, and sporting equipment. It carries virtually anything you'd need to wear for almost any sport in Bermuda. (Almost anything you select here would be appropriate to wear at your local country club when you return home.) Bags by Vera Bradley are also featured. Also available are culinary gift packages including such items as Bermuda fish chowder, fish-based sauces, and island herbs. Open Monday through Saturday from 10am to 5pm.

The London Shop
65 Washington Mall (at Church Street). ☎ **441/295-1279.**

This is the kind of store you might expect to find in an upscale neighborhood of London; it sells men's clothing by Pierre Cardin and a few other prominent designers. Suits range in price from $195 to $500 and sports jackets begin at $75. There's also a collection of dress clothing for adolescent boys. Open Monday through Saturday from 9am to 5pm.

Ruffles
22 Queen St. (Windsor Place Mall). ☎ **441/295-9439.**

This shop specializes in formal clothing for women of all ages. Although the merchandise changes with the seasons, there is a special emphasis on the festivities of the Christmas holiday period. Open Monday through Saturday from 9am to 5pm.

Stefanel
12 Reid St. ☎ **441/295-5698.**

This is the island's only outlet for the clothing of Carlo Stefanel, a well-known Italian designer. Stocking merchandise for both men and women, the store sells tropical-weight men's suits (in cotton and linen) and handmade skirts (some of them knit) with contrasting jackets for women. There's a stylish array of accessories as well. No children's clothing is sold here. Open Monday through Saturday from 9am to 5pm.

Triangle
55 Front St. ☎ **441/292-1990.**

Catering to well-coiffed, well-tailored women who travel, Diane Freis (pronounced "freeze") specializes in easy-care chic but simple women's clothing. The garments,

Hamilton Shops

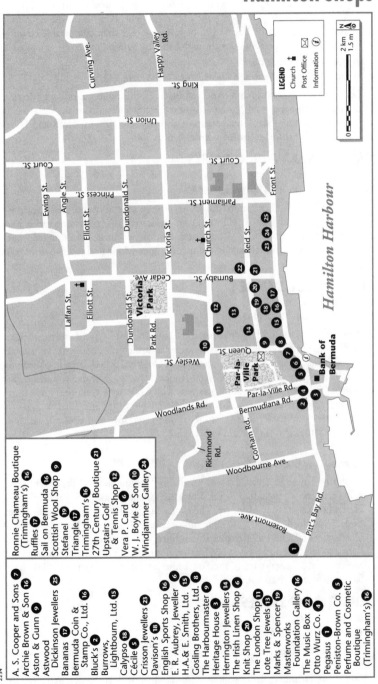

LEGEND
Church †
Post Office ⊠
Information ⓘ

Hamilton Harbour

2234

A. S. Cooper and Sons ⑦
Archie Brown & Son ⑯
Aston & Gunn ⑨
Astwood
Dickinson Jewellers ⑰
Bananas ⑰
Bermuda Coin &
Stamp Co., Ltd. ⑯
Bluck's ②
Burrows,
Lightbourn, Ltd. ⑮
Calypso ⑱
Cécile ⑤
Crisson Jewellers ㉓
Davison's ⑱
English Sports Shop ⑯
E. R. Aubrey, Jeweller ⑥
H.A.& E. Smith, Ltd. ⑮
Gosling Brothers, Ltd. ⑧
The Harbourmaster ⑨
Heritage House ③
Herrington Jewellers ⑭
The Irish Linen Shop ⑥
Knit Shop ⑳
The London Shop ⑪
Lote Tree Jewels ⑬
Marks & Spencer ⑲
Masterworks
Foundation Gallery ⑯
The Music Box ㉒
Otto Wurz Co. ④
Pegasus ①
Peniston-Brown Co. ⑤
Perfume and Cosmetic
Boutique
(Trimingham's) ⑯

Ronnie Chameau Boutique
(Trimingham's) ⑯
Ruffles ⑰
Sail on Bermuda ⑯
Scottish Wool Shop ⑨
Stefanel ⑲
Triangle ⑰
Trimingham's ⑯
27th Century Boutique ㉑
Upstairs Golf
& Tennis Shop ⑫
Vera P. Card ⑥
W. J. Boyle & Son ⑩
Windjammer Gallery ㉔

189

which are usually wrinkle-free, tend to have mosaic-inspired patterns of boldly contrasting colors. The collection includes two-piece outfits, dresses, skirts, and evening jackets. Theoretically, none of the garments ever need ironing. Although pricey, these clothes are believed to be less expensive than comparable clothing in North America. Open Monday through Saturday 9am to 5pm.

27th Century Boutique

4 Burnaby St. (between Front and Church Sts.) ☎ **441/292-2628.**

Long known as a stylish and trend-setting shop, this boutique offers a selection of designer clothing, as well as silver costume jewelry and accessories. The store has a nice collection of shoes—for both men and women—from Canada and London. Open Monday through Saturday from 9am to 5pm.

CASUAL WEAR & SUNGLASSES

Sail on Bermuda

Old Cellar, Front Street. ☎ **441/295-0808.**

A place where the locals shop, this store carries a unique collection of casual wear, bathing suits, and gifts. A poll was taken, indicating that customers feel it has the "best T-shirts in Bermuda." A small addition, called "Shades of Bermuda," has the finest collection of sunglasses on the island. Open Monday through Saturday from 9am to 5pm.

CHINA & GLASSWARE

A. S. Cooper & Sons

59 Front St. ☎ **441/295-3961.**

Bermuda's oldest and largest china and glassware store—and family-owned since 1897—offers a broad range of fine bone china, earthenware, and jewelry. Among the famous names represented are Minton, Royal Doulton, Belleek, Aynsley, Wedgwood, and Royal Copenhagen. The Crystal Room displays Orrefors, Waterford, Royal Brierley, and Kosta-Boda, among others. The Collector's Gallery is known for its limited editions of Bing & Grøndahl, Royal Doulton, and Lladró. A perfume department offers selections from the world's greatest perfumeries. Open Monday through Saturday from 9:30am to 5:15pm.

Bluck's

4 Front St. ☎ **441/295-2296.**

Established in 1844, Bluck's is well known for carrying some of the finest names in china and crystal, including Royal Worcester, Spode, Aynsley, Royal Doulton, and Herend porcelain from Hungary. The choice in crystal is equally impressive: Kosta-Boda, Waterford, Baccarat, Daum, and of course, Lalique, exclusive with Bluck's. Upstairs, you'll find the Antiques Room filled with fine English furniture, antique Bermuda maps, and an array of old English silver. Bluck's has branch shops on Water Street in St. George's and in the Southampton Princess. Open Monday through Saturday from 9am to 5pm.

DEPARTMENT STORES

H. A. & E. Smith Ltd.

35 Front St. ☎ **441/295-2288.**

This store has been selling top-quality merchandise since 1889, at substantial savings over U.S. prices. Smith's comprehensive stock includes sweaters for men and women (in cotton, cashmere, lambswool, and Shetland), British cosmetics, and a collection from the top French parfumeurs. Smith's is noted for its selection of handbags, gloves,

Liberty fabrics by the yard, and children's clothing. It also carries such merchandise as Fendi handbags from Italy, Burberrys rainwear from London, and Rosenthal china. Open Monday through Saturday from 9am to 5:15pm. A subsidiary, "The Treasure Chest," across the street from the main store, carries a full line of French perfumes and gifts.

Trimingham's
37 Front St. ☎ **441/295-1183.**

Family-owned since 1842, Trimingham's specializes in fine European imports, often at considerable savings over U.S. prices. Spode, Aynsley, and Royal Worcester china are featured along with Waterford and Galway crystal. The cashmere, lambswool, and specialty knitwear collection is unrivaled in Bermuda, and Trimingham's own lines of men's and women's wear are known for their quality. French perfumes and European accessories are best buys here, as are fine jewelry, paintings, and gifts. Trimingham's Hamilton store is open Monday through Saturday from 9am to 5pm. Branch shops are found throughout the island and at major hotels.

FASHIONS

Cécile
15 Front St. West. ☎ **441/295-1311.**

Cécile is located near the Visitors Service Bureau and the Ferry Terminal. Well stocked, it is a center for high fashion in Bermuda. Cécile's claims that visiting one of its Bermuda shops is like visiting the fashion capitals of the world— Germany, Mondi; Hong Kong, Ciao and Ciaosport; or Israel, Gottex swimwear. Its sweater and accessory boutique is also outstanding, with many hand-detailed and hand-embroidered styles. Open Monday through Saturday from 9am to 5:30pm. Cécile has branches at the Southampton Princess and Marriott's Castle Harbour.

Marks & Spencer
7 Reid St. ☎ **441/295-0031.**

This outlet, sometimes called "St. Michael," carries reliable quality merchandise from Marks & Spencer in England. You'll find men's, women's, and children's fashions in everything from resortwear to sleepwear, including lingerie. There are also well-tailored dresses and suits, dress shirts, blazers, and British-tailored trousers, as well as swimwear, toiletries, and English sweets and biscuits. Open Monday through Saturday from 10am to 5pm.

FOOTWEAR

W. J. Boyle & Son
Queen and Church Streets. ☎ **441/295-1887.**

In business since 1884, this shop offers footwear for men, women, and children. With the best collection in town, it specializes in brand-name footwear from England, Spain, Brazil, and the United States (including Clarks of England, Bally, and Enzo Angiolini). Open Monday through Saturday from 8:30am to 5:15pm.

GIFTS

Vera P. Card
11 Front St. ☎ **441/295-1729.**

Vera P. Card is known for its "gifts from around the world," including the island's largest collection of Lladró and Hummel figurines. Famous-name watches include

Nivada, Borel, and Rodania. The dinnerware collection features such famous names as Rosenthal, and the crystal department offers a wide assortment of Czech and Bohemian crystal, giftware, and chandeliers. Look for Coalport English bone china, and for the "Bermuda Collection" of 14-karat gold jewelry. Other branches are located at 103 Front Street in Hamilton; 7 Water Street in St. George's, and at the Sonesta Resort and Marriott Castle Harbour hotels. Open Monday through Saturday from 9am to 5pm.

JEWELRY

Astwood Dickinson Jewellers
83–85 Front St. ☎ **441/292-5805.**

Here you'll find a treasure trove of famous-name watches, including Patek Philippe, Cartier, Tiffany, Tag Hever, Tissot, Omega, and Swiss Army, plus designer jewelry, all at prices generally below U.S. retail. From its original Bermuda collection, you can select an 18-karat gold memento of the island, or "The Island Watch" featuring flowers of the island. Another branch is located in the Walker Arcade. Open Monday through Saturday from 8:45am to 5pm.

Crisson Jewellers
55 and 71 Front St. ☎ **441/295-2351.**

Crisson is the exclusive Bermuda agent for Rolex, Ebel, Raymond Weil, Cyma, and Gucci watches, as well as other well-known makers. It also carries an extensive selection of fine jewelry and gems. Open Monday through Saturday from 9am to 5pm.

E. R. Aubrey, Jeweler
19 Front St. West. ☎ **441/295-3826.**

Opposite the Ferry Terminal, this shop has an extensive collection of gold chains, rings with precious and semiprecious stones, and charms, including the Bermuda longtail. Open Monday through Saturday from 9am to 5:30pm.

Herrington Jewellers
1 Washington Mall. ☎ **441/292-6527.**

The leading jewelry store in Hamilton, it offers a nice selection of gold and silver jewelry. It is the authorized dealer for Citizen watches, sells Timex watches, and carries a vast selection of 14-karat gold chains and rings set with precious and semiprecious stones. The Ana-Digi-Temp watch will even tell you the temperature. Open Monday through Saturday from 9am to 5pm.

Lote Tree Jewels
In the Walker Arcade. ☎ **441/292-8525.**

Don't expect the kinds of gemstones carried by conventional jewelers in this unusual jewelry store. The designs here focus on the traditions and workmanship of India, Afghanistan, and the Middle East. The inventory includes necklaces, chokers, rings, earrings, brooches, and a signature kind of ornament designed and distributed by the store's former owner, "Marybeads," crafted from 14K gold and freshwater pearls. Open Monday through Saturday from 9am to 5pm.

LEATHER GOODS

The Harbourmaster
Washington Mall. ☎ **441/295-5333.**

This is your best bet for luggage and leather goods, and the best buys are goods from Colombia—often sold at prices 30% lower than in the United States.

There are also more expensive leather goods from Italy (such as handbags), along with an extensive collection of wallets, and nylon and canvas tote bags. The shop also stocks a number of travel accessories, including luggage carts. Open Monday through Saturday from 9am to 5pm. There is another branch in Hamilton at the corner of Reid and Queen Streets (☎ **441/295-4210**), which carries essentially the same merchandise.

LINENS

The Irish Linen Shop
31 Front St. (corner of Queen St.). ☎ **441/295-4089.**

At Heyl's Corner, near the "Birdcage" police officer, this shop stocks not only table-cloths of pure linen from Ireland, but also a large variety of other merchandise from Europe—everything from quilted placemats to men's shirts in French cotton from Souleiado of Provence. European linens purchased in Bermuda can often save you as much as 50% over American prices. The owners go to Europe twice a year to bring back exceptional items such as Madeira hand embroidery and Belgian lace. Open Monday through Saturday from 9am to 5pm. There is another branch on Cambridge Road in Somerset.

LIQUORS & LIQUEURS

Burrows, Lightbourn Ltd.
87 Front St. ☎ **441/295-0176.**

This store, which is recommended for liquor purchases, has been in business since 1808. You can make your own combination-pack of liquors by asking for a "Select-a-Pac" consisting of any five fifths or two half-gallons. Orders must be placed 24 hours before your departure, except on Sunday, when 48 hours advance purchase is required. The store will deliver your liquor packages to the airport or to your ship. There are two stores in Hamilton, one in St. George's, one in Flatts Village, one in Paget, and one in Somerset. Of course, you can also buy liquor to drink while in Bermuda. Open Monday through Saturday from 9am to 5:30pm.

Gosling Brothers, Ltd.
Corner of Front and Queen Streets. ☎ **441/295-1123.**

This large competitor of Burrows, Lightbourn has been selling liquor in Bermuda since 1806. Here's where you can buy Gosling's Black Seal dark rum, perhaps one bottle to sample on the island and another as an "in-bond" purchase to take home with you. The bottle you drink on the island is likely to cost 50% more than the "in-bond" bottle. If you want to purchase liquor to take home for your duty-free allowance, you can arrange to have it sent to the airport. Open Monday through Saturday from 8:30am to 5:30pm.

MUSIC

The Music Box
58 Reid St. ☎ **441/295-4839.**

By almost any estimate, this is the largest and most complete record store in Bermuda, with an exceptionally large selection of pieces by local musicians whose live performances you might have heard in some of the island's hotels. Owned by Eddy De Mello, one of Bermuda's most influential music agents, this store stocks albums of the music we recommended earlier, as well as a large variety of classical and popular music from other idioms. There are also recordings by musical stars from the

Bahamas and such Caribbean islands as Jamaica and Trinidad. Open Monday through Saturday from 8:30am to 5:30pm.

NEEDLEPOINT PATTERNS
Knit Shop
48 Reid St. ☎ **441/295-6722.**

This is the place to go if you knit, embroider, or sew. There is a large variety of needlepoint and cross-stitch patterns with Bermudian themes, all of which are also available in kits. The shop also carries craft supplies with kits for jewelry making and glass making. Open Monday through Saturday from 8:30am to 4:30pm.

PERFUMES
Peniston-Brown Co.
23 Front St. West. ☎ **441/295-0570.**

Opposite the Ferry Terminal, this shop carries almost all of the world's most popular perfumes. The shop's "fragrance specialists" will be happy to teach you something about the art of choosing and wearing perfume. Open Monday through Saturday from 9am to 5pm.

The Perfume and Cosmetic Boutique
In Trimingham's Department Store, 37 Front St. ☎ **441/295-1183.**

Located on the ground floor of Bermuda's largest department store, this is the island's most comprehensive emporium of every imaginable brand of perfume and cosmetics. Look around as much as you like, but it is hard to resist purchasing something on impulse by Estée Lauder, Clinique, Van Cleef & Arpels, Issey Miyake, Chanel, Boucheron, or Dior. Open Monday through Saturday from 9am to 5pm.

SILVER
Otto Wurz Co.
2 Vallis Building, 3–5 Front St. ☎ **441/295-1247.**

Otto Wurz is located at the western end of Front Street past the Ferry Terminal and the Bank of Bermuda—between Par-la-Ville and Bermudiana Roads. It specializes in articles made of silver, including jewelry, charms, and bracelets. One section of the store is devoted to gift items, such as pewterware, cute wooden signs, and glassware which the store can engrave. Open Monday through Saturday from 9am to 5:15pm.

SPORTSWEAR
Upstairs Golf & Tennis Shop
26 Church St. ☎ **441/295-5161.**

Everything you'll need for the tennis courts or the golf links is sold in this amply stocked store. For golfers, there is merchandise by Ping, Callaway, Titleist, Lynx, and Spalding. Tennis enthusiasts will recognize products by Dunlop, Slazenger, and many others. There is also men's and women's rainwear from Scotland, which is suitable for Bermuda's rainy winters. Open Monday through Saturday from 9am to 5pm.

STAMPS & COINS
Bermuda Coin & Stamp Co. Ltd.
In the Walker Arcade, Front St. ☎ **441/295-5503.**

Philatelists and numismatists will enjoy this shop, where they can browse among a wide selection of stamps and coins—some of which are real treasures.

Commemorative groupings are also offered. Open Monday through Saturday from 10am to 4pm.

WOOLEN GOODS

Archie Brown & Son
49 Front St. ☎ **441/295-2928.**

In business for more than half a century, this shop features sweaters for men and women in cashmere, cotton, lambswool, and Shetland; for women, there are matching skirts. Colors range from neutral to spectacular. Open Monday through Saturday from 10am to 5pm.

English Sports Shop
95 Front St. ☎ **441/295-2672.**

This shop, established in 1918, is one of the island's leading retailers of quality classic and British woolen goods for men, women, and children. Open Monday through Saturday from 9am to 5:30pm.

Scottish Wool Shop
7 Queen St. ☎ **441/295-0967.**

This shop carries a wide range of tartans for men, women, and children—all imported from Great Britain. Many woolen and cotton goods were made especially for this shop. There are women's accessories; children's toys; and Shetland, cashmere, lambswool, and cotton sweaters. Special orders can be placed for more than 500 tartan items. Open Monday through Saturday from 9am to 5:30pm.

3 Shops Around the Island

As you leave Hamilton and tour the island, you may want to continue looking for typical Bermudian items—at one of the shops listed below.

For other shopping suggestions, consider the **Bermuda Craft Market** and the **Bermuda Arts Centre** (see "Ireland Island," in Chapter 7, "What to See & Do"). Those interested in Bermudian art might also want to visit the **Birdsey Studio** in Paget Parish (see "Paget Parish," in Chapter 7, "What to See & Do").

HAMILTON PARISH

Bermuda Glass-Blowing Studio and Showroom
16 Blue Hole Hill, Hamilton Parish. ☎ **441/293-2234.**

Bermuda's only glass-blowing studio employs both locally trained Bermudians and European glassblowers. Although some of the studio's glass pieces have been commissioned, most of them have been inspired by cutting-edge developments in the art glass world. Pieces on display in the showroom range in price from $5 to $1,000. The minimum commission accepted is usually in excess of $500. Open daily from 9am to 5pm.

IRELAND ISLAND

Island Pottery
Royal Naval Dockyard, Ireland Island. ☎ **441/234-3361.**

At this popular attraction, visitors can see a workshop with Bermudian craftspeople. The spacious stone-built warehouse has a gift shop in one section and the workshop in the other. Artisans in traditional aprons toil over potter's wheels, turning out their wares. There's also a glassware artisan. Since the pottery is made in Bermuda, it is duty-free. Open Monday through Friday from 9:30am to 5pm, Saturday and Sunday from 10am to 5pm.

Kathleen Kemsley Bell

Bermuda Arts Centre, 4 Freeport Rd., Ireland Island. ☎ 441/236-3366.

Mrs. Bell's work is displayed exclusively at the Bermuda Arts Centre at the dockyard. Working from her studio in Paget, she creates papier-maché dolls with historically accurate, hand-stitched costumes. Each doll is signed as an original work of art. Mrs. Bell has sold top-of-the-line dolls, known for their expressive faces, to collectors in both Europe and North America. Prices begin at $350, and can go much higher. Mrs. Bell will work on commission; for this purpose, she can visit a buyer at any hotel. Call for an appointment.

PAGET PARISH

Art House

80 South Shore Rd., Paget. ☎ 441/236-6746.

The Art House specializes in original paintings and hand-signed lithographs by the Bermuda-born artist Joan Forbes. After studying in Massachusetts and Canada, she returned home to create watercolors and lithographs of Bermudian landscapes. Prices range from $10 to $50 for lithographs, and from $75 to $3,000 for original watercolors. Ms. Forbes also sells a variety of island-made craft and gift items. Open Monday through Friday from 10am to 4pm, Saturday from 10am to 1pm. Closed January and February.

ST. GEORGE'S PARISH

Bridge House Gallery

1 Bridge St., St. George's. ☎ 441/297-8211.

Situated in one of the parish's oldest buildings—a two-story 18th-century building that was home of several of the island's governors, and is now maintained by Bermuda's National Trust— this may be the best-stocked emporium on the island's East End. It carries a wide selection of antique and modern Bermudiana, including old lace, Christmas ornaments, imported English porcelain, antique maps, old bottles, postcards, and unique mementos of Bermuda's unusual geography and history. One corner of the building has been set aside as the studio and sales outlet of local artist Jill Amos Raine. Since the gallery is actually a sightseeing attraction, it is listed as such in Chapter 7, "What to See & Do." Open Monday through Saturday from 10am to 5pm, Sunday from 11am to 5pm.

Carole Holding Studios

Town Square, St. George's. ☎ 441/297-1833.

Carole Holding is known and well respected for her skill in what might be Bermuda's most-loved art form, watercolor painting. Many of Ms. Holding's works depict the peace and serenity of Bermuda's homes and gardens. A few of her works were commissioned by individuals; more frequently, however, the subjects of her paintings came from her own inspiration. Although Ms. Holding's works can be found in other gift shops around the island, most of them are here in her own shop on Town Square in St. George's. Open daily from 10am to 5pm.

Cow Polly

16 Water St., Somers Wharf, St. George's. ☎ 441/297-1514.

Named after a rather unpleasant-looking fish that abounds in Bermuda waters, this is an upscale gift shop which prides itself on its collection of unusual objects imported from virtually everywhere. The gift theme is aquatic designs, often inspired by fish and underwater mythology. Items for sale include handpainted shirts, jackets, costume jewelry, and unusual neckties. Open Monday through Saturday from 10am to 5pm.

Frangipani

Water Street, St. George's. ☎ **441/297-1357.**

This is a world of fun, color, and fashion for women. You'll find a large selection of comfortable cottons, bright silks, soft rayons—all with that island feeling. There is also a fine collection of swimwear and unusual accessories. Open Monday through Saturday from 10am to 5pm.

Somers Gift Shop

King's Square, St. George's. ☎ **441/297-1670.**

Located in a historic old building, this gift shop offers a nice selection of sterling silver jewelry and T-shirts. Open Monday through Saturday from 10am to 5pm, plus Tuesday and Wednesday evenings from 7:30 to 10pm.

SOMERSET

The Old Market

Main Road, Mangrove Bay, Somerset Village. ☎ **441/234-0744.**

Occupying premises that date from 1827, the Old Market was formerly a private home. This unusual boutique offers everything from old coins, brass, and crystal to costume jewelry and casual clothes. Open Monday through Wednesday from 9:30am to 7pm, Thursday through Saturday from 9:30am to 8pm.

SOUTHAMPTON PARISH

Desmond Fountain Sculpture Gallery

Mezzanine of the Southampton Princess Hotel, 101 South Shore Rd., Southampton Parish. ☎ **441/238-8840.**

Perhaps the most prominent Bermuda sculptor, Desmond Fountain has created some of the island's most visible public art. However, much of his work in recent years has been commissioned for upscale private homes and gardens around the island. Some of his sculptures, including a depiction of a woman seated on a bench reading a newspaper, can be viewed on the grounds of the Lantana (see Chapter 5).

11

Bermuda After Dark

Nightlife in Bermuda may not be the island's main attraction, but there is a lot of it, even though it seems to float from hotel to hotel. Thus, it's hard to predict which pub or nightspot will have the best steel-drum band or calypso music at any given time. Many of the local pubs feature sing-alongs at the piano bar, a popular form of entertainment in Bermuda. Most of the big hotels offer shows after dinner, with combos filling in between shows for couples who like to dance.

The tourist office and most hotels distribute free copies of such publications as *Preview Bermuda, Bermuda Weekly,* and *This Week in Bermuda* to inform visitors of scheduled activities and events. There is also a calendar of events in the *Bermudian,* sold at most newsstands.

You might also tune into the local TV station, which constantly broadcasts information for visitors, including cultural events and various nightlife offerings around the island. Furthermore, a local radio station, 1160 AM (VSB), broadcasts news of Bermuda cultural and entertainment events from 7am to 12:30pm daily. Discount tickets are almost never offered; although students and senior citizens are sometimes offered discounts to various entertainment events, discount tickets are not commonplace.

1 Cultural Entertainment

BERMUDA FESTIVAL

Bermuda's major cultural event is the **Bermuda Festival,** staged for two months (January and February). Outstanding artists, including classical and jazz, perform and there are major theatrical entertainments. During the festival, performances are given every night except Sunday. Tickets for these events range in price from $15 to $35, and most performances are held at City Hall Theater, City Hall, Church Street, Hamilton. For more information and reservations, write to: Bermuda Festival, P.O. Box 297, Hamilton HM AX, Bermuda (☎ 441/295-1291; fax 441/295-7403).

MAJOR PERFORMING ARTS COMPANIES

The **Bermuda Philharmonic Society,** conducted by Graham Garton, presents four regular concerts during the season. In addition, special outdoor "Classical Pops" concerts are presented at the end of May in St. George's and the Royal Naval Dockyard. Concerts usually feature both the Bermuda Philharmonic orchestra and choir with guest soloists. Tickets and concert schedules may be obtained from the Harbourmaster, Washington Mall (☎ **441/ 295-5333**). Tickets generally range from $18 to $20; seniors and students are often granted discounts, depending on the performance.

Ask at the tourist office if the **Gombey Dancers** will be performing during your stay. This local dance troupe of highly talented men and women often performs in winter. This is the island's single most important cultural event of African heritage; once considered part of the "slave culture," this tradition dates from the mid-1700s. On all holidays, you'll see the "gombeys" dancing through the streets of Hamilton in their colorful costumes.

In addition, the **Bermuda Civic Ballet** presents classical ballets at different venues on the island. Again, ask at the tourist office if any performances are scheduled at the time of your visit.

The **Gilbert & Sullivan Society of Bermuda** continues the musical legacy of these English favorites, staging a production each year, usually in October. Sometimes this group will stage a popular Broadway musical. All events are well publicized.

2 The Club & Music Scene

Clay House Inn
77 North Shore Rd., Devonshire Parish. ☎ **441/292-3193** for reservations. Mon–Wed, $22.50 per person, including two drinks; Thurs–Sun, $10. Bus: 10 or 11.

Although calypso and steel band music originated on islands south of Bermuda, this nightclub offers up those musical forms with panache. You're likely to be entertained in a folkloric celebration of island dances with both vocal and instrumental music— a carefully contrived package of Caribbean-style nostalgia. The folkloric shows are presented every Monday through Wednesday year-round. Other nights of the week, the Clay House Inn makes no attempt to cater to a tourist audience; instead, it becomes a local hangout for jazz, reggae, and blues bands. From Monday through Wednesday, drinks are included in the entrance price. On other nights, drinks go for $4 each and are not included in the entrance price. Regardless of the venue, the music and/or show begins at 10:15pm, nightly, with no exact closing time.

The Club
Bermudiana Road, city of Hamilton. ☎ **441/295-6693.** Nonmembers $15. Bus: 1, 2, 10, or 11.

With its red velvet, mirrors, and brass, this club is sometimes favored by an older group of Bermuda business and professional people. It's located above the Little Venice restaurant, which has an understated mirrored entrance that reflects the two stone lions at its portals. Dress is "smart casual." There is dancing, but drinks cost extra. Admission is free if you dine at the Little Venice, the New Harborfront, or La Trattoria restaurants. Open daily from 10pm to 3am.

Club 21
Royal Naval Dockyard. ☎ **441/234-2721.** Cover varies according to the jazz band performing.

If the night is right, this joint can be rocking. That's especially true when it's dedicated to jam sessions for local musicians and singers. You get hot jazz Tuesday through Saturday from 9pm to 2am and on Sunday from 8pm to 2am. Always call first to make sure that it's open. A pint of lager costs from $4.50.

The Hollywood Connection

Film buffs may be surprised to discover that Bermuda has an indirect link to *The Wizard of Oz,* the 1939 movie starring Judy Garland and a host of memorable, magical characters. It is Denslow's Island.

This privately owned island is named after W. W. Denslow, who created the original illustrations for the book on which the movie is based, *The Wonderful Wizard of Oz* (1900) by L. Frank Baum; thus, Denslow's pen gave form to many of the characters depicted on the screen. Denslow lived in Bermuda at the turn of the century. The island, however, is off-limits to visitors.

Several major films were shot in and around Bermuda. The most famous is *The Deep* (1977), starring Jacqueline Bisset, Nick Nolte, Robert Shaw, and Lou Gossett—a visually arresting movie about a lost treasure and drugs and, of course, scuba diving off the island's coast. For one of the scenes, a lighthouse near the Grotto Bay Beach Hotel was accommodatingly blown up.

Part of the movie *Chapter Two* (1979), starring James Caan and Marsha Mason, was filmed in Bermuda. Based on the successful play by Neil Simon, it is the story of a playwright's bumpy romance soon after the death of his wife. The Bermuda scenes were shot at Marley Beach Cottage.

The Gazebo Lounge

In the Princess Hotel, 76 Pitts Bay Rd., city of Hamilton. ☎ **441/295-3000.** $5 to $30, depending on the show. Bus: 7 or 8.

The largest and most prestigious hotel chain in Bermuda prides itself on the array of talent that parades through the bar/lounges of each of its two hotels. The same type of entertainment is presented at the Neptune Club in the Southampton Princess (see below).

Depending on the venue, the season, and the availability of the artists themselves, some type of entertainment is presented Monday through Saturday at each of the two hotels. The schedule changes periodically, but music and comedy acts tend to begin around 9pm and continue, with breaks, up until around midnight.

Dinner/show packages are available, with dinner served in one of the dining rooms followed by a move into the bar/lounge just before the entertainment begins. Artists are likely to include singers, dancers, comedians, or dance troupes, all of whom work hard to keep their respective rooms alive. Also popular within both hotels are 90-minute plays presented by a local repertory company, whose schedules vary seasonally.

Henry VIII

South Shore Road, Southampton Parish. ☎ **441/238-1977.** No cover. Bus: 7 or 8.

This establishment, previously recommended as a restaurant (see Chapter 6), also functions as the premier comedy club of Bermuda. Live comedians are imported, usually from England, for performances Thursday through Tuesday from 9:30pm to 1am. Intermissions in the long-running comedy monologues are sometimes filled with rowdy audience participation. The stage is visible from the pub and from one of the restaurant's three dining areas. Bottles of beer in the pub cost $4 each.

The Oasis Nightclub & Back Room Bar

In the Emporium Building, 69 Front St., city of Hamilton. ☎ **441/292-4978.** Cover $15, including entrance to both the Oasis Club and the Back Room Bar. Bus: 3, 7, or 11.

One of the leading nightlife venues on the island, the Oasis Club is reached by riding a glass-encased elevator to the second floor of a stylish commercial building in the center of Hamilton. It has been renovated into New York warehouse–style. Extensive work has improved the sound system and added lots of special-effects lighting. TV monitors are widely used throughout the nightclub to provide background video effects. The extensive music repertoire includes the latest Top 40 dance music. The Back Room Bar still provides karaoke-style entertainment, but the emphasis is on live bands. Top North American club bands complement local bands playing a variety of rock and blues. The cover charge includes entrance to both establishments, which are open daily from 9pm to 3am. Drink prices range from $4.95 to $5.60.

Neptune Club

The Southampton Princess, 101 South Shore Rd., Southampton Parish. ☎ **441/238-8000.** Cover $5. Ferryboat from Hamilton.

This newly renovated club offers both guests and nonresidents hours of entertainment with a live show. One of the most popular entertainers on the island, Jimmy Keys, a comedian/impressionist/singer performs at the club. Call for hours and details, which are subject to change.

3 The Bar Scene

Casey's

Queen Street (across from the Little Theater), city of Hamilton. ☎ **441/293-9549.** No cover. Bus: 1, 2, 10, or 11.

Casey's aficionados claim it as their neighborhood bar. At least 90% of the clientele are Bermudians; the remainder are welcomed as newcomers. No food is served, but a pint of lager costs around $4.50, and the bar has the best jukebox on the island. The club is open Monday through Saturday from 10am to 10pm. Friday night is the busiest. There is no live entertainment—just the jukebox.

Frog & Onion

The Cooperage, Old Royal Naval Dockyard, Ireland Island. ☎ **441/234-2900.** No cover. Bus: 7 or 8.

Converted from an 18th-century cooperage, a barrel-making factory, this British-style pub lies within the Royal Naval Dockyard. (See Chapter 6 for its restaurant review.) Operated by a "frog" (a Frenchman) and an "onion" (a Bermudian), it is open March through November daily from 11am to 1am; from December through February it is open Tuesday through Monday from noon to midnight. You can enjoy bar snacks throughout the afternoon and evening.

Hog Penny

5 Burnaby Hill, city of Hamilton. ☎ **441/292-2534.** No cover. Bus: 1, 2, 10, or 11.

With a name that Clint Eastwood might have invented for one of his California bars, this is the best-known pub in Bermuda (see Chapter 6 for its recommendation as a dining choice). There is nightly entertainment from 9:30pm to 1am, and dress is casual—often very casual. Between drinks and the music, you can order such pub grub as "bangers and mash" or even steak-and-kidney pie. Although dark and smoky, the place always seems to be full. A pint of lager costs $4.50.

Hubie's

Angle Street (at Court Street), city of Hamilton. ☎ **441/293-9287.** No cover. Bus: 1, 2, 10, or 11.

Well known as a neighborhood bar, this drinking and social outlet is the territory of Hubie Brown. Hubie's been known to play the drums at infrequent intervals during the jazz session on Friday nights from 7 to 10pm, and the only price aficionados pay is the cost of a drink. Otherwise, the rest of the week—from 10am to 10pm every day—the site functions solely as a bar—no food, no music, just the neighbors getting together over drinks. Beer costs $2.50 during normal hours; $3.25 after the music begins.

Loyalty Inn

Mangrove Bay, Somerset Village. ☎ **441/234-0124.** No cover. Bus: 7 or 8, or ferry from Hamilton to Watford Bridge.

If you're out in the West End at night, this 250-year-old home overlooking Mangrove Bay has one of the most popular bars in the area and there is nightly entertainment. (For a dining review, see Chapter 6.) Find a captain's chair and enjoy a pint of lager for $4.50 or, in nice weather, take your drink outside on the terrace. The bar is open daily from 11am to 1am.

Swizzle Inn

3 Blue Hole Hill, Bailey's Bay, Hamilton Parish. ☎ **441/293-9300.** No cover. Bus: 3 or 11.

The home of the Bermuda rum swizzle, this bar and dining choice lies west of the airport near the Crystal Caves and the Bermuda Perfume Factory. (See Chapter 6 for details on dining.) The Swizzleburger and fish and chips can be ordered throughout the day. Sports aficionados usually enjoy playing a game of darts. In the old days you might have run into Ted Kennedy here; now his present wife steers him to more sedate places. The jukebox plays both soft and hard rock. The tradition here is to tack your business card to any place you can find a spot, even the ceiling. A pint of lager costs from $4.50. The inn is open daily from 11am to 1am. It is closed, however, on Mondays in January and February.

Wharf Tavern

Somers Wharf, St. George's. ☎ **441/297-1515.** No cover. Bus: 3, 10, or 11.

For swizzling glasses of tropical rum punch and for talking of sailing the high seas, this is the preferred spot in St. George's. In a converted warehouse from the 1700s, you can enter the darkly paneled bar area where a pint of lager costs from $4.50. The tavern is also a dining choice (see Chapter 6 for food recommendations). But you can also come here just to drink, as many do. The bar is open daily from 11am to 1am.

Ye Olde Cock and Feather

8 Front St., city of Hamilton. ☎ **441/295-2263.** No cover. Bus: 1, 2, 10, or 11.

Located in a converted warehouse, between Burnaby Hill and Queen Street, this is one of the most enduring pubs and restaurants in Bermuda (see Chapter 6 for a dining review). Considered at times the busiest watering hole along Front Street, it resembles both a jazzy English pub and something you'd find along the Florida Keys. The most sought-after place to eat is the balcony upstairs overlooking the harbor, but these tables go quickly. From April through November, live entertainment is presented in the bar. A pint of lager costs $4.50.

Index

FROMMER'S COMPLETE TRAVEL GUIDES

(Comprehensive guides to destinations around the world, with selections in all price ranges—from deluxe to budget)

FROMMER'S FRUGAL TRAVELER'S GUIDES

*(The grown-up guides to budget travel, offering dream vacations
at down-to-earth prices)*

Australia from $45 a Day	India from $40 a Day
Berlin from $50 a Day	Ireland from $45 a Day
California from $60 a Day	Italy from $50 a Day
Caribbean from $60 a Day	Israel from $45 a Day
Costa Rica & Belize from $35 a Day	London from $60 a Day
Eastern Europe from $30 a Day	Mexico from $35 a Day
England from $50 a Day	New York from $70 a Day
Europe from $50 a Day	New Zealand from $45 a Day
Florida from $50 a Day	Paris from $65 a Day
Greece from $45 a Day	Washington, D.C. from $50 a Day
Hawaii from $60 a Day	

FROMMER'S PORTABLE GUIDES

(Pocket-size guides for travelers who want everything in a nutshell)

Charleston & Savannah	New Orleans
Las Vegas	San Francisco

FROMMER'S IRREVERENT GUIDES

(Wickedly honest guides for sophisticated travelers)

Amsterdam	Miami	Santa Fe
Chicago	New Orleans	U.S. Virgin Islands
London	Paris	Walt Disney World
Manhattan	San Francisco	Washington, D.C.

FROMMER'S AMERICA ON WHEELS

*(Everything you need for a successful road trip, including full-color
road maps and ratings for every hotel)*

California & Nevada	Northwest & Great Plains
Florida	South Central &Texas
Mid-Atlantic	Southeast
Midwest & the Great Lakes	Southwest
New England & New York	

FROMMER'S BY NIGHT GUIDES

(The series for those who know that life begins after dark)

Amsterdam	Los Angeles	New York
Chicago	Miami	Paris
Las Vegas	New Orleans	San Francisco
London		